NEW YORK INSTITUTE OF FINANCE

Growing Rich with Growth Stocks

NEW YORK INSTITUTE OF FINANCE
NEW YORK • TORONTO • SYDNEY • TOKYO • SINGAPORE

Kirk Kazanjian

Library of Congress Cataloging-in-Publication Data

Kazanjian, Kirk.
    Growing rich with growth stocks / Kirk Kazanjian ; foreword by Don Phillips.
      p. cm.
    Includes index.
    ISBN 0-7352-0061-0
    1. Stocks. 2. Investments. 3. Corporations—Valuation. 4. Rate of return.
  I. Title.
  HG4661.K34 1999
  332.63' 22—dc21   98-56048
                                                          CIP

Acquisitions Editor: *Ellen Schneid Coleman*
Production Editor: *Sharon L. Gonzalez*
Formatting/Interior Design: *Robyn Beckerman*

© *2000 by Kirk Kazanjian*

Printed in the United States of America

10 9 8 7 6 5 4 3 2 1   *10 9 8 7 6 5 4 3 2 1*

ISBN 0-7352-0061-0 (c)   **ISBN 0-7352-0153-6 (p)**

 NEW YORK INSTITUTE OF FINANCE
Paramus, NJ 07652

On the World Wide Web at http://www.phdirect.com

To my mom, Linda Kazanjian,
with thanks for making so many wonderful
investments in my life

About the Author

Kirk Kazanjian, Director of Research and Investment Strategy, for one of the nation's largest independent fee-only financial planning and investment management firms is a nationally recognized investment expert, stock and mutual fund analyst, best-selling author and lifelong entrepreneur.

Kazanjian developed a passion for the stock market after buying shares of Disney at the age of five. He spent several years as an award-winning television news anchor and business reporter, and frequently offers advice on radio and TV stations across the country, including CNBC, CNNfn, and Bloomberg. Kazanjian is the author of many books, including *Wizards of Wall Street* and the annual investment guides *New York Institute of Finance Guide to Mutual Funds* and *Wall Street's Picks*. He is a popular teacher and speaker on investment topics, and has been featured in numerous publications, including *Barron's, Your Money, USA Today, Entrepreneur, Mutual Funds Magazine, First,* and *The Christian Science Monitor.*

He welcomes your comments and feedback, and can be reached at KirkKazanjian@aol.com.

Acknowledgments

This book would never have been possible without the help of a long list of talented people. To begin with, I want to thank each of the experts profiled in these pages and their able assistants for sharing their time and wisdom with me. I feel deeply honored to know Don Yacktman, Bob Stovall, Shelby Davis, Roy Papp, and Liz Bramwell; I am sure you will find their insights to be as valuable as I did.

Thanks also go out to Don Phillips, who is arguably the most influential voice in the mutual fund industry and an extremely nice guy to boot. I am grateful to Don for writing the book's foreword and for his support of this and many other projects I have been a part of.

Finally, I want to applaud the fine folks at Prentice Hall, including my editors Ellen Schneid Coleman and Barry Richardson, for doing such a great job of shaping this book into what it is today. Because of our collective hard work, readers around the world will now know the secrets to "Growing Rich with Growth Stocks."

Contents

Foreword

I started investing when I was 14 years old. That's when my father bought me shares in the Templeton Growth Fund, explained how the fund worked, and showed me how to look up its price in the daily newspaper. While that gift didn't cause me to stop reading *Boy's Life* in favor of *The Wall Street Journal,* it did make a lasting impression.

By giving me this fund, my father not only introduced me to Sir John Templeton, one of the twentieth-century's greatest investors, but he also established himself as an important role model. He taught me that investing was a part of his life and could be a part of mine, too.

In time, I came to see investing as an activity for all responsible adults. By setting aside today's gratification to ensure tomorrow's well-being, we demonstrate our maturity. These are hard lessons to learn. The temptation to spend today is always great. I'm constantly reminded of this lesson as I watch my sons grow up. Seeing the world through their eyes reminds me of how many messages we receive on how to spend and consume. Commercials, fast-food promotions, the toys of friends—all send countless messages about the instant gratification of consumption.

Apart from me, I often wonder where my sons will get lessons on the discipline of saving and investing.

Too many of us grow up without investment role models. The subject rarely comes up even in schools. We spend a lifetime fine-tuning our shopping skills, but we don't work nearly as hard at our investment skills. The same person who will drive across town to save 50 cents on a six-pack of cola will throw thousands of dollars at a stock or a mutual fund on the basis of a hot tip or an unsubstantiated rumor. We are, despite much well-intended educational efforts, a nation of investment illiterates.

We need help. We need role models.

That's where Kirk Kazanjian's *Growing Rich with Growth Stocks* comes in. Kirk has gone right to the best investment role models out there: top, time-tested managers such as Don Yacktman, Liz Bramwell, and Shelby Davis. These experts share their secrets with Kirk, who in turn has translated their collective wisdom into a sound agenda for any investor looking to learn the ropes. In a field still too dominated by get-rich-quick schemes, Kirk has sought and found a different breed of investor, one who accumulates money through diligent research and patience. The advice of these managers isn't flashy, but it works.

Investing is a simple activity at its core. Buy low and sell high isn't a tough lesson to learn. It's just phenomenally difficult to put into practice. If you're going it alone, it can be maddening. With the counsel of these great investors at your side, however, the road will not only be smoother, it should also be much more profitable.

My best to you on your journey. May you truly grow rich with growth stocks.

—Don Phillips

Introduction

The roots of growth stock investing are very rich indeed. Among the sport's earliest players was T. Rowe Price. This venerable Wall Street legend preached the merits of buying quality companies with accelerating earnings, even if it meant paying a slight premium for the privilege. Price was among the most influential portfolio managers of the early twentieth century. He went on to build a mutual fund empire that has grown exceedingly faster than most of the stocks he ever owned. While many of his peers agreed with his philosophy, few followed it as religiously as he did. As a result, their performance suffered, while his earned widespread praise.

Growth stock investing has come a long way since Price rose to prominence. Among the more modern-day practitioners of this art are billionaire Warren Buffett, arguably the most successful and admired living investor, and former Fidelity Magellan manager-turned-author Peter Lynch. It is clearly the investment discipline with the widest following on the Street today, largely for one important reason: It works.

Unfortunately, most who proclaim to follow the tenets of growth stock investing never reap its rewards, for finding companies with lasting staying power is no easy task. They come in every size and industry. But failing to separate the genuine growers from the one-hit wonders leads many investors astray. That's why so many professional money managers fail to even keep up with the computer-run stock market indexes. Surely their performance would be greatly enhanced if only they knew the 12 rules for successful growth stock investing, as revealed in this book.

These rules are based on lessons I have learned through interviewing and observing five of the top growth stock managers watching over other people's money today: Elizabeth R. Bramwell, Shelby Davis, L. Roy Papp, Robert H. Stovall, and Donald Yacktman. These luminaries have more than 170 years of combined investing experience and have amassed some of the most impressive performance records on public display. Investment professionals of this caliber are precious indeed, for they are few and far between.

While each investor has a slightly different way of choosing companies for his or her portfolio, they all share a dozen key traits. In this book, you'll discover their secrets. If you take the time to learn and master each rule, something that is clearly within your reach, you can begin to share in the tremendous financial rewards bestowed upon those smart enough to know a promising investment when they see one.

Before we begin this journey into successful stock picking, let me briefly introduce you to the five minds behind the concepts. (You will get to know them in greater depth as you read their "One-on-One" profiles throughout the book.)

Donald Yacktman is president and chief investment officer of Yacktman Asset Management in Chicago. Before starting his own firm in 1992, he managed the Selected American Shares fund for almost a decade. Yacktman likes to buy growing, and often boring, companies when they're beaten down and selling below their estimated intrinsic value. In other words, Yacktman is a growth investor who uses value techniques for choosing stocks. He favors big companies and believes in holding a concentrated portfolio.

Robert H. Stovall first began observing the Wall Street scene as a 14-year-old messenger boy for the brokerage firm Reynolds and Company. After taking time out for military duty in Italy during

World War II, he earned two business degrees and has been involved in money management ever since. He was one of the first investment analysts to earn the prestigious CFA designation and is a popular panelist on the PBS program *Wall $treet Week With Louis Rukeyser*. Most of Stovall's clients are retired and therefore quite conservative, which means he tends to be more risk-averse than some of the others featured in this book. He concentrates on locating attractive growth stocks in undervalued sectors while hunting for companies expected to benefit from his broad-based observations of leading trends around the world.

Shelby Davis comes from an impressive bloodline of investment geniuses. His father was a well-known insurance stock analyst whose personal equity portfolio grew from $100,000 to $50 million in less than eight years. Davis started the New York Venture Fund in 1969. It has easily eclipsed the Standard & Poor's 500 index during its profitable history. The Davis investment philosophy calls for identifying long-term trends early while focusing on high-quality companies with good growth prospects that sell for reasonable prices. His emphasis is on research and getting to know management. Davis doesn't believe in market timing and strives to be a long-term owner of every stock he buys.

L. Roy Papp is like the jolly old grandfather every kid would love to have. This folksy investment manager from Arizona has more than four decades of experience under his belt, including a stint as the American director of and ambassador to the Asian Development Bank in Manila under President Gerald Ford. Papp graduated from the Wharton School and worked his way up through the ranks at the growth-investment shop Stein Roe & Farnham in Chicago. He started his own firm in the early 1980s and now has some $1 billion under management. Papp's pioneering investment philosophy calls for buying American companies with a decidedly international theme, to safely capture some of the incredible profits enjoyed by doing business overseas. To make Papp's buy list, a company must get at least 35 percent of its sales or operating earnings abroad, show increased earnings and dividends in each of the last ten years, have a high return on shareholder equity, and sport only a small amount of debt.

Elizabeth R. Bramwell is among the most successful women ever to work on Wall Street. Following her early days as an analyst, she teamed up with her business school classmate, Mario Gabelli, to start the Gabelli Growth Fund in 1987. During her tenure as manager, she consistently bested the performance of her boss, which created a lot of tension between them. She ultimately quit and went out on her own. Bramwell follows smaller stocks than Yacktman and Davis, and holds a more diversified portfolio. Her investment style can best be described as "eclectic." She is both a top-down and a bottoms-up manager, who begins by analyzing broad secular trends before hunting for individual companies that stand to benefit. She attends plenty of analyst meetings and prefers well-financed businesses with growing market shares, ready access to capital, and good managements.

The "One-on-One" profiles, which are interspersed between the chapters, contain complete biographies of each of these five living investment legends. One thing you'll learn from their personal stories is that past life experiences have had a definite impact on the way they choose stocks. You'll also discover each investor's ten favorite growth stocks for the twenty-first century. These are companies poised to make you rich for decades to come.

I would encourage you to not simply skim through the list of rules, which are fully summarized in "The Bottom Line" briefings at the end of each chapter. Rather, read each one carefully to gain a greater understanding of the rationale behind these principles. Otherwise you will be left flying an airplane without knowing how each of the buttons on the cockpit's control panel really work. If you digest the underlying reasons behind every rule completely, by the time you finish reading *Growing Rich with Growth Stocks,* I'm convinced you will have the tools you need to greatly improve your investment results. You will never buy stocks the same way again. Instead, you will enter the game with more discipline and the knowledge you must have to stay ahead of the crowd on Wall Street for the rest of your investment life.

—Kirk Kazanjian

Rule 1

FORGET ABOUT
THE MARKET

As you step inside Donald Yacktman's downtown Chicago investment firm, it's easy to forget about the hubbub of activity taking place on Wall Street less than 800 miles away. The muted color furnishings make you feel at home, yet give no indication you've entered an area responsible for managing around $1 billion of other people's money. There are no frantic traders running around shouting buy and sell orders. No flashing Quotron screens or television monitors relaying the latest market gossip. And no hyper portfolio managers yelling into their phones in search of late-breaking information. In fact, this place is so quiet and free of outside distractions, you could easily take a nap, which Yacktman does on a regular basis. The most gaudy decoration in the entire place is a ceramic Christmas display in the conference room. It was loaned to him by the president of one of his largest holdings, Department 56, which designs and manufactures products like this.

The employees of Yacktman Asset Management don't dress up for work. In contrast to the dark three-piece-suit uniform common among financiers, Yacktman and his crew prefer a more casual approach. This means a simple dress or pantsuit for women, and slacks with a button-up shirt (no tie) for men. Boring committee meetings are also a rare occurrence. The day I visited, Yacktman and his staff of ten gathered for their monthly luncheon meeting to discuss the latest company news. After a brief update on the progress of winning over some major new accounts, the rest of the talk focused on sports, upcoming vacations, and other subjects you'd expect people to chat about in a coed locker room. It's almost like the conversation one has at a family dinner. In a way, that's what this is. One of Yacktman's sons works for him. The rest of his associates have been with him so long they're arguably closer than blood relatives. While gobbling down turkey sandwiches and potato chips, the closest thing to a conversation about the market comes from Yacktman's son Brian, who's filling in as a summer intern. "Are we up or down today?" he asks. "We won't know until this afternoon," Yacktman replies, in almost an "I don't care because I'm in this for the long haul" sort of way.

Yacktman's personal office is equally placid. It houses little more than a desk, coffee table, and a few chairs, most of which he bought from his former employer for pennies on the dollar. Occasionally, he likes to stroke the computer to his right, although he admittedly still feels more comfortable with a plain old calculator. By turning his head in either direction, Yacktman has a towering view of downtown Chicago from 19 stories above his Madison Street address. The scene is both beautiful and serene. It's also a source of inspiration for many of Yacktman's investment decisions. "Sometimes the most intelligent thing a person can do is pause and just look out this window for maybe 30 minutes, think about what he's going to do and make sure he's focused on the right priorities," he says. "Too many people go through the day without taking time out for things like that."

These simple surroundings are typical of Yacktman's personal and professional style. He's a mild-mannered man who doesn't let things like a constantly fluctuating stock market get in his way. "I like to say that my dad fell asleep on crash day in 1987," reveals son Stephen, who is now an assistant portfolio manager at his dad's firm. "He's very calm because, when you think about it, nothing's really changing with the companies we own. There's nothing new to get worked up over. My father regularly takes an afternoon snooze, and he wouldn't let something like a stock market crash interfere with that."

Yacktman views predicting the direction or level of the market as a rather fruitless exercise. "Instead, my objective is to buy shares of good businesses at relatively low prices and to execute this strategy regardless of where the market is," he insists.

FOCUSED ON "THE MARKET"

Sadly, most investors are not like this. They get worked up over what's happening with the Dow, Standard & Poor's 500, Nasdaq, Wilshire 5000, or the myriad of other benchmark indexes created over the past several decades. Almost every nightly newscast spouts off at least where the Dow Jones Industrial Average of 30 blue-chip stocks closed out the session, while this information is relayed even more frequently on the radio, Internet, and business section of the daily newspaper.

Since the media spend so much time reporting on "the market," it seems logical that it's something investors should pay attention to. But it's not. Savvy pros know it is nothing more than distracting noise that can prevent you from doing what's really important: focusing on picking quality companies and keeping track of them.

"If I were an individual investor, I'd read the weekend press coverage and that's about it," says Robert Stovall. "Don't look at what's going on every day. I have some clients who will buy something one day, and if it goes down the next morning they'll call and tell me to sell it. I have to quiet them down and explain that if you take a position in a company that you have conviction in, you shouldn't sell out after the first two down days. People like that would be better off not reading the newspaper at all. Getting all worked up about the events of the moment turns you into your own worst enemy. The buy-and-hold investor is the successful investor. This is the person who does his or her homework, has patience, and lets time work for him or her."

Market Watching from Worlds Away

In Roy Papp's early days as a money manager with Stein Roe in Chicago, he spent time not only watching the market, but also trying to react to it. He was a shorter-term thinker, as was the firm, in terms of shifting assets in and out of stocks depending on which direction he thought the market was headed. After leaving Stein Roe & Farnham in 1975, he went overseas to become a U.S. representative to the Asian Development Bank in Manila. Once he got his own personal portfolio in order and scooped up shares of a number of small companies that got clobbered during the 1973–1974 bear market, he headed overseas, intending to follow his investments from abroad.

"When I was in Manila, I was never awake when the New York Stock Exchange was working," he says. "I got *The New York Times* about ten days late. I was forced to make some changes. I couldn't make investments on a short-term basis. I realized I had to have a long time horizon of three to five years. I bought many dirt-cheap small stocks that were good quality companies with no problems other than that they had been beaten down. I made a lot of money from them." Among his biggest winners were book publishers Scott Foresman, John Wiley & Sons, and Richard Irwin. "I bought Irwin for $11 a share and a few months later Dow Jones bought it out for $26," he says.

Investing the Phoenix Way

In retrospect, Papp believes that leaving Stein Roe and accepting the Manila assignment was the smartest investment move he's ever made. "Going to Manila gave me a chance to do a lot of thinking on my own," he says. "It taught me to take a longer-term view. It also taught me that life doesn't have to be so frantic. You can slow down. That's why I like living in Phoenix. We probably work only 85 percent as hard as people in New York and Los Angeles, yet the results are almost the same. I think people in Manila work much less than that, particularly those in the international bureaucracies. But I learned you don't have to break your back to be successful and happy. Running around in the rat race isn't the smartest thing to do. A lot of that is just spinning wheels. I also learned to take a very long-term view of the horizon."

Nowadays, Papp rarely checks to see if the Dow is up or down, nor does he trouble himself with keeping track of the constantly fluctuating values of the stocks in his portfolios. In fact, as I spent the day talking with Papp in his opulent office, I noticed he never once turned on his computer. Long after the stock exchanges had closed and we were preparing to leave for the night, I asked, "Don't you follow the market at all? To that he replied, "I don't have a Quotron in the office. I knew where the market was when I picked you up at the airport this morning and I know where it closed. If I have an ongoing order for certain stocks, I'll monitor it periodically throughout the day to see if it gets filled. If we have a day when the market is down big, I might look for things to buy. Otherwise, I don't pay attention to it. A drop in the market is usually an opportunity, not a crisis. It's easier for me to buy when the market's going down 500 or 1,000 points because it's cheaper, unless there's an accompanying problem, like an oil shortage or war. You don't necessarily want to buy right in the middle of a fall, though. I normally prefer to wait until I have some idea of what is causing the drop, to find out if it's a temporary or permanent problem. The worst thing you can do is panic out."

This Glass Is Always Full

Shelby Davis insists he doesn't believe in market timing because, as an optimist, he thinks of the glass as always being half full, not half empty. "I once asked my father, 'When is the best time to invest money?' " he reflects. "Dad answered, 'Son, the best time to invest money is when you have it.' He told me to just make it a habit, like eating and sleeping, and to invest every week. He insisted that if you invest for a lifetime, you will become rich." Nevertheless, Davis offers the following prediction: The Dow Jones Industrial Average will be trading at around 50,000 by the year 2030. "So if you have 30 or 40 years to invest, why worry about the next 1,000 or 2,000 points?" Davis asks.

Why worry indeed. If you need more proof that market timing is for the clueless, just look at the track record of those who have tried to do it over the years. Almost every mutual fund, investment newsletter, and adviser claiming to practice market timing has a performance record not even a mother could love. There are many reasons for this. For one thing, the market has an upward bias, meaning it goes up a lot more than it goes down. Therefore, by being out of the market, you are more likely to lose out on potential gains than you are to avoid any steep losses. Second, the market tends to move widely in both directions on only a select number of days. Therefore, if you're out during the few most profitable sessions of the year, your overall returns will plummet.

One often-cited study shows that from 1980 to 1990, the annual return on stocks in the Standard & Poor's 500 index was 17.6 percent. During that period, if you were on the sidelines during the top ten trading days, your return would have dropped to 12.6 percent. Had you been in cash on the 20 best days, your increase would have been a mere 9.3 percent. If you were unfortunate enough as to miss the 30 best sessions, out of a potential 3,650, your return would have been cut by almost a third, to 6.5 percent.

Sure, sometimes these market forecasters will be right. Several correctly called for a fall in 1987, then harped on continuously about the accuracy of their prediction. However, many of these same folks continued to forecast Armageddon throughout the ensuing decade, while the market kept rising higher and higher. Besides, even when the market does little or nothing, there are always individual stocks that go up. Warren Buffett knows that. He has said many times that he can care less about the market. He buys carefully selected companies and follows *them,* not the Nasdaq and Dow.

HAVE I GOT A SYSTEM FOR YOU

The reality that market timing doesn't work, which has been proven time and time again, still hasn't stopped people from putting out newsletters and books revealing supposedly "foolproof" techniques for forecasting future stock price movements. These systems are based on everything from wave patterns to the astrological lining of the stars. There's even the remarkable "Super Bowl" stock market predictor. This one dates back to 1967, when the NFC's Green Bay Packers beat the AFC's Kansas City Chiefs 35–10 at the Los Angeles Coliseum. "Here's how that predictor works," Stovall offers. "It simply states that the market will close the year higher if the Super Bowl is won by an 'original' National Football League team, while it will decline if the game is won by a team from the now-vanished American Football

League." This predictor has had an 89 percent accuracy rate. But since sports results have no direct relationship to money flows into equities, Stovall attributes its uncanny record mostly to chance. "The only coincident weighting that makes it less perplexing is that there are more teams in the NFC than in the AFC, and the stock market goes up more years than it goes down," he surmises. "Various academic studies in recent years have brought the conclusion no closer than that."

There are a number of political market forecasting theories swirling around as well, most of which are based on the quadrennial cycle of the U.S. presidency. The crux of these arguments is that the first two years of any president's term will be rough for equities, while the final two should be much better. "The basic reasoning behind this is that the administration and Federal Reserve Board are usually at their 'tightest' during the early quarters and at their 'most accommodating' during the later quarters of the four-year cycle," Stovall points out. "Since the William McKinley election of 1900, a definite up, down, and up again stock pattern has accompanied each U.S. president's term. This 'pendulum pattern' can be explained, too simply perhaps, as initial enthusiasm for a new president, a subsequent period of disillusionment, followed by a rally from the previous low, either because a popular president seems likely to be returned to office for another four years, or an unpopular one is in the process of being turned out to do other things."

One final and graphic form of proof that market timing doesn't work can be seen by looking at "The Investment Decision-Making Process" chart on the following page. It shows how investor sentiment is often a contrary indicator. When the market is going up, and everything looks great, this can cloud your vision about what's really ahead. Likewise, when prices are down, and the market seems dreary, it may be just the time to start investing more money. You never know. That's why second-guessing the direction of the market almost always fails. "Market timers are slow to get in and never the first to get out," Stovall notes. "They never buy at the bottom, because they wait for signs of strength before making a commitment. Then they won't sell out until they see a serious break point." Stovall got this chart in 1970 from the late Ken Ward, a senior technical analyst he hired when he was at Reynolds Securities. "It is a good reminder of human fallibility. The market will do what the market will do," Stovall adds.

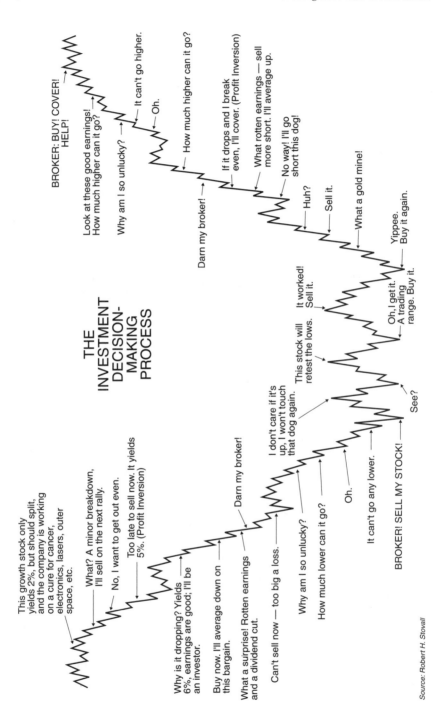

Source: Robert H. Stovall

WILL THE REAL MARKET WATCHERS PLEASE STAND UP?

One of Wall Street's dirty little secrets is that even those who caution against following the market still pay attention to it themselves. After all, it really is hard to ignore. Robert Stovall admits to keeping a constant eye on the direction of the major indexes throughout the day. You'll find his eyes glued to CNBC most mornings, regardless of whether he's in his New York office or at one of his homes sprinkled along the East Coast. It's not that he reacts to each move of the ticker. Instead, watching the tape has become a habit-forming way of life. "I think it's partly because my job has always been to know what's going on from moment to moment," he rationalizes. "For 30 years, I worked as the up-front spokesperson for major brokerage firms and was expected to constantly have an opinion on the market. Even today, clients and reporters call all the time to ask, 'What happened today?' or 'Where will the Dow be at the end of the year?' It's part of the short-term mentality of both the media and most investors. But I am the first to acknowledge that it's hard to be right about the direction of the market. I think I'm on the money a bit more than half of the time, which is pretty good. The fact is, no one can call it correctly all or even most of the time. It just can't be done." That's why Stovall, like the others I interviewed for this book, view watching the tape as more of a distraction than anything else.

DON'T SELL WHEN THE DOW IS DOWN

While he usually knows whether the major indexes are up or down, and by how much, Stovall insists he doesn't normally make investment decisions based on these numbers, with one exception. "I don't like to sell on down days, and I rarely buy on up days," he reveals. "Let's say the market is down 100 points on Wednesday. I won't sell into that kind of market, because I know I won't get a good price for my shares. By contrast, that might be an environment to do some buying in. If, on the other hand, the market is strong on Thursday and Friday, and I've been thinking about getting rid of some stock anyway, those would be good days to unload it, assuming my particular companies are benefiting from the positive momentum."

Besides, when it comes down to it, Stovall claims he's really a buy-and-hold investor anyway, not a trader. "I watch the market and listen to TV business shows because it's both enlightening and entertaining," he says. "I know how to keep it in perspective and not react irrationally to the developments of the moment. Most people don't, so they would be better off leaving their TVs off. The truly successful investors I've watched or worked with over the years are those who know how to sit on their assets. They get themselves into several good positions and aren't shaken out just because the market has a weak season."

Stovall also points to Warren Buffett as a great example. He's built his multibillion-dollar stock market fortune by ignoring the indexes and focusing on individual company selection instead. In fact, there's a good chance Buffett rarely tunes in to CNBC, CNN, or any other financial news station. Buffett has long espoused the belief that you should purchase shares of stock in a business the same way you would if you were buying the entire company, thus taking out the worry of what "the market" will do. "It makes great sense," Stovall insists. "If you time the market, you might not want to buy shares of XYZ now, even though you feel it is a good value, simply because, let's say, your work indicates this will be a lousy year for stocks because of the strong dollar overseas. However, would that be a factor in your decision-making process if you were buying the entire company? Would the strong-dollar worry be any more relevant? Probably not. I once heard Buffett on a television show say it makes no difference to him whether 100 other security analysts agree or disagree with his opinion about a company. The only thing that counts is a company's ability to generate earnings from the assets employed in the business. Short-term fluctuations in the price of a company's stock are meaningless to him. The price of a stock on a given day is only what others think the company is worth."

Elizabeth Bramwell agrees. While she doesn't invest based on the overall market, she does pay attention to it. She follows the progress of the major indexes and her individual holdings throughout the day on her computer, keeping an eye out for possible trading opportunities. "The computer can be very distracting," she admits. "But on the other hand, look at all the information I can get from it." What's more, with the explosion of online information,

Bramwell notes that investors today must be prepared to make instantaneous decisions.

NEVER FORGET WHAT'S IMPORTANT

Shelby Davis cautions that paying attention to day-to-day variables, outside of those that directly impact the companies in your portfolio, can be extremely costly. "A narrow investment period and approach often can be the worst enemy of a growth stock investor," Davis says. "Short-term swings, while scary at times, should sometimes be overlooked so that more meaningful long-term stock market growth trends have an opportunity to provide real investment results. Too often, an investor sells his or her shares at or near the very bottom of a down-market cycle. That same investor often fails to get back into the stock market when it begins to recover because there is usually an assumption that the market will decline again."

Nevertheless, although Davis fancies himself a long-term investor who places more emphasis on a company's management team than on its latest trading price, he does stay focused on his Bloomberg terminal, which gives him up-to-the-minute market news and information. He feels that in a runaway market like the one we've experienced in the 1990s, this is the only way to keep track of when his favorite stocks become available at bargain prices.

"What I'm trying to do is pick off pressure points in the companies I like," he reveals. "When I see any stock I own on my screen down 5 or 10 percent, it triggers an interest in me to either call the company and find out what's going on or to buy it. Granted, I don't just do this mechanically. I try to find out why the stock is down and whether the crisis of the day creates an opportunity. I think all good managers have their quote machines on all the time, even if they don't acknowledge it. After a long bull market, the only way you're going to get a bargain is when there's some controversy or short-term event that creates doubt in the minds of investors. In these days of instant information and high volatility, short-term disappointments or the threat of adverse developments can have a huge impact on a company's stock price and create buying opportunities. For example, President Clinton's plan for health-care reform in 1992 created a panic that caused first-rate pharmaceutical companies to trade down 40 to 50 percent, even though they stood to benefit greatly from the aging baby boomers."

OTHER THINGS TO IGNORE

By the way, it's not just the market that you should forget about. "I spend virtually no time trying to predict the economy, interest rates, or inflation either," Don Yacktman adds. "I feel it is a far more valuable use of my time to look for large disparities between the value of a business's property and its current price in the marketplace. My objective is to buy high return businesses at favorable prices and wait patiently for the market to upwardly revalue them, instead of focusing on whether the economy, interest rates, or the market are forecast to go up or down. By reducing the number of variables in my analyses and avoiding economic guesstimates, I believe I am effectively reducing risk."

The rationale behind Yacktman's blasé attitude is straightforward. "In investing, as in coaching a basketball team, certain events can be controlled and others cannot," he offers. "I believe good coaches (and investors) focus on the controllable and lose little sleep worrying about factors outside their control. If I do my homework and buy high-return businesses at big discounts, these outside influences should be relatively insignificant in my decision process."

Roy Papp couldn't agree more. "When investing, you should take a long-term point of view and ignore the weekly expert opinions, forecasts, one-month figures, and views of very experienced analysts who have been in the industry for as many as two years," he maintains.

THE BOTTOM LINE

Take a long-term view of investing and ignore the day-to-day fluctuations of the economy, interest rates, and overall stock market. These constantly changing variables have little or no impact on the companies in your portfolio.

If you can't help but pay attention to how your stocks and the market averages are doing, at least resist the temptation to panic in or out based on the events of the moment. Instead, use this information to your advantage. For instance, if you see the price of a company you own or have been eyeing get slammed by the market for an irrational reason, this may be an opportune time to buy. What's more, it is generally best to avoid purchasing stocks on days when the market goes up significantly, while you are normally advised not to sell in the middle of a fall. Instead, sell on strength and buy on weakness.

Rule 2

INVEST LIKE A TORTOISE, PROFIT LIKE A HARE

Donald Yacktman likes to compare himself to the tortoise in that famous story about the tortoise and the hare. You remember how it goes. The tortoise can't run as fast as the hare, but by staying on course, it still manages to win the race. Likewise, although Yacktman has never been one to churn out a quick buck in the market, he's made his shareholders rich over time. He sticks with his discipline in tough times. In fact, his investment style has been out-of-favor for the past several years, causing the performance of his funds to significantly trail the overall market in both 1997 and 1998. Nevertheless, Yacktman insists he's not about to change his ways. "Like the tortoise, I may appear to be a little slow at executing my strategy at times," he says. "But that's what happens when you're looking to give investors the highest possible return with a minimal amount of risk. After all, I believe investing is a marathon, not a sprint. Consequently, I have a longer time horizon."

Yacktman looks for similar characteristics in the companies he invests in. He prefers to own steady, predictable businesses he can hang on to for years, if not decades, to come. He doesn't want to worry about whether their products will soon become obsolete. For that reason, he often avoids small and unproven companies, especially those in the technology arena. "To me, they're like Roman candles and shooting stars," he says. "What's popular today might not even be around tomorrow."

That's one reason why Yacktman also stays away from generic financial stocks. "They generally have mediocre businesses," he rationalizes. "A standard run-of-the-mill bank or insurance company, for instance, doesn't appeal to me, although I've been in Freddie Mac, Sallie Mae, United Asset Management, Salomon Brothers, and Morgan Stanley before. It's really a matter of returns. The more generic a business is, the harder it becomes to get high returns. A lot of times, a generic bank or insurer produces mediocre returns, meaning I wouldn't want to own it for a long time. They're what I call conduit companies. The same product they take in the back door is sold through the front door. Retailers are another example. They sell the same product as the guy down the street, so the only way they can make more money is by becoming the lowest-cost producer, which is tough to do in a generic business.

"Some of the biggest mistakes in my investing career have been with financial companies," Yacktman adds. "At one time, I was willing to buy some businesses strictly on the basis of asset values, as opposed to cash flow. I found some financial companies that looked very cheap on an asset basis, but were really low-return businesses. The problem with financial companies is that they often create assets with the stroke of a pen. The assets are no better than the person who wrote the loan or made the deal. Because they are leveraged by a factor of 10 or 20 to one, book value can quickly disappear.

"Probably the single worst investment I ever made was buying First Executive Life back in 1989," he adds. "I turned it down twice, but this broker kept pestering me about it. The stock was selling below book value, but never really earned a high return on equity. When junk bonds declined, regulators overreacted and forced the company to sell the bonds it owned at the bottom of the market. First Executive's book value evaporated and the investment was a disaster. Now I'm more cautious and always look for good long-term buys. I'm proud to say that since I've been running Yacktman Asset Management, I've never bought what turned out to be a bad business. I haven't always beaten the market, but I've virtually avoided any permanent losses by sticking with my positions. Granted, the market price of any stock will change daily, and you could have a gain or loss at any given time. But if the process is done correctly and enough effort is put into it, a person should hardly ever experience a permanent loss investing in carefully selected stocks over the long haul."

SLEEPING WHEN THE WIND BLOWS

You can think of Yacktman's philosophy as being similar to the young man who once applied for work as a farmhand. The farmer in charge asked, "What are your qualifications, son?"

The man replied, "I can sleep when the wind blows."

That didn't make a lot of sense to the farmer, but the man was physically strong, so he was hired for the job. A short time later, a terrible storm crept up in the middle of the night, complete with thunder, lightning, and treacherous winds. The farmer was so shaken and worried about his crop, he jumped out of bed and ran up to his young assistant's room, only to find him fast asleep. The farmer shook the farmhand fiercely, until he finally opened his eyes. "How could you possibly sleep through this terrible storm?" the perturbed farmer asked.

"Don't you remember what I said when you hired me?" the man replied. "I told you I could sleep when the wind blows."

"But what about the livestock?" the farmer shouted.

"They're taken care of in the barn and the hay is covered," he said. "There's no reason to worry. Everything is the same as it was before, except you're a little more excited."

Yacktman believes all investors should be like this young, yet wise farmhand. They should sleep when the wind of the stock market blows. Yacktman insists this is his attitude, and his staff will attest to it. He is known for taking an occasional afternoon nap and has told employees not to disturb him, even if the market comes crashing down. His rationale? Even though the herd may be in a panic, he rests assured that the outlook for his companies remains the same.

No Guarantees

Yacktman's the first to admit, however, that you can never be totally certain about a company's prospects, nor whether it is being led by a capable management team. "Many people feel it's the number of hours you put in at the office in this business that makes the biggest difference," he observes. "That's simply not true. This is a judgment business. Stephen Covey wrote a book called *The Seven Habits of Highly Effective People*. At one point, he talks about the four quadrants. Quadrant two is where very important and long-term-oriented decisions are made. I think I spend a lot of time in quadrant two. I try to concentrate on what's really important, which is why my office is so calm. Unfortunately, most people in this business focus only on the short-term. In my opinion, that kind of attitude just amounts to a lot of wheel spinning."

Instead, Yacktman takes great pains to ignore all the noise that distracts many investors. "Remember, there are four things I pretty much avoid spending time on: the stock market, interest rates, inflation, and the economy," he insists. "Those subjects are like noise in the background. They take away from what I do best. It makes the job a lot easier if I spend all my time looking for dollar bills that I can buy for 50 cents, which is how I view my investment process. I also think making a to-do list is helpful. I once knew a man who wrote down the seven or ten most important things he planned to do the next day. He then ranked those tasks in order of priority. He started with number one. When he got through with that, he went on to number two, and so forth. Most people don't do that. They end up spending their time on C and D tasks. As a result, they go home at the end of the day and feel like they haven't accomplished anything. I'm not saying I'm perfect. But I am focused on getting the important tasks done first. I think that's why I've been able to achieve a lot in a relatively short period of time." Without question, Yacktman is what you would call a true buy-and-hold investor.

This outside "noise" is what causes many investors to constantly trade in and out of their positions. Blame it on human nature. When we own shares in a company that's the subject of a negative story on the news, our tendency is to sell. Yet history tells us this instead is often an opportune time to buy. If you own good businesses, you should simply accept that their share prices will fluctuate greatly up and down from day-to-day, week-to-week, and month-to-month. What's important is that over time, as earnings rise, stock prices will follow.

In addition, thanks to recent tax law changes, staying put makes more sense than ever before. Until you sell shares of a stock, you have no tax liability, except for dividend income, which is often either low or nonexistent. This makes owning individual stocks akin to having a legal tax-deferred IRA account for your nonretirement plan dollars. And when you keep a holding for 12 months or more, you incur taxes at the much lower capital gains rate of 20 percent, which can represent a huge discount from ordinary rates.

"I hate to pay commissions and especially taxes," Robert Stovall insists, noting that with Internet brokers offering to trade stocks for pennies a share, the commission penalty is not as high as it once was. "But taxes are still a major issue, especially for older investors," he adds. "When they get to be 80-plus years old and have a long list of great companies that have gone up in value by ten times or more, selling triggers an enormous capital gains liability. If you're selling for personal reasons, like to pay for medical costs, that's understandable. But to sell just because your broker thinks it's a good idea is often a mistake. This is especially true if an older person is trying to grow their portfolio as a legacy to leave to their loved ones or designated charities. After all, when they die, the cost basis becomes the date of death, and the huge capital gains liability suddenly disappears."

INVESTING FOR THE LONG HAUL

The term "buy-and-hold investing" has become almost a cliché. You've no doubt heard experienced professionals dole out this advice time and again. It's simple, it works, and it's easy to understand. Unfortunately, few people heed this counsel. As a result, their returns suffer. As Shelby Davis puts it, you should go into every investment with the intention of sticking with it forever.

"I like to buy stocks that I call core holdings rather than trading in and out of the market," he says. "As a long-term investor, I measure success by the long-term wealth I build. I strive to create an environment in which compounding can flourish. One way I do this is by sticking with a universe of companies growing between 7 and 15 percent a year, selling for 10 to 15 times earnings. That range is attractive because time is your friend in the compounding process. Nobody thinks twice about investing in a 30-year bond. Likewise, they think nothing of buying a house and owning it for 20 or 30 years. A stock is just another way to invest your cash. I feel that over time if the Dow compounds at just 7 percent a year, it will trade for between 50,000 and 60,000 in 30 years. Compounding is really the eighth wonder of the world. Using the rule of 72, you can easily calculate the number of years it will take to double your money. You simply divide the rate of interest into 72. In this case, 7 into 72 equals about 10 years. In other words, if you can compound your money at a rate of 7 percent, it will double every 10 years, quadruple in 20 years, and be up eight times in 30 years."

STAY PUT AND IN THE MARKET

By the same token, Roy Papp not only holds on to his companies for years, but also stays as fully invested in stocks as he can. "I normally keep less than 1 percent cash in my fund," he reveals. "The only time I carry more is when I'm cautious about the market. It's not that I'm nervous, but I want to make sure I have enough money on hand to meet shareholder redemptions." This goes back to the principle of avoiding market timing. If you're a long-term investor, as you should be, and the fundamentals of your companies are sound, there is no reason ever to panic out of equities altogether just because you are fearful of "the market."

THE BOTTOM LINE

The real message for investors is this: On Wall Street, you truly get rich slowly. Don't be a trader. Buy quality companies and stick with them for the long haul. By doing so, one day you'll wake up and realize you have more money than you know what to do with. Without question, traders die poor, while investors prosper. Besides, as Peter Lynch often said, most of his money was made in the third or fourth year he owned a stock. Sometimes it took even longer.

DONALD
YACKTMAN

$\mathcal{D}$onald Yacktman has been an expert at math and playing with numbers since he was a little boy. As a preschooler, he was cared for during the day by a childless old woman he called "Nanny." He remembers sitting on Nanny's floor counting pennies by the hundreds. Then, in the first and second grades, he was the top math student at his Catholic school. The nun who taught his class would hold races to see who could add up long columns of numbers the fastest. The winner got to compete head-on with her. Yacktman easily defeated his fellow students and proved a formidable challenger to the nun.

One of the great ironies in Yacktman's life is that he and his wife, Carolyn, were both born in the same Chicago hospital just nine days apart, but they didn't meet again until they were in college. "I kid her about the wink she gave me in the nursery. Our mothers were both in the hospital for about ten days," he explains. An only child, Yacktman spent his early years in a two-flat home near Chicago's Rose Hill Cemetery. His parents divorced after 17 years of marriage when he was eight. He then moved with his mom to Salt Lake City and returned to Chicago each June to spend the summer with his dad.

FROM RAGS TO RICHES

Although both of his parents came from impoverished backgrounds, Yacktman's father's life was a modern-day Horatio Alger story. His given name was Ignatz Yacktman, but he often went by the more Americanized "Victor," the male version of Victoria, which was his mother's name. Victor's father immigrated to the United States from Poland. His mom had been a chef for the Waldorf Astoria hotel in New York. In 1909, when Victor was five, his father disappeared, and he and his half-sister were sent to Poland to live with their aunt. Four years later, they returned to New York, and lived with his mom and a man named William Morsdorf, who was "Grandpa" to Don. Yacktman doubts Victor ever had a very close father-son relationship with Morsdorf. "Dad was a hard-charger, and Morsdorf was more laid back and not financially successful," he says.

People used to say Victor looked a lot like former President Dwight D. Eisenhower. Yacktman remembers him as a rather slim man of average height with a balding head, much like his own, who was critical of those around him. "I think all his life he was trying to get acceptance from his mother," Yacktman surmises. "He felt she was very critical, and that bothered him. According to Dad, she used to say, 'No girl would want to have you.' Perhaps that's why he married the first girl who fell for him right out of high school." He started college at the University of Southern California. But before he even had time to learn his way around campus, both of his legs were broken when a car he was cranking went into gear and slammed him against a wall. At about the same time, he found out his wife was pregnant. Since he had to make a living for the family, he went to work selling magazines door-to-door. As Yacktman puts it, "At that time, direct marketing was an honorable profession for a college student." (Victor and his first wife were later divorced.)

In 1930, during a sales trip through Utah, Victor went to the Salt
Air dance hall in Salt Lake City and met the woman who would
become Yacktman's mother. (This marriage, too, ended in divorce.)

Victor always made a decent living in direct sales, but didn't
strike it big until the early 1950s, when he cashed in the money he
had accumulated over the years and began buying real estate. He
learned about this business the hard way. "Following World War II, he
bought an old building in Chicago, which he remodeled. It was an
economic disaster," Yacktman recalls. "The next time around, he purchased 120 acres near Glenview and made a killing on it. He ended
up helping three people develop it. He did all of the financing. The
estate had a home and three horse barns on it. Typical of my dad, he
remodeled the primary barn and turned it into office space. He also
created a water company, which was sold off after he died."

Yacktman's mother, Matilda Mable Chamberlain, was of British
and Swedish extraction. She was born in 1909 on the west side of
Salt Lake City, which has always been the poor part of town. Her
father was an artist, who died when she was nine. She never had
much money. Matilda's mother made a living as a janitor at the
Larkin Mortuary. Til, as Matilda was known, was also good with
numbers, and after going to business college, became a secretary.
After the breakup of her marriage to Victor, she married an engineer
for the Western Pacific Railroad. His father, too, subsequently remar-
ried, and Yacktman has two stepbrothers, a half-brother, and a half-
sister. Because of their age differences, he was never extremely close
to any of them.

Til didn't learn to drive until she was almost 40. "She always
preferred public transportation," Yacktman recalls. "She wound up
buying a duplex in Salt Lake City right next to the bus stop. She
thought it was ideal." Til worked for an optometrist for several
years before becoming an assistant to the executive director of the
Utah Pharmaceutical Association. "She was a very organized, neat,
and tidy person. The first man she worked for at the Association
was the total opposite," Yacktman says. "He was sort of a back-
slapping Irishman. The two were a great pair. He was messy; she
was so organized, and he really appreciated her. He would set up
the pharmaceutical conventions, and she supported him from the
sidelines. She worked there for more than 20 years, until she was
in her seventies."

A Religious Experience

Religion has always been extremely important to Yacktman. He joined the Church of Jesus Christ of Latter-Day Saints at the age of 15. His mother was a Mormon, but she was not active in the church during Yacktman's early years. He was raised Catholic, like his paternal grandparents, and attended Catholic school. Then, after his parents divorced, he got involved with scouting. Since most of his fellow scouts were Mormons, he developed a desire to learn more about the Mormon church. "I started to have certain questions, and as I searched for the answers, I decided that joining the church was the right decision for me," he says. "I'm a very bottom-line oriented person, and look at results. I saw the strong family environment enjoyed by my friends who went to the church. As I began to learn more about the LDS teachings, it all made so much sense. The gospel was logical, and I could relate to the things it taught."

He was also searching for Mormon male role models, which the church provided. "We have a program called 'home teaching,' where a younger man is assigned to an older man, or companion," he explains. "We go out together and visit about four families each month to see how they are doing. The way the church is organized, we have a bishop, and he has two counselors in the ward, which is what the congregation is called. All of them are volunteers. At different times, I had each of the counselors in our ward as my companion. I saw so much dedication among them and their families. I remember going home with one and watching as they knelt in family prayer before dinner. I had never seen that before."

Although divorced, Yacktman's parents were both loving and nurturing, which helped to shape him into the man he is today. "My mother was very caring and protective toward me," he says. "Even though she had her own problems, I always knew where I stood with her and that she loved me a lot. My dad was a very successful entrepreneur. He taught me to have a good work ethic and also cared about me in his own way."

The Mission

After graduating from Highland High School in Salt Lake City, Yacktman spent his freshman year of college at the University of

Utah. He then went on a church mission. (Each male member of the Mormon church is asked to go on a two-year mission once he reaches the age of 19. The young men can be sent anywhere in the world.) Yacktman's assignment was to minister in the southern states, which he jokingly describes as, "The only foreign-language English mission in the United States." Although the mission included Alabama and South Carolina, he spent most of his time in Georgia. "I knew the little towns of Georgia like the back of my hand," he says. "Atlanta was the headquarters, and I spent about six months there as secretary for the mission. I also ended up in places like Augusta and Savannah, along with Brunswick and Marietta." Most missionaries travel around on foot or on bikes, but Yacktman had a car, perhaps because he had so far to travel. In local areas, most of his work was done on foot. He started out going door to door, hoping to find receptive housewives who would listen to the message he and his partner were there to deliver.

"We learned to accept a lot of rejection," Yacktman admits. "In the south, we ran into people who were a little more well-mannered and hospitable than they were in some other areas. Many of them would say things like, 'Ya'll come back now.' We'd go back at the appointed time, and they'd usually listen to what we had to say. In 1960–1962, a lot of women were still working at home. Many times we'd get to talk to the woman during the day, and if she was interested, you'd come back in the evening. But there were times when we'd knock on the door and all of a sudden the lights inside would mysteriously go off. Other times we'd return to find the woman's husband had no interest and wouldn't let us through the front door. It was really like looking for needles in a haystack. The overall percentage of people we got to spend time with wasn't high, so we had to knock on a lot of doors. I would guess that over a two-year period, my companions and I helped bring about 50 people into the church." The mission experience changed the nature and direction of Yacktman's life.

As a boy, Yacktman had spent summers watching his father's entrepreneurial exploits. Although this experience lit the business bug that lurked deep inside, Yacktman's real academic strengths were always in science and math. Not surprisingly, therefore, he originally planned on becoming an electrical or chemical engineer. "The late 1950s were the Sputnik period, when anybody who was good at science or math sort of got pushed into engineering," he remembers. "I didn't like life science that much, but I studied it anyway. I was always intimidated by going to the chemistry lab and having to find out what elements were in the samples we were required to analyze. I got A's, mind you, but it intimidated me."

After returning home from his mission, Yacktman knew he wanted to do something else, something that involved working around other people. "I felt if I went into engineering, I would be more oriented toward working with things rather than people, and I really loved the idea of working with people," he explains. "Before I began college, I had taken this exam, which shows the professions that are best suited for your own personal interests and aptitudes. When I returned from my mission, I looked at it again. To my surprise, I was in the 30 or so percentile for engineering, but in the 90-plus percentile for business. I knew right then I wanted to get an MBA and switched my major to economics. It was as if a light bulb went off in my head once I started taking those business courses. They were really fun and enjoyable."

LOVE CONNECTION

Yacktman remained active with the Latter-Day Saints throughout college, both in Utah and Illinois. It was during a summer trip to Chicago that he was first introduced to his wife, Carolyn, a beautiful girl with short blonde hair, who has been a lifelong Mormon. Her dad was a commercial artist in Chicago, whose best-known project was designing the signature logo for Sunbeam. It's the same one that's used today. "I met her at one of the young-adult meetings," Yacktman recalls. "She was going to the University of Wisconsin and came home for the Labor Day weekend to visit her folks. I thought she was pretty and vibrant and we chatted on the phone. I figured she'd be married by the time I saw her the following year, but she wasn't."

The next summer, Don and Carolyn traveled with a church group to hear the Mormon Tabernacle Choir in Milwaukee. They then went to the church's Palmyra Pageant near Rochester, New York. "Carolyn and I were holding hands at the Sacred Grove in Palmyra," he says. They've been together ever since. "Our first official date was to see *The Unsinkable Molly Brown* movie here in

Chicago," he shares. "I remember we were holding hands coming out of the theater and this guy came along and took our picture. He said, 'You're a nice young married couple.' But it was our first date. We were obviously close at that point. I think we both knew early on we were meant for each other."

Don and Carolyn married the year he graduated from the University of Utah, in 1965. He went straight to the Harvard Business School for his MBA. Carolyn was working as a medical technologist and took a job at the Veteran's Hospital in Boston. Today, in addition to being a full-time and very busy mom, she's an artist who specializes in making porcelain dolls. Like many Mormons, Don and Carolyn have a large family, with seven children, five boys and two girls (and so far three grandchildren). Their oldest, Donald, 31, is in the software-development field and lives in Utah. He created the Internet site for Yacktman Asset Management. Next is Stephen, 28, who is a portfolio manager for his dad's firm. Daughter Jennifer, 25, is an elementary school teacher in Indianapolis; his fourth child Melissa, 21, is a student at Brigham Young University studying performing arts. Nineteen-year-old Brian also attends BYU and interns at the investment firm during summer breaks. The two youngest children, Robert, 17, and Michael, 11, still live at home. "Mormons are encouraged to have large families because they're great blessings," Yacktman says. "I have to tell you, after being an only child, it's been an interesting yet wonderful experience. My wife is great at handling the home front, although it's a challenge. Our life definitely revolves around our children. I don't spend a lot of time at the office on weekends. Instead, I see a lot of Little League games, school plays, and things that involve our kids."

So far, Yacktman's been able to convince only one of his kids to join his firm. But he wouldn't want it any other way. He has never pressured any of them to enter the investment field. "Carolyn and I told all of our children to look into the mirror, choose what they wanted to be, and then be the best at it," he says. "The first four have all gone in different directions."

Son Stephen remembers buying his first stock on a momentous day: Monday, October 19, 1987. The previous Friday, the market sank some 200 points. He asked his father to run out and buy some shares of Sears. "I called Monday afternoon to see if he had done it, and dad told me he had some good news and some bad news,"

Stephen recalls. "He said the good news is you didn't pay $40 for the stock, which is where it opened in the morning. You got it for $36. The bad news is Sears ended the day at $32." Stephen earned his undergraduate degree in economics at Brigham Young in just two years, after testing out of many general education courses by taking a series of advanced-placement tests in high school. He also has an MBA from BYU. At first, he planned to get into investment banking, but after a bit of prodding, decided to join his father's firm instead.

COLLEGE AND THE FIRST INVESTING EXPERIENCE

Before going to Harvard, Don Yacktman earned his undergraduate degree in economics at the University of Utah and was a senior-class officer as well as commencement speaker. His first investment in stocks took place a couple of years earlier, in 1963. "After my mission, I stopped in Chicago on my way back to Salt Lake and found my dad had started investing in stocks," he says. "I thought it was fascinating. Dad subscribed to *Wright Investor's Service,* which consisted of little green sheet reports on different companies. It was very statistically oriented, detailing things like PE ratios and whatnot. To be honest, I can't remember the first company I bought, but it was probably Fram Filters. When I returned to Salt Lake City, I went down to the local Merrill Lynch office and met a nice stockbroker. He was very typical. He tried to get me to buy the hot stocks of that time."

Although Yacktman had his own ideas, he spent a lot of time talking with the broker and listening to what he recommended. "Then I discovered this company called Community Discount, which rented space in my dad's shopping center," he says. "It was a discount store, and its stock was real cheap, like $1 or $2 a share. The company was just barely profitable, but after watching it for awhile, I bought and sold it a few times and made some nice trades. From there, I did a lot of experimenting with charting and various other technical indicators. I eventually took an investment class during my senior year of college. The professor's name was William F. Edwards. He worked in the trust department at First Security Bank and was a value-oriented investor. He asked us to do a report on a single stock as our research project. I chose General Tire. I remember some of my classmates were doing Zenith, which was the trendy name of that time."

While Yacktman had an ongoing fascination with the stock market, it wasn't until his senior year in college that he realized he wanted to spend his entire career on Wall Street. "I went through this period, as most people do, when I thought about life and doing things for society," he reflects. "The perception of those around me was that investing in stocks didn't really create anything useful for society. I disagree. An investment adviser is entrusted with people's savings and can provide them with an opportunity to earn a fair return, thus preparing them for the future."

Although investment management is among the most highly paid professions in the world, money was of little concern to Yacktman when he started out. "Part of what intrigues me about this business is that we're constantly learning about new opportunities," he says. "I think I'd be bored if I worked for just one company and had to learn how to efficiently make a single product. In a way, I think of myself as a consultant to the companies I invest in. I talk with them about strategic issues. A few months ago, I was chatting with the president of Department 56 (one of his largest holdings as this book was being written). It's fun to look at the display she left us in the conference room. It helps me to understand the concept of how and why the company makes so much money. I'm continually being challenged and learning new things. When I go into a store and see an exciting new product, I'll turn it over to find out who makes it. This passion for investing is like fire in the belly. Either you have it or you don't. I also say there are three essential ingredients one must have to be a success in this industry. I call them the three I's: Integrity, Intelligence, and Intensity. A person either does or does not have them."

Does he think most people in the investment field have the three I's? "In a majority of cases, yes, at least in the investment advisory field," he replies. "I think integrity is of foremost importance, because people are trusting us with their money. There are few things people have a higher regard for in this life than their money. People must trust their investment manager. It's not always easy to figure out if your manager has integrity. Even if you spend time with him or her, you can occasionally be snowed. Going back to the three I's, a wise person once said if someone doesn't have the first one (integrity), but has the other two (intelligence and intensity), regardless of the profession, that person can do enormous damage. The problem I see in the investment business is there's too much superficiality out there. A lot of people have this casino mentality. Instead of viewing what they own as little pieces of businesses, they view the stock market as a series of trends. They rely on chart patterns or are driven by momentum, instead of looking at the underlying companies."

OFF TO HARVARD

During his first year at Harvard, Yacktman decided to get a summer job in the investment field so he'd have something to put on his resumé. Not knowing whom to contact, he went down the list of investment advisers in the Boston Yellow Pages. "I didn't hit pay dirt, to say the least," he says. "Then I found a posting on the bulletin board from the Keystone Funds. I got a job there as an analyst. My partner and I were assigned to cover uranium. We made a lot of money for the firm with a company called Utah Construction and Mining, which was bought by General Electric several years later. It was a big miner of uranium. We studied the whole business at a time when utilities were just starting to build nuclear plants. Nobody on Wall Street was following this area. I guess we were ahead of our time." This job allowed Yacktman to get through the doors of some major brokerage firms and companies. "We talked with many analysts and corporate executives," he says. "I got to meet a lot of people."

Students at the Harvard Business School are placed into various sections of around 100 students each. Early on, they begin to form study groups of about six people so they can bond and work together on various projects. "This fellow named Dan Barr was watching everybody, and on about the third day of class, he put together a study group, which he asked me to join," Yacktman recalls. "I accepted. About a month later, Dan's father died and he flew home to Seattle to help run the family business of selling yachts. Of the six people left behind, five of us were Baker scholars or had graduated with distinction. All went on to be very successful. One was Joe Kasputys, who is now the CEO of Primark, a database management company. Another was Jack Gabarro, who became a professor at the Harvard Business School."

LIFE AFTER HARVARD

After graduation, Yacktman took a small detour. "My dad was an entrepreneur, and I always thought it would be neat to use my education to work with him," he says. "But I really liked investing. Since my dad and Carolyn's folks both lived in Chicago, I decided to get a job there. I interviewed at several places during my senior year at Harvard. I had a couple of offers in Boston, with Putnam and Keystone. Stein Roe & Farnham in Chicago also wanted me. I was more impressed with the top people at Continental Illinois Bank, however, and ended up taking a job in the commercial-lending department. I wanted to be in the trust department, but my colleagues at the bank advised me against it. They told me it was like the bank's stepchild. I was never happy in commercial lending. I think part of it was the training program, which was very slow and boring. I was eager to do something. It got so bad, I almost moved back to Boston to work for Keystone. Instead, I went to Stein Roe and asked if they still wanted me. They did, and I started there in May 1968."

THE STEIN ROE YEARS

Yacktman was frustrated with his job at Stein Roe early on because the firm would either let you be a research analyst or a portfolio manager, not both. "As a result, their portfolio managers didn't have research backgrounds," he laments. "They also tended to be very sales-driven on the portfolio management side. We were encouraged to sell the Stein Roe approach and bring in new accounts. I was hired to be on the portfolio management side. Unfortunately, I felt like a fish out of water. Their investment style was very momentum-driven. In addition, we were expected to focus solely on portfolio management, and I was very research oriented. It was tough because I enjoyed the research, yet I didn't want to be an analyst all my life, which is how I thought it would be if I joined the research department."

Yacktman immediately began managing money for some private accounts under the direction of one of the firm's partners. "We would work with a senior partner at first, and they would gradually transfer new accounts over to us," he explains. "Initially, we would put together a recommended portfolio based on the stock-rating committee's approved buy list." Eventually, Yacktman became a partner at the firm and was named a member of that committee. "The analysts would come in and present their recommendations to us," he shares. "We would then make a decision one way or another as to whether the stock would be approved as a buy, hold, or sale on our recommended list. Everything at Stein Roe was done by committee. I think this was the firm's way of protecting people. It was a very political organization."

In Stein Roe's early days, managers used research-based techniques for picking growth stocks. Unfortunately, by the time Yacktman got there, the top people making these investment decisions were moving on. "For a long time, Stein Roe was a very stable partnership," he notes. "About the time I came aboard, it became a revolving door. People were leaving left and right during the 14 years I was there. The partner who ran the firm in the 1970s was very momentum-oriented. I was more analytical. By 1980, the firm began picking stocks using computer-based models. I referred to it as 'the Bonsai Pipeline.' It was very similar to the system used by William O'Neil (founder of *Investor's Business Daily*), *Value Line*, and what was then known as Twentieth Century mutual funds (now American Century). It was a system that focused strictly on changes in earnings and price changes. It looks good on paper, but I always found myself saying, 'Here's a great company that's been beaten down in price.' Of course, it wouldn't show up on the momentum screens. It was on the opposite end of the spectrum. But that's what attracted me to it. I remember buying Bandag stock for some clients because it was a good company selling at a depressed price. It promptly went down another 10 percent. At that time, the company had diversified a little too much and had a number of short-term problems to work through, but it was cheap and I wanted to add to my position. To my dismay, the stock committee pulled it off the approved list. I had no choice but to sell it. This was a great business that was slightly down in price, and they pulled it off the list. It frustrated the daylights out of me. As it turned out, the stock went up more than 1,000 percent after that."

So how did this man who espoused value and abhorred momentum survive at Stein Roe for so long? "That's an interesting question," Yacktman admits. "I think part of it was I simply enjoyed the business. The firm had a lot of young guys who were my age and I liked their company and companionship. But there was certainly a lot of friction. I'm a pretty autonomous guy, and we didn't have much freedom in making investment decisions. When they offered me a partnership and more responsibility, I felt better for awhile. As luck had it, they gave it to me after I had been there for about six years, right after the market tanked in 1974."

A CALL FOR CHANGE

The day Yacktman's dad died, October 27, 1981, he was supposed to have lunch with Bill Goldstein, who helped to manage a small brokerage firm in Chicago. "Bill and his firm wanted to start up an investment advisory subsidiary called Vincent Chesley Advisors. He asked me to head the operation," Yacktman says. "Bill was my personal broker, so he understood how I made investment decisions. We went out to lunch frequently and knew each other quite well. He really wanted me for the position. I questioned whether I was the right guy. I guess I didn't have a lot of self-confidence at that point because of my frustration with Stein Roe. I wasn't sure I could sell myself to potential clients. I later realized I couldn't sell Stein Roe because I didn't believe in their investment strategy. About this time, the partnership at Stein Roe was kind of tired of me, too, and I knew they wouldn't be upset to see me leave. So I resigned and joined Bill and his firm on April 1, 1982."

That summer, Vincent Chesley Advisors hit the jackpot. Ferris Chesley, one of the firm's principals, had an assistant whose husband managed the Selected Special fund. The Selected funds were run by a subsidiary of Lincoln National and had been around since 1933. In 1968, they were sold to the International House of Pancakes, during which time they floundered in mediocrity. "The funds had become true orphans because the people in charge had all since left the company," Yacktman explains. "In the ten years that Lincoln National ran Selected American, assets went from $210 million down to $76 million by the end of 1982." The fund had eight outside and two inside directors, who had privately reached an agreement that it was time to change the fund's investment adviser. They interviewed three potential candidates, including Vincent Chesley, Stein Roe, and Kemper Financial. "One major advantage we had over the competition was that these funds were very big for us. They were small potatoes to the others," Yacktman surmises. "We were also willing to compensate the former manager by purchasing some computer equipment and software from them. The bottom line is we were selected to manage the funds the day the market bottomed, Friday, August 13, 1982. We officially started running them on January 1, 1983."

Bill Goldstein, Yacktman's boss, took over Selected Special, a small-cap fund, and gave Yacktman Selected American to run. "He said it was made for me," Yacktman recalls. "It was clearly my style. At the time, it was a balanced fund. I didn't like that aspect of it, but I loved the idea of managing my own fund. It was what I really wanted to do. When I left Stein Roe, I felt it was an opportunity for me to prove myself. Either I had it in me to manage money on my own, or I didn't. My salary had always been secondary. Actually, I took a pay cut when I left Stein Roe, but the opportunity was there. I didn't realize how big the opportunity would turn out to be."

LIFE AT SELECTED AMERICAN

Six months after taking over Selected American, Yacktman convinced the board of directors that balanced funds were a thing of the past. "I really felt it was a cafeteria-style investment environment," he says. "People wanted either an equity or a fixed-income fund, and I didn't like bonds to begin with. The directors bought my argument. I guess they figured they had nothing to lose. I mean, this fund was in the bottom decile of performance at the time and assets had run down to almost nothing. At my first directors' meeting, I remember walking in, and I'm sure their mouths were agape, because I told them my ten-year goal was to get the fund up to $1 billion in assets. They had seen it go from around $200 million to

$76 million, so I imagine they thought I was crazy. They probably hoped I would just keep it stable, and if we got an increase, that would be great. I didn't quite get it up to $1 billion, but I didn't exactly make the ten years either."

After switching from a balanced fund to a stock fund, Selected American shot the lights out, in terms of relative performance, rising 14.9 percent in 1984, compared to a gain of 6.3 percent for the S&P 500 and a *loss* of 2.1 percent for the general equity fund index. "One day, I got a call from a researcher in Pennsylvania," Yacktman says. "He was at a university and said, 'I want to understand your investment style.' I thought it was incredible that we were already being noticed for our great performance, because I told the directors once we developed a record, and people saw we were making money for the right reasons, the money would follow. As I started to tell this guy about my process, he interrupted. 'No,' he shouted, 'the reason I'm calling is because you're in the bottom 10 percent of all funds over the past decade, and I want to know the difference between those that are in the top 10 percent and those that are in the bottom.' I explained that the fund had been run by someone else for most of that time, but it really discouraged me to hear him say that. I thought he wanted to praise the work we were doing. Instead, he was oblivious to it."

Nevertheless, Yacktman did turn Selected American into an equity fund just as the market was taking off, and his performance sparkled. The following year, as the market cooled down, the fund remained hot. "My style and philosophy have always been to get the highest return consistent with taking a minimal amount of risk," he says. "The next year, our fund was up and the market was down. We really began to show up on a lot of radar screens, so to speak, because it was clear we had something good. This performance got the ball rolling, in terms of attracting new assets into the fund."

SELECTED PASSES ON

As Selected American was being converted from a dog to a shining star, Vincent Chesley got a deal it couldn't pass up. "Kemper Financial, through its 80-percent-owned subsidiary Prescott Ball and Turben, wanted to buy the firm out for three times book value at the beginning of 1984," Yacktman says. "The owners were at a point in their lives where they were willing to sell and did. I found out later that Prescott never really wanted the money management business. They were more interested in the brokerage operation. But they kept us anyway, and the president of Prescott gave me a bonus to stay on."

The new firm had offices in Chicago, New York, Cleveland, and Sarasota. "It was like ships passing in the night," Yacktman says of the situation. "We'd be on conference calls with each other twice a week. They put together this group of money managers who were totally disparate and independent. At least I still had autonomy and could do what I wanted. They left me alone and let me build a business as long as I was bringing in assets. A few years later, one of the firm's principals, Ron Ball, was assigned to manage the Selected Special fund. Before that, Ball was with Bank One and Central National Bank of Cleveland. His investment philosophy was similar to Yacktman's and the two became close friends and confidants.

In the mid-1980s, Kemper decided to add a 12b-1 marketing fee to the Selected funds, so brokers could get an ongoing commission for recommending them to clients. Before, the funds had been pure no-loads. "Prescott was trying to figure out a way to attract more assets," Yacktman says. "About that time, I was unhappy because I felt I was being undercompensated for what I had done. After all, Selected American was performing well and bringing in a lot of money. So I approached John Goldsmith, who was the head of Prescott Ball and Turben. We solved things in about five minutes. He agreed to give me a percentage of the revenue from the fund management fees. I was happy; he was happy. The agreement was truly a win-win deal and lasted until I eventually left. As far as I was concerned, life was wonderful. I was managing a top-performing fund, making money for the company, and earning a nice income for myself.

"In 1990, Kemper decided to join all of the brokerage firms it owned and put them under one umbrella called Kemper Securities. Kemper also bought out what it didn't own of Prescott Ball and Turben. The company then decided that since my division was in the money management business, it didn't belong with the brokerage operation. So, it was moved back underneath the Kemper Financial subsidiary on July 1, 1991. My new boss was like a loose cannon on the deck in dealing with the Selected board. It was like being at Stein Roe only worse. The people I had worked with at Prescott and I were totally frustrated. I told Kemper I needed two things in order to stay: autonomy and the same compensation plan that was in place prior to the reorganization."

They didn't see things that way and what's more wanted to decrease Yacktman's compensation. "In essence, they said, 'We love what you're doing so much we want to reduce your autonomy and lower your pay.' The bureaucracy was awful," he claims. "While I was on vacation, they moved into this new 24,000-square-foot building across the river. I walked in when I got back and thought it was a joke." Ironically, just a few years earlier, he had watched a new building being erected down the street at 303 West Madison, which he wasn't very impressed with. "I kept thinking how ugly it looked because of the turquoise high up on top," he says. "I didn't like it at all." Little did he know he would one day call that building home.

GETTING THE NUDGE . . . AGAIN

Once more, Yacktman's history of getting nudged when a firm tired of him remained intact. "Kemper essentially wanted to stall my compensation plan, and I said no," he says. "My boss refused to negotiate. In fact, he guaranteed me I would earn less in 1992 than I did the previous year. At that point, I decided I had to go. In March 1992, they hired a new fellow to be the chief investment officer. I guess they figured if I left, they'd have someone to run the fund. They handed me an agreement to sign, which basically called for me to step aside and be co-portfolio manager in name only for about six months. After that, I would manage only private accounts. Basically, they were trying to find a way to get rid of me in a legal way so I wouldn't sue them. The agreement also called for me to keep everything that was happening confidential. Imagine that. I was supposed to be the portfolio manager of Selected American in name only and keep it a secret. I knew I couldn't sign that agreement. I asked if the board of directors knew what was going on, and my superior said, 'No they don't. I'm the one running the funds.' I knew he would be in for a rude awakening."

Preparing for the Worst

It had been clear to Yacktman that trouble was on the horizon for him at the firm for some time. As a precautionary step, in July 1991 he created Yacktman Asset Management, so he'd at least have the shell of a new company ready in case his worst fears came true. He also had written a rough draft of his form ADV (the document one must file with the Securities and Exchange Commission in order to start an investment advisory firm). "I knew if something happened, I wanted to be in a position to land back on my feet quickly," he says. "My first hope was that things would work out with Kemper, because I had nine years of my life tied up with Selected American. That fund was my baby."

Deep in his heart, however, Yacktman knew his career at Kemper was over. Ironically, this was at the same time he was rapidly turning into a star manager. In early 1992, fund-rating service Morningstar crowned him "Fund Manager of the Year for 1991." But there was nothing that could be done to salvage his career at Kemper. He resigned his post and teamed up with former colleagues Ron Ball and Jon Carlson to get Yacktman Asset Management up and running. "My idea was to set up an investment advisory firm that had a minimal amount of work done in-house," he shares. "In other words, I wanted to farm out a lot of the administrative work. Jon and I had already put plans in motion for starting the Yacktman Fund because we didn't want to be out of business very long. When I resigned from Kemper, I laid out my plans to the Selected board of directors. I think they wanted me to continue managing the fund, but they were afraid I didn't have the support staff in place to do all of the necessary back-office paperwork. If I had gone to work for another established firm, and simply stayed on as the fund's subadviser, I feel they would have accepted that arrangement. At one point, they even asked if I would be willing to work with Shelby Davis (who later took over full management of the Selected funds)."

The Selected board questioned whether Yacktman would halt plans to start his own fund if they retained him as an adviser to Selected American. He agreed. In the midst of this turmoil, they sent out a letter to shareholders stating that Yacktman was still president of the fund. In the end, however, the board decided not to go with him. "As much as I wanted to run Selected American, it was clear that the best thing to do was press forward on my own," he says. "So we put the process in high gear, and the Yacktman Fund was ultimately launched on July 6, 1992."

THE YACKTMAN FUND

Within days of Yacktman's departure from Selected American, some $200 million poured out of the fund. A year later, Kemper lost the Selected management contract to Shelby Davis. Before the contract was awarded to Davis, Yacktman also talked to the chairman of the board again about getting it, but they weren't interested, essentially for many of the same reasons as before. "I think part of it was the board of directors had this vision of Selected becoming a large family of funds, but it never really worked out," Yacktman surmises. "I believe they wanted to be more like a Kemper, Fidelity, or Vanguard. In other words, they wanted a whole series of offerings. Before the brokers were merged into Kemper Securities, Selected had a money market fund with more than $1 billion in assets. When Kemper combined its brokerage operations, it insisted that brokers put their free cash in Kemper money market funds, which virtually wiped out the Selected offering. I'm convinced that, in the end, things worked out for the best. I have my own fund and a great board of directors. Several of the directors at Selected didn't even have any of their own money in the funds. I remember some criticism years ago about this. After that happened, one of the directors decided to put some money in right before the proxy statement went out so it would get listed and make him look good. The next day, he sold all of his shares. The proxy showed that he had a position, but he really didn't. I thought that was very deceiving."

A QUICK START-UP

Right after leaving Kemper, Yacktman struck a deal with the son of one of his clients who ran a small Chicago investment advisory firm. The man let Yacktman temporarily come on as an employee until Yacktman Asset Management was approved by the SEC. This allowed him to immediately get back into business. "Within a couple of days,

I had office space and was a registered adviser, thanks to these great people," he says. "I called every client I had within 24 hours of leaving Kemper. All of them brought their accounts to me. My son Stephen and one of his classmates came down to help set up a computer system for my accounts. It was kind of embarrassing because we were taking over this little office. I felt so guilty. Jon Carlson and our marketing director Diane Kotil were working out of the basement of his home. Once Yacktman Asset Management was approved by the SEC about a month later, Ron came with me. The first building we were shown was at 303 West Madison, that same one I thought was so ugly. Well, that's where we wound up. Incidentally, I was wrong about the building. It's really very nice."

A TRAILBLAZER

Yacktman's departure from Kemper was a momentous event in the mutual fund world. It marked the first time a high-profile fund manager had left a large conglomerate and successfully started his own fund from scratch. It was a groundbreaking move that would pave the way for many more entrepreneurial managers in the years to come, including Elizabeth Bramwell. Not that others hadn't tried it before. They had. But most resigned their previous jobs with little fanfare. Some quickly failed, since the economies of scale in the industry are such that a fund must have a significant amount of assets to justify the high cost of running the operation. Others stayed afloat, but didn't attract enough money to receive much public attention.

Because Yacktman was charting new territory, he had a ton of homework to do, especially since he didn't have much time to get his business set up in the first place. "Before, I had only dreamed about having my own fund," he reveals. "It was nothing serious though. I remember the first time I thought about it was in July of 1991, right after my boss at Kemper had first proposed a salary-reduction plan. My son Stephen was working at Quaker Oats in Barrington, Illinois, that summer, and we went to Brian's ball game together. I remember telling him that night, 'I wonder what it would be like to have the name Yacktman down at the bottom of the list of mutual funds in the paper.'"

Yacktman's decision to start his own fund, by his own admission, was predicated by a combination of determination and stubbornness. "I just really felt I had been wronged by Kemper," he shares. "Yes, I wanted to run Selected American. But if that wasn't an option, the next best thing was to use the other name most people associated with that fund, which was Yacktman. It really wasn't an ego trip. Calling it the Yacktman Fund, instead of something else, was just an inexpensive, value-added marketing idea."

THE SUCCESS OF SUNSTONE

Unfortunately, there is more to running a fund than simply picking good stocks. You have a lot of administrative details to tend to, like keeping track of each shareholder's account, fulfilling requests for prospectuses, answering the phones, and mailing out annual reports. It's very time-consuming and cumbersome work that can easily distract from the most important goal of each fund manager—making money for his or her shareholders. Remember, one reason the Selected board decided against hiring Yacktman's new firm to continue management of the funds was because they feared he wasn't equipped to handle the enormous administrative paperwork mandated by law. Truth be told, he wasn't. He certainly couldn't do all this work himself, and he didn't have a large enough staff to handle these details either. So he farmed out all of the administrative duties to a Milwaukee company called Sunstone Financial Group and employed Firstar to act as the fund's custodian and transfer agent. "I really wanted to see how small we could keep the operation," Yacktman says. "At first, I didn't even know these things could be farmed out. I was delighted to find they could."

You might say Yacktman was instrumental in Sunstone's enormous success. The company was started by Miriam Allison, who had previously worked for Firstar. She, like Yacktman, had a vision that as more independent managers and smaller investment boutiques got into the fund business, they would want to outsource as many administrative functions as they possibly could, in order to save both time and money. With her former employer's blessing, Allison founded Sunstone in 1991 with just nine employees. Today, the company has grown to a staff of more than 150 and is the primary source smaller fund families turn to for taking care of the many tedious yet necessary aspects of running a fund.

ON HIS OWN

While launching his own fund was both a costly and risky move for Yacktman, especially since he was a rising star in the industry and could easily have gone to work for another established firm, he decided the chance to be out there on his own was worth it. "I had enough money saved up by that time that I really didn't have any particular financial risk," he says. "When my dad died, I got very little. It was all basically passed on to my stepmother. I had earned my money by saving and investing over the years. I built up enough of an estate that I felt, financially at least, that there was very little risk things would go wrong."

Once the Yacktman Fund was up and running, the major challenge was attracting assets. While Selected American had wooed the brokerage community and tried to reach out to the general public, Yacktman realized early on there was another source that not only had plenty of money, but also was loyal and didn't do a lot of switching around. "When I was managing Selected American, I put together a 15-page report for the board of directors outlining what I saw as a different way to market the fund," he says. "The Kemper people wanted to do it with ads. I suggested that we go out and target independent investment advisers. They resisted this idea. But when I went out on my own, it was a natural fit."

A NEW DISTRIBUTION CHANNEL

Then Yacktman learned about Charles Schwab's OneSource mutual fund program, which was still in its infancy. Schwab had created a distribution channel that allowed both financial advisers and individual investors alike to set up one account in which they could buy or sell no-load funds from numerous different families, in some cases without paying any transaction fees. Instead, Schwab charged participating funds a distribution fee of 25 cents to 35 cents for every $100 that was brought in. Funds that didn't want to pay this fee could still be purchased at Schwab, but shareholders would be charged a small commission for the trade, to compensate Schwab for its trouble. Although many fund families were reluctant to sign on at first, Yacktman saw it as a great opportunity for gaining instant national distribution. He also knew that instead of keeping accounts with a dozen or more different fund companies, the independent adviser community would surely embrace OneSource, since it made monitoring client portfolios a breeze. OneSource has since become a huge success, and most of Schwab's competitors now have similar fund supermarkets of their own.

"Schwab started the network in June 1992, right before I was up and running. I wanted to be part of OneSource, but Schwab decided to let only a handful of funds in at first. I started too late," Yacktman recalls. "So in the beginning, advisers had to pay a fee to buy my fund. A year later, they let me join the no-transaction-fee group. From the very start, I made a conscious effort to target the investment adviser community, not individuals. I do zero advertising. My investment philosophy is more sophisticated than the message you can get across in a 30-second ad. I like investment advisers because they are great about educating people on what I do and why. They are, in effect, like a sales force. They go out and tell their clients how Yacktman manages money, and they explain my process. I never wanted people to buy my fund simply because of a performance number touted in an ad."

Furthermore, Yacktman saw the growing popularity and reliance on the Morningstar ratings system as another step toward educating both professional and novice investors about how important individual managers were to the overall performance of a fund. "Morningstar elevated the idea that it's the manager who's running the fund, not the firm, that is important to getting good results," he says. "Kemper didn't buy that. What's funny is the press did all of these articles about me during 1991, when Selected American was having a great run and was up 46.3 percent for the year. It was wonderful for business the following year. I don't think Kemper liked to see me get all this attention because they knew it would be even more difficult for them once I left."

By the time Yacktman departed Kemper, he and marketing director Jon Carlson had developed a strong mailing list of investment advisers, and they immediately began to target them. "We knew where many of the significant advisers and bank trust departments that used mutual funds were," Yacktman says. "We had been gradually building up a database for some time. I had no idea at first that you could go into a place like Kalamazoo, Michigan, or Indianapolis, Indiana, and find people managing $50 or $100 million through mutual funds. The significance and influence of the small adviser was an eye-opener for me." Today Yacktman gets close to 60 percent of his money through Schwab's OneSource program. He's also part of every other discount broker's no-transaction-fee supermarket. "It's a big check we write out every month to participate," he admits. "But it's a great partnership and well worth it." In addition, 80 percent of his shareholder accounts are managed by professional financial advisers.

OFF TO A BAD START

Since it seemed Yacktman could do no wrong in 1991, everyone had high expectations when he went out on his own. Many, including the media, were sorely disappointed. The Yacktman Fund fell 6.6 percent during its first full year, compared to a gain of 10 percent for the Standard & Poor's 500 and 13.8 percent for the average growth fund. All of a sudden, the same reporters who were praising Yacktman's stock-picking prowess months earlier were writing headlines such as, "What Happened to Don Yacktman?" A $10,000 investment in the Yacktman Fund on the day it was launched was worth only $9,783 on December 31, 1993. By comparison, that same $10,000 invested in the S&P 500 would have grown to $11,756. In his 1993 annual report, Yacktman wrote, "Even though the fund suffered short-term pain earlier in the year as the market prices of several great businesses we own fell to very low levels, we clearly now see the beginning of long-term gains. Many of our earlier investments are now showing gains as investors are starting to realize how valuable these businesses are."

In retrospect, Yacktman blames the lousy performance on Wall Street's delay in recognizing the value of the beaten-down drug and consumer stocks that accounted for roughly half of his portfolio. "It was typical of my style—short-term pain for long-term gain," he insists. "I go through the same thing every time the market shoots straight up. In that kind of environment, I tend to lag badly." That's easy to say now, but this was a man who had just gone out on his own and was desperately trying to attract assets. Since investors, especially novice ones, tend to follow performance, it makes sense few would want to buy a fund that showed up at the bottom of the rankings. That's exactly where the Yacktman Fund found itself during its rookie year of operation. "Honestly, we did answer the phone a lot in 1993 fielding questions from people who were worried," he now admits. "But I truly felt my investors were more sophisticated and understood that this bad period was just part of my process. My only real fear in 1993 was that people who put their money in during 1992 would take it out at a loss. I didn't want this to happen, because I knew my performance would come back. The process I follow is logical and sensible. It's a low-risk approach to making money, but it requires patience. As it turned out, more money came in than went out. I'm sure there were people who redeemed their shares when the fund was down. That decision made me feel bad because I don't like to disappoint anyone." Those who stuck with Yacktman had watermelon smiles the following year. In 1994, the Yacktman Fund rose 8.8 percent, compared to a loss of 1.7 percent for its peers.

The number of shareholders in the Yacktman Fund now stands at around 40,000. What's it like knowing that the financial futures of all those people are riding on your back? "I think about it a lot," Yacktman says. "I feel good, though, because I'm convinced my investment process allows people to sleep well at night." Interestingly, even though Yacktman never achieved his goal of attracting $1 billion in assets at Selected American, he did it with the Yacktman Fund in less than five years. "I called and left a message with the Selected board chairman the day it hit the $1 billion mark to let him know I made it," he exclaims, like a child who has just won a prized contest. "It's not often you reach a 14-year goal like this, and the chairman had been hearing me talk about it for several years."

The assets in both of Yacktman's funds were much larger before he had a bitter falling-out with marketing director Jon Carlson. Carlson was also one of the independent directors for Yacktman's funds. After Yacktman fired Carlson in June 1998, Carlson and three other fund directors staged a high-profile proxy battle to remove Yacktman as manager of the funds. This dispute grabbed headlines in the financial media and caused several prominent shareholders to pull their money out until the dust settled. In the end, Yacktman was triumphant and his funds now have a new board of directors.

EQUITIES FOR EVERYONE

Without question, Yacktman is a big believer in equity investing, regardless of one's age. In fact, he has a 90-year-old client who has some 90 percent of her portfolio in stocks, the value of which is more than ten times her cost. "She has a great lifestyle directly as a result of investing that way," he says proudly. "I would never buy bonds. They just don't provide a high enough return for the level of risk you take. Besides, the bond contract is very slanted in favor of the creditors. If you look at probabilities over any short period of time, one, three, five, or even ten years, there's a 70 percent chance equities will outperform bonds or cash. Over a 20-year period, that number jumps to 100 percent. We have a very long-term approach to investing. I believe that over a decade, some of the investments I make will grow five to ten times what I paid for them. That's the kind of goal I have. Given that, why would I want to be in bonds? I believe common stocks will continue to outperform bonds. Thus, I want to be an owner of a business, not a creditor (bond holder), particularly when business investments (common stocks) are available at attractive prices. I believe the main issues are what stocks to buy and what price to pay, not whether investors should own stocks."

Yacktman sums up his philosophy on asset allocation (deciding how much of one's investment dollars to put in various instruments) like this: "Pay off all of your debts first, including your credit cards and mortgage," he suggests. "That will put you on a solid foundation, because they can't take your house away. Then gradually put the rest of your money in stocks. This way you'll be an owner, not a creditor, in life. That's not to say you shouldn't own stocks if you have a mortgage. You should. All of your tax-sheltered profit sharing, 401(k), IRA, and other investment accounts should still be in stocks. After-tax savings dollars can also be put into stocks if you do it conservatively and are able to understand and accept the risks.

The important thing to remember is that if you've already paid off your home, your overall risk is less.

"The two questions one must ask when it comes to purchasing equities are, 'What do I buy?' and 'What do I pay for it?'" Yacktman continues. "It's not a matter of *if* you ought to own stocks. It's only when you buy the wrong stocks or pay the wrong price that you can have bad results." Yacktman eats his own cooking. He doesn't have a mortgage, and his entire portfolio is invested in the stock market. "I think the idea that all older people should keep some of their money in bonds is malarkey," he contends. "The key variable is the annual cash needs of the investor, not his or her age. Likewise, if someone just throws money into an index fund when the market is high, I think that person is taking an inordinately high level of risk. However, this is much different than looking at individual stocks and buying them at low prices. The alternative would be to invest in a lower-volatility mutual fund. The bottom line is that investing should be a logical process."

A Triangular Approach

When it came time to design a logo for his investment firm, Yacktman opted to go with a triangle with three layers, which represent the three essential elements he looks for in each company he buys: a good business, shareholder-oriented management, and a low purchase price.

Later in life, Yacktman discovered that his mother also had a talent for using these value techniques. "My mom was frugal in a funny way," he reveals. "After she died in May 1988, we went through some of her things and found $1,000 worth of clothing that still had tags on them. The prices had been crossed out about three times on each one. We discovered she was buying them for like 25 cents on the dollar. I try to apply the exact same principle when buying stocks."

Understanding Capitalizations

Wall Street's fixation on the market capitalizations of stocks during the 1990s is something that has Yacktman concerned. In essence, some traders have been buying companies based solely on their market capitalizations (the number of shares outstanding multiplied by the current market price) instead of their underlying fundamentals. The last decade has seen the creation of micro-cap, small-cap, mid-cap, and large-cap funds, all of which buy stocks, not merely on their merits, but also on their market capitalizations. For example, a stock with a capitalization of less than $500 million might be considered a small-cap, while one with a capitalization of $5 billion or more is often classified as a large-cap.

"Investors in funds like this are more concerned about the size than the value of a company, which makes no sense," Yacktman maintains. "Some say small-caps earn higher returns than large-caps over time. I would argue there's not a lot of logic to that argument. Here's why: If a stock goes from being a large-cap to a small-cap because the price drops, investors will say it was a large-cap laggard. However, when the company gets its act together and the price bounces back, it will then be viewed as an outperforming small-cap as it once again becomes a large-cap stock. I think investing by buying value rather than size makes much more sense."

NOT SELLING OUT

As this book went to press, one of Yacktman's top holdings was United Asset Management, a conglomerate of 49 money-management firms around the world. UAM is famous for buying up small boutique investment firms, such as Yacktman Asset Management, allowing them to maintain their independence and giving them marketing incentives. Yacktman admits UAM has talked with him about selling out, but maintains he's not interested. "I wouldn't consider it for two reasons," he shares. "One is the autonomy issue. Even though UAM's current management does give each firm a great deal of independence, who's to say that won't change in the future? I've been through that before with my previous employers. The second thing is I've already got the next generation in place here. One of the reasons people are willing to sell out is to capture all of the value they've created for their estate over the years. In my life, money is not nearly as important as autonomy. I think the same will be true for my son Stephen and everyone else who's here. If I were going to drop out of the business and had no children who were going to come work here, selling out would be a wonderful way for me to capture all of the value I've put together throughout my life. But that's not my situation."

HAVING FUN

Away from the office, Yacktman enjoys taking a rare spin on his 17-foot powerboat and remains active in the Mormon Church. "I have a great assignment now," he says enthusiastically. "I was a bishop for five years and have served on what's known as the high council since 1985. Now I'm what's called a young men's president. My responsibility is to oversee the young men's program, which is for 12 to 18 year olds. Specifically, I work with the 16 to 18 year olds in the local church and teach them on Sunday. I have had two of my own boys with me in the room. The rest of the kids in the class have become like sons as well."

Another of his favorite pastimes is reading the biographies of great people. He's constantly trying to uncover the secrets to what makes them tick. "I think the person who has had the biggest influence on my investing life, even though I have never met him, is Warren Buffett," Yacktman reveals. "Buffett isn't really a portfolio manager. He's a businessman who often buys pieces of companies through the stock market. That's because the businesses may either not be for sale outright or he finds their stock to be extremely undervalued. I think conceptually Buffett really understands what a good business is. Too many people separate the price of a business in the stock market from what it would sell for in the private market. That's a mistake. When you see how much some of these companies are trading for in the stock market today, you can only conclude that it's ludicrous. Buffett knows how to do it right. Most investors don't."

DONALD YACKTMAN'S
top 10 GROWTH STOCKS

FOR THE 21ST CENTURY

1. Philip Morris

2. First Data

3. Franklin Covey

4. Department 56

5. United Asset Management

6. Intimate Brands

7. Luxottica Group

8. First Health

9. Jostens

10. Dentsply

Rule 3

BUY THE BEST AT BARGAIN PRICES

If I offered to sell you a Lexus for the same price as a Ford, you'd probably think I was crazy. You'd also agree it was a great deal. Unfortunately, such opportunities don't come along very often in real life. But they are constantly available in the erratic stock market. This is a huge advantage for savvy investors who know how to spot a good bargain. As Warren Buffett would say, buy good companies when their share prices are temporarily down for bad reasons.

This rule makes a lot of sense, although the natural tendency among investors is to follow the crowd by rushing into stocks when they are going up, not down. This is but one reason why market timing is so dangerous. Human nature entices you to buy when prices go up and sell when they fall, which is the opposite of what you should do.

GROWTH INVESTING WITH
A VALUE BENT

Don Yacktman once followed the herd, investing in the hot stocks of the moment without regard to quality or staying power. "I went through a period in college where I started to chase stocks, like the airlines," he says. But after losing a lot of money, he had a change of heart. "It wasn't me. I'm really built as a value investor and always have been. When I had been in this business for about ten years, I sat down one night and said, 'Yacktman, what have you learned?'" he shares. "I concluded there were really two major camps in investing. The growth camp and the value camp. The growth camp tended to own better-than-average businesses, but there was no price discipline. The value camp, on the other hand, had a style I really admired. I liked their attitude of buying on weakness, when things were on sale. I also appreciated their price discipline. Unfortunately, it seemed as if they always ended up owning residual fuel oil. They owned the worst and most mediocre businesses. I decided there must be a way to bring these two disparate parts together."

Over the following years, it became clear to Yacktman that he was better off owning good businesses, bought at a fair price, since their stocks acted more like escalators (always rising in price) than moving sidewalks (cheap to buy, but without much upward movement). As an investor, you can put this concept into practice by purchasing quality companies when their prices are temporarily on sale in the stock market for one bad reason or another. It might be a scandal that's big news today, but of little concern in the long run. A good example is what happened to Intel in 1994. Word leaked out that the company's Pentium chips had a slight flaw. Even though it impacted only a handful of customers, the story became front-page news around the country, causing shares of Intel to come careening down. The company offered to immediately replace any defective chips, and once Wall Street put its commonsense cap back on, Intel shares continued their upward rise. Those who bought on the day this news hit the wires are very happy campers. Those who immediately panicked and sold missed out on a huge opportunity.

WHY STOCKS GO ON SALE

Many times, stocks fall in price for one of three reasons: a market decline, a threat to the cash flow, or a short-term problem that Wall Street views as terminal. "A market decline always tends to shake things up," Yacktman rationalizes. "It's sort of like when you shake the apple tree, a few always fall to the ground. When companies have a threat to their cash flow, it's usually a case where some outside force is threatening the company, like the current pending litigation against tobacco producers or potential government regulation of the drug companies in 1993. In effect, these events serve to shrink the capitalization rates of all stocks in the industry, making them go down or sideways. This trauma requires really keen judgment. In other words, you must make an educated determination that, based on current profitability and future cash flows, the company is worth a lot more than it's selling for in the marketplace."

When a company does have a short-term setback, which might impact earnings only in the next quarter, traders often see the slide as being eternal. "Cash flow can fall due to some temporary problem and often does," Yacktman emphasizes. "In that case, you've got to say, 'Yes, I understand there's a problem right now. But, on a normalized basis, this situation really doesn't exist.'"

PREPARING YOUR SHOPPING LIST

Robert Stovall loves to buy quality businesses when they are under temporary pressure. "This is the only time a company is 'for sale' at a bargain price," he says. "Sometimes it's an entire industry that's under a cloud for some reason. The essence of Warren Buffett's thinking is that the business world is divided into two groups. The first group consists of a small number of wonderful businesses that are well worth investing in at a price. The second group is full of mediocre or bad businesses that from time to time become attractively priced, but are generally not worth owning because they are not good, long-term holdings. This second group, in Buffett's opinion, consists mostly of mature companies that make up the Dow Jones Industrial Average."

CHARACTERISTICS OF A GOOD BUSINESS

According to Buffett, Stovall, Yacktman, and everyone else in this book, a good or wonderful business has at least a majority of the following characteristics:

- It earns a high return on capital without accounting gimmicks or a lot of leverage.
- It generates cash profits.
- It posts predictable earnings.
- It is not a natural target of regulation.
- It is led by owner-oriented management.
- It follows an understandable business model.
- It owns strong franchises, thus having the freedom to success-fully raise prices when necessary.

"A good business is one with a high return on tangible assets," Yacktman says. "In other words, it must be profitable. I like businesses that have low asset intensity. I look at how many times a company turns over its fixed assets, for example. Then I examine the income and cash-flow statement to see what kinds of returns it has generated. You can analyze a building the same way you analyze a stock. It's just that one requires much less maintenance than the other. Essentially, I want to see the private market value growing."

Yacktman also likes companies with strong market shares in their principal products or service lines, a need for relatively low-capital, long product cycles, and excellent positioning in global markets. Three typical businesses he owns are unique professional service companies (which have low start-up and maintenance costs), media providers (because of their sparse competition and low capital requirements), and guaranteed franchises (which require little capital and derive a substantial percentage of revenue from a growing pool of service fees).

Good businesses aren't always glamorous or immediately recognizable. Yacktman likes to tell the story of the guy who went to his twenty-fifth class reunion at the Harvard Business School. He drove up in a limo, walked down the red carpet, and was immediately greeted by his fellow classmates. They asked what he had been up to.

"You know, I barely made it into this school in the first place," he told them. "I worked my tail off for the entire two years I was here. It was clear to me I couldn't compete with you for any of those fancy consulting or finance jobs. So I went back to my small hometown in Ohio and started this little manufacturing company. We develop a device that every automobile in America must have. We make the product for $1 and sell it for $4. You'd be amazed at how that 3 percent adds up." The guy obviously didn't get his math right. He barely made it through business school, after all. But he clearly had what Yacktman would call a good business. Low capital intensity, high profit margins, and a product with extremely strong demand. If this guy ever takes his company public, you can bet Yacktman would be an interested investor.

Davis's Top Ten

Over the years, Shelby Davis has developed a list of the ten most important characteristics he looks for in every company he invests in. Although almost no corporation has every one of these qualities, he searches for those that exhibit at least a majority of them:

1. *First-class management.* "When I visit a company, I look for management with a record of doing what it says it's going to do."
2. *Insider ownership.* "Just as I invest heavily in my own funds, I look for managers who own significant stakes in the companies they run."
3. *Strong returns on capital.* "I seek companies that wisely invest their capital and reap returns on that investment."
4. *A lean expense structure.* "Companies that keep their own costs low are in a much better position to compete, especially in difficult times."
5. *A dominant or growing market share in a growing market.* "A firm that is increasing its share of a growing market has the best of both worlds."
6. *A proven record as an acquirer.* "When a specific industry or the entire stock market goes through a downturn, I want to be invested in companies that can take advantage of low prices to build their own positions through inexpensive acquisitions."

7. *A strong balance sheet.* "Strong finances give a company stay-ing power to weather difficult economic cycles."

8. *Products or services that do not become obsolete.* "Many investors are left high and dry because they have invested in firms with products that eventually are replaced by a competi-tor's stronger offerings."

9. *Successful international operations.* "A proven ability to expand internationally reduces the risk of being tied too closely to U.S. economic or business cycles."

10. *Innovation.* "The savvy use of technology in any business—from a food company to an investment bank—can help reduce costs and increase sales."

We'll delve into each of these characteristics in greater detail later in the book.

BIG IS BETTER (USUALLY)

Although you can occasionally spot a diamond in the rough among small-cap issues, the truly good businesses are almost always blue chip, established corporations. That's because start-ups often sell based on promising stories and hype, as opposed to good earnings and a strong balance sheet. Yacktman normally won't consider a com-pany unless it has at least $100 million in reported earnings, since a business of that size is hard to kill, even if a major recession comes along. "If a company has six cylinders, or six divisions, and one of those divisions is currently in trouble, it's not going to impact the earn-ings or cash flow nearly as much as if it has just one product segment or business," he reasons. "If a company doesn't have multiple busi-nesses and experiences a shortfall for some reason, the stock will likely go down because people on Wall Street are so short-term ori-ented and focused on what's happening with earnings right now."

Roy Papp is convinced that after a decade of restructuring and downsizing, the world's largest conglomerates are not only safer investments, but are also potentially more rewarding. "The large-capitalization companies have seen their stocks go up more than the small-capitalization companies during the 1990s, so many people think the reverse will be true in the future," he notes. "I strongly disagree, because people aren't buying large-cap companies. They're buying companies with the best global growth prospects."

Elizabeth Bramwell is perhaps the only investor I interviewed for this book willing to use initial public offerings on an ongoing basis, although she puts them through greater scrutiny than their larger-cap brethren.

WHICH PRICE IS RIGHT?

Now that you have an idea about what to look for in evaluating whether a stock is even worth considering for purchase, you must determine whether it is selling for an attractive price. Figuring out how much to pay is an age-old dilemma for investors. It's what keeps the market moving. Someone must be willing to buy in order for another to sell. In raging bull markets, traders are often so anxious to jump in, they'll pay almost anything for the fad of the moment. That's what happened in the early 1970s, when a concept called "One Decision Investing" was born.

"It grew and became popularly known as the 'Nifty 50,' " Papp recalls. "The idea was to buy the best companies in the world and just sit on them. Some of the stars were Polaroid, Xerox, Avon, IBM, and several drug and food companies. They were the biggest and best around. Like a chain letter, the concept caught on and institutions poured money into the 'Nifty 50' during 1971 and 1972. These stocks were selling at 30, 40, even 50 times earnings, even though they were growing only about 15 percent a year. It was a tremendous party atmosphere and only the supposed dummies didn't participate. But like a chain letter, the day eventually arrived in 1973 when some people began to realize 'The Emperor Has No Clothes.' The day of reckoning came and these stocks declined by as much as 60 to 80 percent from their highs. When the disaster finally settled, people realized that pouring all that money into 50 stocks was pure insanity."

Robert Stovall remembers that period well. Now, he often creates a shopping list in his head full of stocks he would love to buy, but only if the price is right. "When you've been at this for as long as I have, you develop an enormous memory bank in your brain full of companies you would like to own, but are willing to wait for to avoid paying too much," he explains. "General Electric is a good example of a stock I think everyone should have a little bit of in their portfolio. The price of GE frequently fluctuates, and I have certain price points in my mind where I'm comfortable adding to my position in this company. You already know I'm not a fan of market timing and advise against it. However, the one benefit to paying attention to the market and the direction of the tape is that you can instantly see when the stocks you are eyeing come down to the levels you want to pay for them."

LOOK FOR HIGH GROWTH, LOW PEs

One of Stovall's mantras is that he likes to invest in companies with high growth rates compared to their price-earnings (PE) ratios. "Unfortunately, that's difficult to do these days, especially with the large well-known corporations, because they've been picked over so well," he laments. "However, if you can find a stock selling for 18 times earnings with an underlying annual growth rate of 22 percent, that's certainly more attractive than an 18 percent grower selling for 22 times earnings."

Roy Papp has a similar discipline. "I am oriented toward high-quality growth stocks, and I don't want to pay impossibly high prices for them," he says. "I want to purchase them at roughly a market multiple. On the other hand, if I buy damaged goods or companies in real trouble, I can get them cheaper. But then I have other problems and risks to deal with," such as the fact that the price might go much lower. Specifically, Papp looks for stocks with earnings-growth rates of 12 to 15 percent selling at the same PE multiple as the S&P 500. "Obviously the more growth the better, but I'm not willing to pay 35 or 40 times earnings for it," he explains. "When you're willing to pay only a market multiple (which is around 25 as this book goes to press), you're not going to find stocks growing at 35 percent a year. Those companies are much more expensive. The trouble is, if you pay 30 times earnings for a stock, chances are that growth won't be sustained. Something will come along to interrupt it, and the stock will really get hit. That's why I stay away from them. If I can buy a superior company at roughly a market multiple, I'm happy."

This market multiple guideline isn't always a practical one to follow. For example, banks as a group normally sell at a below-market multiple anyway, as do many automakers, restaurants, and utility companies. Therefore, the nature of a company's business may force you to reevaluate your definition of a fair price. For this reason, Papp often compares the valuation of a particular company with that of its closest competitors to see how the multiple and earnings growth rates of the two businesses compare. In some cases, the result causes him to buy another firm in the industry instead.

INDUSTRIES TO AVOID

"There are many companies and industries I simply won't touch," Papp reveals. "For 40 years, the airline industry has never made any money, so that's a good one to stay away from. I don't want to own steel or extraction companies either, because I don't think there's a lot of growth there. I further don't want to own commodity businesses, because you have no control over prices. And if a stock sports a price-earnings ratio above the overall market, I normally won't buy it."

In addition, since Papp is convinced market timing doesn't work, he avoids cyclical companies altogether. "Take paper manufacturers," he suggests. "You play the cyclical game by buying these stocks when they are priced low and selling them when prices rise. That's the same thing as market timing, only you're confining yourself to one stock or industry. It's very hard to be right twice on both the buy and the sell decision. I believe if you stick with growth stocks, you can buy and hold them for a very long time. That way, you're not constantly subjected to making the tough calls of when to get out."

CALCULATE PRIVATE MARKET VALUE

Yacktman has a slightly more complicated formula for evaluating whether a stock is selling for the right price. He tries to buy companies trading below their so-called private market value, defined as what an intelligent businessperson would pay for the entire company. The number is computed by applying the following formula:

operating cash flow (after depreciation)
× capitalization rate
= total private value
− net debt
= private market value

Operating cash flow is the amount of cash generated from operations after taking care of capital spending. You can think of the capitalization rate as the inverse of a company's discount rate. (Yacktman generally plugs in a number between 10 and 15 here. If you use a lower capitalization rate, you'll get a more conservative private market value.) Net debt is a company's long-term debt minus available cash. By subtracting this number from the total private value, you'll find out what the firm owes its debtors. You then divide the result by the number of outstanding shares to get the per-share private market value. One thing to keep in mind is that this formula assumes the company will generate the same cash flow every year. Therefore, it works best for consistent, steady growers, as opposed to more cyclical operations.

"I try to be as objective as I can when calculating this," Yacktman says. "It's really a blended number. In other words, you take each segment of the company, break it apart, and decide how much it's worth based on cash flow. Then you bring all of those parts back together, add them up, and get a net result. I'm trying to get as close to the private market value as I can. Nobody knows exactly what that is. I'm not attempting to cut it to the exact decimal. I can only hope to be close. What I really want to do is make sure I don't overpay for the stock."

IGNORE BOOK VALUE

Book value also used to be a traditional measure of whether a company was cheap. The thought was that if you could buy a company at or below book value, you were getting a good deal. It was a theory popularized by Benjamin Graham, a man who is often thought of as the father of value investing. But Yacktman and the others I interviewed all agree this measure of value is no longer relevant. "When you concentrate on book value, you wind up buying asset plays, which I view as moving sidewalks," he says. "Will buying based on book value work over time? Yes, if you consistently purchase companies that aren't disasters. But I feel you can enhance this approach through buying good businesses at cheap prices, not necessarily at book value. You'll almost never get a truly good business for book value. Freddie Mac, the financial services company that packages and resells mortgages, dropped down to that level in 1990. But situations like this are extremely rare. They are so rare, I don't think you could run a portfolio based on those parameters alone. While I use some value techniques, I consider myself to be a growth manager. Value managers will buy a stock at a low price, even if it's not growing. Over time it's hard to make money that way. The classic example of this is General Motors versus Philip Morris. These are both stocks in the Dow Jones Industrial Average. Since 1965, when the market first hit 1,000, General Motors has maybe doubled. Philip Morris, on the other hand, is up about 250 times. General Motors is the moving sidewalk. It sells for a low PE and closer to book value. Philip Morris is the escalator. I'd take Philip Morris over General Motors any day."

Accordingly, Yacktman argues that the real core of a company's value isn't the physical assets on the balance sheet, but rather its ability to earn a high return on assets over a sustained period of time. "The economics of the business are what matter," he says. "I like companies with what I call an unfair competitive advantage. They have some unique feature that allows them to stand apart from the crowd. I didn't fully appreciate this concept until I had been investing in stocks for several years. The common thread among my biggest winners is that they have all been good businesses with low-capital intensity."

ONCE A BARGAIN HUNTER, ALWAYS A BARGAIN HUNTER

Yacktman traces his affection for low-priced stocks back to his childhood, when his mom pinched every penny she could. This discipline was also driven home to him by a finance professor in college. "A colleague recently told me, 'The problem with value investing is that it permeates your life,'" he shares. "I think it does. A consultant came into my office once and commented that he liked to visit his potential money managers in person because their surroundings set a tone as to what kind of person they are. When you look around my office, you'll notice it isn't an opulent place. We have nice furniture, but it's nothing fancy. I got most of my equipment used for a song and had it refinished and recolored to look more modern. That's just how I've always purchased things for myself. If I'm looking to buy a particular item, I'll go to three or four places to see who has the best price. My kids are the same way. When my son Stephen went shopping for a new dining room set recently, he negotiated hard to get a cheaper price. This search for value truly permeates our lives."

Yacktman claims that 90 percent of the time when a stock he already owns declines further in price, he's buying more instead of unloading it with the crowd. "If I've done my homework right, I know what the private market value is, and that's not going to change much in the short term," he maintains. "Therefore, as the stock goes down, it creates more of a gap between the public and private-market value. One of the toughest things for investors to do is buy stocks that have gone down. They are consumed by too much superficiality. There's no substitute for knowledge. Once your knowledge level is high enough, you can look at a stock that has gone down and say with relative certainty it is an even more attractive buy than it was at a higher price."

This attitude may seem like common sense, and it is. After all, if you're attracted to a shirt at the store selling for $30, wouldn't you like it even more if it went on sale for $25? It makes you wonder why so many investors are foolish enough to get rid of good stocks just because of the headlines of the moment. Yacktman has a reasonable explanation for this. "Probably 70 percent of all investors in this country play the momentum game," he estimates. "A lot of them are driven by trivial things. As a result, they're buying what has been good, as opposed to what may be good in the future. I'll grant you this approach works better than mine in a racing bull market, especially when the market is up 10, 20, or 30 percent in a quarter. But over the long term, the market's a weighing machine, not a voting machine. The votes of today carry the market only in the short term. That's why we do very well when the market is flat or down, as opposed to when it's going straight up." This is not to say Yacktman's stocks won't go down in a bear market. They will and did during the 1998 correction. But he insists they won't fall nearly as hard as the darlings of the momentum players.

TAKING CUES FROM COMPANY MANAGEMENT

Before investing in any company, Elizabeth Bramwell likes to talk with top management. She is most interested in collecting information to help her project a company's future growth prospects. "I want to know whether this growth will come from new products, new markets, price increases, product upgrades, or changes in the mix," she explains. "I also need to understand whether expenses are growing as quickly as revenues, whether gross margins are expanding, what the company's tax rate is going to be, how much is being plowed back into research and development, and whether costs are being cut to expand earnings. In the drug industry, for example, there are a lot of new drugs in the pipeline. I need to know when they are likely to be approved. In any business, I want to make sure the balance sheet is adequate to support future growth. Otherwise, more money might have to be raised. Once I am able to figure out these variables and project earnings out a year or so from now, the picture starts to come together, allowing me to make an informed decision about whether I want to own the company."

With that number in mind, she can calculate an appropriate price for the stock. "My basic assumption is that over time stock prices are going to move with earnings growth," she surmises. "Buying companies at close to one times their future growth generally allows for expansion in the PE multiple relative to the general indices, assuming that interest and inflation rates stay low." To make it into her portfolio, a company usually must have good management, be number one or two in its industry, and enjoy growth of between 15 and 30 percent a year. "The level of risk increases with the growth rate, so I don't have too many companies growing at more than 30 percent annually," she points out. "I really like companies that are well run, make strategic long-term decisions, and execute their plans well."

IMPROVING YOUR ODDS

When it comes down to it, though, knowing whether you've paid too much for a stock is really a judgment call every investor must make each time he or she buys a stock. As any professional will admit, it's impossible to ever buy at the exact low, unless you're extremely lucky (and it truly does come down to luck). But using these tools will certainly stack the odds in your favor.

One way Stovall tries to improve his chances of getting a good deal is by doing what he calls sector analysis research. This involves looking at how whole sectors are priced compared to the overall market. It's the kind of work his son Sam specializes in. Sam is the sector analyst for Standard & Poor's. "I try to find groups that are overpriced, which I avoid, and those that are underpriced, which are worth looking at," Stovall explains. "When I find an underpriced group, I then look further at its past historical relationship with the market, along with whether it appears to be entering a turnaround. If so, it may be attractive for purchase."

To put this into more understandable terms, let's say Stovall notices that the airline sector is selling at an overall multiple of 11 times earnings, while the S&P 500 trades for 20 times earnings. On the surface, the airlines look like a steal. Stovall then digs deeper to discover the airline sector's historical multiple range. If it is 9 to 11 times earnings, the current valuation is no bargain, since the group usually sells for a low relative PE anyway. However, if the sector's historical PE range is 12 to 18, it's a great buy at 11 times earnings. From there, Stovall goes on to handpick companies within the sector. By doing additional homework, he often finds individual stocks that are even more reasonably priced. "Once I have the sector that I want to examine further, I look at the industry's top and bottom line growth, to see what's going on with sales and profits," he says. "Often this explains why the discount is so dramatic. Nevertheless, some companies in the sector are always stronger than others. Those performing better than average have a definite leg up on the competition. I next examine each stock's price-earnings ratio, see whether it pays a dividend, and perform additional due diligence from there."

THE BOTTOM LINE

Buy good businesses at the right prices. It is also often wise to concentrate on large, established companies with first-class management teams, predictable earnings, diverse product lines, pristine balance sheets, lean expense structures, and successful international operations.

One useful guideline for making sure you don't overpay is to stick with stocks you can purchase for PE multiples below the companies' overall growth rate. In other words, look for businesses growing by 25 percent a year that you can buy for 20 times earnings. Also, try not to purchase a stock selling for a PE multiple that's greater than the PE multiple of the S&P 500 index.

Rule 4

TAKE A GOOD LOOK AROUND YOU

Great investments are everywhere. That's why you must always be on the lookout for potential opportunities. Your next best investment could be on one of the aisles in your grocery store, the sports page of the newspaper, your child's Christmas wish list for Santa, or even on the beach during your trip to a tropical resort.

FOCUS ON THE BULL'S-EYE

Robert Stovall first learned the importance of incorporating the events and trends around you when searching for promising investments as an undergraduate at the University of Pennsylvania. "I had a professor at the Wharton School named Julius Grodinsky who made this concept so clear to me," Stovall reports. "He didn't think I was very smart, and maybe he was right. But he made a favorable impression on me, especially when he explained what I call the 'bull's-eye concept.'"

Stovall teaches this same technique in his own classroom at New York's Stern Graduate School of Business today. "I draw a big bull's-eye on the blackboard to represent a given event," he explains. "Let's use El Niño as an example. El Niño is the outer circle of the target, or big picture. We all know what this is, what it does, and what it might do. It's a recurring weather pattern that warms sea temperatures in the Pacific, which can trigger droughts in the Pacific basin or unleash hurricanes in some areas of South America and Southern California. Let's say forecasters predict we're in for the biggest El Niño in a decade or maybe this century. That forecast forms the foundation of our theme or concept. Now we take at look at what it might mean for investors. Which companies or industries stand to benefit or be hurt from El Niño if this prediction proves correct? Fire and casualty companies are sure to be affected. But they could be helped or hurt, depending on what actually happens. If we know these bad storms are supposed to hit southern California, Mexico, Arizona, and the Southwest in general, while leaving the east and gulf coasts unharmed, insurers could be helped. The reasoning behind this is that there are more people and assets, and therefore a preponderance of insurance policies, on the east and gulf coasts. If insurers have to pay reduced damage claims in those states, they would benefit financially.

"Keeping with our El Niño bull's-eye, I might then turn my attention to food processors, who will be helped or hurt depending on whether or not crops are damaged," Stovall continues. "Then I would look at fertilizer stocks. If El Niño causes a serious drought in the Asian basin and parts of Latin America, that will reduce crop yields and result in more fertilizer being laid down in the temperate zones, such as Argentina, Canada, and the United States. These areas would have to plant more crops to make up for the grain shortfall. As a result, prices of agricultural commodities would rise and the stocks of farm equipment companies could also go up. So the big picture is El Niño. The middle picture is the potential consequences from it, namely damage and droughts, and the resulting impact of those events. Then, you move to the smaller picture, or actual bull's-eye, to find which specific stocks you might want to buy that would likely benefit from the full development of this concept. Assume I believed insurance damage was going to be minimal and that a resulting drought would cause a rush on fertilizer.

That might cause me to purchase shares of Chubb and Potash Company of Saskatchewan as a play on El Niño."

Granted, this technique requires some educated guessing on your part, but it is based on factual data. "I use this process every day," Stovall adds. "Each time I read the paper, or see something on TV, I say to myself, 'Which companies will be helped or hurt by this?'" This is something you, as an individual investor, can do as well. The next time you watch your favorite news program, pay attention to every story, especially those about hot new trends, promising products, and revolutionary discoveries. Let the stories be your emerging target. Then ask yourself which industries might be helped or hurt by them. Finally, go out and find individual companies that specifically stand to benefit from the consequences of this bull's-eye. Later in this book you will learn various techniques for evaluating the attractiveness of a stock. However, you must first have a shopping list of names, and using the concentric circle (or bull's-eye) method is a great way of compiling one.

Shed Pounds, Make a Profit

Sometimes good investment ideas are staring you in the face, even though you don't immediately realize it. Perhaps you have been trying to get in shape and lose weight. You probably didn't know this laudable effort can not only trim your waistline, but also fatten up the profits of many corporations in the physical fitness business. "This is a theme I picked up on some time ago," Stovall notes. Nevertheless, part of your job as an investor is to decide whether your bull's-eye observation is a long- or a short-term trend. "For instance, there has recently been a resurgence in the use of cigars and cocktails," Stovall observes. "I haven't invested in this trend, because I think it is transient and won't last long."

This doesn't mean investors can't profit from a short-term trend. You can, if you're quick to spot it and react accordingly. Since you never know how long a short-term trend will last, however, you must always stand ready to pull the trigger, to avoid getting creamed once your temporary bull's-eye gets clobbered. Therefore, the pursuit of such quick gains doesn't much interest Stovall. He'd rather concentrate on enduring themes that can remain intact for months or even years to come.

So would Shelby Davis. "Since I am a long-term investor who stresses 'research, research, and more research,' I look for secular investment themes that will drive a decade, not five weeks or five years," he says. "My research wouldn't do me much good if I owned stocks for only five weeks. The market is a discounter that's paid to look ahead—it's a barometer, not a thermometer. If you take a longer time frame, that creates opportunity."

Short-term trends also make it much more difficult to spot which specific companies are destined to benefit from them. If, as in Stovall's example, cigars remain popular for only a short time, it's hard to tell which cigar makers will get the brunt of the business before this craze is extinguished. If the fascination with puffing on rolled leaves continues for some years, however, many companies will have a chance to capture a piece of the action by creating a continuous stream of new and improved cigars.

Interesting Ideas from Boring Places

Roy Papp gets his ideas from all over the place, including such unlikely sources as the weekly magazine *Morbidity and Mortality,* which his son Harry subscribes to. He also pays close attention to the world around him and is always sniffing around for profitable opportunities. He found one recent investment while he and his wife, Marilyn, were on a cruise to the Baltic. "Marilyn and I have taken a dozen cruises, and we always notice that the women go nuts over the spas and beauty parlors on board," he says. "They're on the ship with a boyfriend or husband and want to look beautiful. They're competing with everybody else and are willing to spend money to look good. On our latest trip, I saw this up close and found out there is one company, Steiner Leisure, that supplies 80 percent of the beauty parlors and spas on the world's cruise ships. I then started to do my homework."

Sure, Papp called the company and asked for more information. But he also read-up on the industry to find out how many new ships were scheduled to come on line in the next few years and how many of those would buy their spas and parlors from this company. "I found out that capacity's going through the roof, and 80 percent of them will use Steiner Leisure's products," he shares. "What's more, these new ships are bigger, which is a good sign. By reading the company's annual report, 10-Qs and 10-Ks, I found out Steiner Leisure had zero debt on the balance sheet. I also learned that it had a 40 percent market share until 1994, when it bought its biggest competitor. If the market grows as expected, Steiner Leisure should do very well. It has been in business a long time, has a dominant position in a rapidly growing industry, and (as this book goes to press) is trading at 20 times earnings, less than the market. That's my ideal stock. It's unknown, nobody understands it, it's attractively priced, and it has a lead position in its industry."

The reason Papp does so much ancillary research is that initially he's more interested in the philosophy than in the particulars of a single company. "If you're not following Wall Street, which I'm not, you've got to do all of this work yourself," he says. "Then you concentrate on the specifics of the stock. Is it loaded with debt? Are the earnings real and sustainable? What's the competition like? I noticed Steiner Leisure had some tough times before 1994, but people were scared of losing their jobs then and cruise ship activity was low. Now they're going gangbusters. I don't expect a depression in the next couple of years, so it should be smooth sailing for this company."

Viewing what was going on in his own industry led Papp to another one of his top holdings, State Street Bank. "I was looking for something that would benefit from the stock market's continued rise," he explains. "Forty-three percent of all mutual funds house their assets with State Street. The other thing that makes it great is the company has gone abroad in a major way. It is becoming a world leader in the custodian business. If the globalization trend continues, as I expect it will, this company will be a big winner. The other thing I noticed is that State Street used to sell at a bank multiple, but it's not a traditional bank. Wall Street is beginning to realize that, and the multiple has expanded."

Like a kid in a candy store, he goes on to talk about another trend he's been following. "Right now, we're looking at a company that I think may turn out to be a great stock," he exudes. "It makes these little connector boxes that you plug computers into to protect against power surges. Our country has been blessed in that we don't have many brownouts or power failures. But in about three years, I guarantee you we're going to have them. As our utilities become competitive and nonmonopolistic, they will start competing, and that will cause a number of problems. But forget about the United States. Computer sales are picking up in Europe, Africa, and southeast Asia too. The power's not so reliable over there." He then points out that his one concern is there are many competitors in the field, and since power-surge protectors don't need to be replaced that often, this huge demand he predicts must materialize for earnings to grow.

"Manpower is an additional stock we got into through the back door," Papp continues, scratching his balding head. "We liked it because its biggest market is in France. The French have such stupid regulations. If you fire or lay off a worker over there, you've got to pay them for two years. The same is true in Sweden and all of Germany. You can't just lay anybody off. The net result is companies won't hire any permanent workers. They want temporary help. Who benefits from that? Manpower. Sure, we could go buy shares in a foreign outplacement agency. But buying Manpower, a U.S. company, is much safer."

LOOKING FROM THE TOP DOWN

Before Elizabeth Bramwell considers buying a specific stock, she takes a broad look at both the world and the economy. It's what's called a "top-down" approach. In other words, she wants to find out the direction of inflation and interest rates, along with the shape of the global political landscape and how the U.S. dollar stacks up against foreign currencies.

From there, she comes up with a list of themes that are likely to do well in the future. For example, Bramwell expects technology to lead the way for growth in the twenty-first century. Specifically, she is attracted to companies that use technology well to gain a competitive advantage. "Technology accounts for about half of all U.S. capital spending," she says. "The ability to use technology effectively allows you to increase both your revenues and productivity. The bigger you are, the more you can use technology to achieve economies of scale." Using these themes, she looks for individual companies that will prosper if her hypotheses are correct. Specifically, she searches for leaders in their respective industries that can be bought at a reasonable price. "I'm looking for individual stocks," she adds. "I don't try to run my portfolio on a sector basis. If I have a lot of stocks in any one area, it's because that's where I think the opportunities are."

Bramwell gathers ideas from many sources, including personal and anecdotal observation, the general press, and the brokerage community. She also reads various research reports, goes through several daily newspapers, and scrounges through the mounds of information that arrive in her office each day. Is it good information? Not always. That's why Bramwell must rely on sound judgment and her own diligent research before making any buy or sell decision.

GET THE EARLY EDGE

Whether you manage millions of dollars, like the experts in this book, or a small personal portfolio worth much less, the way you make big gains in growth stocks is by being the first to recognize and understand a new theme. In other words, you want to buy shares in the next Microsoft or Wal-Mart before it gets "discovered" by the rest of Wall Street. That's because if you're in early, and hold for the long haul, you'll get to sit back and watch the value of your shares grow as traders bid them higher and higher. Therefore, keeping a constant eye out for new ideas and perceiving an emerging trend before the rest of the crowd gives you a substantial edge over the rest of Wall Street. Unfortunately, in a stock market as efficient as ours, that's easier said than done.

"We get an edge by looking beyond the horizon, not just at three days, weeks, or months, but three years," Shelby Davis confides. "I just listened to a conference call the other day for Citicorp. I don't know whether they're bluffing or not, but they were talking about having one billion customers by 2005. If you consider that there are only six billion people in the world, you'll realize we're talking about a grandiose goal. They'll have to do some mergers to get there. But at least they have a vision of where they want to go. I like companies with a vision. I enjoy seeing management set out an earnings goal several years out and then try to hit it." The company is well on its way. Shortly after this call, Citicorp announced a merger with Travelers Group. The combined financial giant is now known as Citigroup.

CULTIVATE YOUR INNATE CURIOSITY

To succeed in the investment business, Bramwell insists, one must have both intellectual curiosity and flexibility. "Having set opinions will hurt you," she warns. "For example, technology is continuously changing. Look at what Dell has done for computers. It initiated the direct-sales model that has totally changed how other companies market and distribute their products. Amazon has done the same thing, only with bookselling."

Bramwell adds that it's essential to be aware of what's going on around you. "It's helpful to listen to your children, to see what they think of Nike or Coke," she advises. "What are they buying? You should also look at where the crowds are lining up at the mall." Bramwell practices what she preaches. In the late 1980s, she went to a lecture about women in Russia and the appalling conditions they live under. What she heard prompted her to buy Tambrands, the world's leading maker of tampons and other feminine sanitary products, believing it would benefit from economic gains in the Soviet Union. (Tambrands was acquired by Procter & Gamble in 1997.) "The trick is to find companies that are underfollowed and to be early," she adds. "I have owned Washington Mutual for a long time. It was once underfollowed, given its then-remote location in the Pacific Northwest. Now it is viewed as a play on one of the fastest growing areas of the country."

Although her views are subject to change, Bramwell is concentrating on the following investment themes, which she believes will benefit from the continuation of a slow-growing economy into the next millennium:

- *Financial services.* "This industry enjoys favorable demographics as aging baby boomers expand the market for financial products. Economies of scale and technology favor consolidation."

- *Geographic plays.* "The Pacific Northwest is growing faster than the rest of the United States as technology companies, in particular, expand in the region and as trade with the Pacific Rim grows."

- *Global expansion.* "Rising personal income and an expanding middle class, especially in emerging countries, create opportunities for global brands."

- *Innovation.* "Companies that create their own growth and markets by introducing new products and services will prosper."

- *Intellectual property.* "Companies with proprietary data and knowledge that can leverage their know-how across various media [have an edge over the competition]."

- *Outsourcing.* "The need to improve productivity and global competitiveness continues to drive outsourcing for manufacturing components, personnel, and data processing."

Robert Stovall has a similar list. Looking toward the future, he predicts the greatest investment themes (or bull's-eyes) for the twenty-first century are environment, health care, energy, and communications, all of which are powered by advances in technology.

DEVELOPING A CIRCLE OF COMPETENCE

Davis assembles his portfolio by combining top-down themes with bottom-up stock picking. He has developed what he calls a circle of competence in the financial services industry, probably because he grew up working with his dad, who was a well-known insurance analyst on Wall Street. Davis believes every investor should develop his or her own circle of competence. In other words, find one or two areas of the market or industries that you know and understand like the back of your hand. By cultivating a close relationship like this, you will be better able to make intelligent investment decisions, while keeping up with changing trends in the field. Davis's son Chris has also developed a circle of competence in the financial services area, namely with banks and insurance companies. His other son Andrew's goal is to become the dean of real-estate investment trusts.

Your circle of competence could be the industry you work in. If you're a computer programmer, for example, you might decide to follow software stocks. You presumably already know the business well. You live and breathe it every day. So when you hear about a company in your field that sounds promising, you'll be able to make a rational decision as to whether it's a good investment, since you understand the conditions under which it operates. This doesn't mean you buy only stocks of computer software developers. You would never want to concentrate all of your money in one area. But you can make this sector a healthy part of your portfolio.

THE BOTTOM LINE

Always be on the lookout for promising investment ideas. Keep an eye on what products you use the most and what your kids are buying. Then, figure out how you can profit from them. In addition, look for broad trends in the economy and determine which companies are likely to benefit from them the most.

ROBERT H. STOVALL

*R*obert H. Stovall is about as all-American as they come. He's a twelfth-generation Yankee, who traces his roots back to a Quaker named Bartholomew Stovall. Bartholomew arrived from the little town of Albury in Surrey, England, as an indentured servant at the Hampton Roads seaport area of Virginia in 1684. In the 1790s, Robert's branch of the Stovall clan migrated west to what is now Kentucky. His dad, Harold, was born in 1893 to a family of Kentucky farmers. Stovall's mom, the former Agnes Hinkle, was three years younger than his dad. She is the descendent of German-Americans, a group whose members are still numerous in Louisville and the Ohio valley. "Mom's people came to America in the 1840s," Stovall shares. "That was when a lot of Germans fled to the States to escape squabbles among all of the baronies, dukedoms, principalities, and the various revolutions taking place in their native land."

Stovall's parents met at a party in Louisville during World War I. They courted for years, but didn't get mar-

ried until both were in their late twenties. "Their families objected to
the union because they came from different religious backgrounds,"
Stovall explains. "My father's people were Masons and Baptists,
while my mother's were Roman Catholic." They eventually tied the
knot in 1923. Stovall was born three years later. He has a younger
sister, Joanne Perrot, who is four years his junior. "She is a former
art historian for the Corning Museum of Glass," Stovall says. "Joanne
married the Corning Museum's then-director Paul N. Perrot. He's
also an art historian and conservationist who spent 12 years as the
assistant secretary of the Smithsonian Institution. He was later director of the Virginia Museum of the Arts, and is currently chair of the
visitor's committee of The Getty Museum."

FROM FEED STORE TO WALL STREET

When Robert Stovall was born, his dad worked as a clerk at a
Louisville feed store. After it burned down in the late 1920s, he took
a job clerking with a local brokerage firm called C. D. Barney, the
predecessor of Smith Barney. Three of his colleagues at the firm were
members of the Reynolds Tobacco and Reynolds Metals dynasties.
"They were cousins of R. J Reynolds, the tobacco baron," Stovall says.
"The metal company grew out of the tobacco operation. Reynolds
Metals' early products included tin foil to wrap around their tobacco
cousins' Camel cigarettes and tin cans to put Prince Albert tobacco
in. Prince Albert was a very popular pipe tobacco. As a kid, I remember one of our favorite telephone pranks was to call a store and say,
'Do you have Prince Albert in a can?' When the clerk said, 'Yes,' we
would laughingly reply, 'Let him out, please.' But that's how
Reynolds Metals got started. The two companies had major operations in Louisville that produced both metal and tobacco products."

One of the Reynolds boys, Richard S. Reynolds, Jr., decided to
set up his own brokerage house in New York following the 1929
crash. He called it Reynolds and Company. Later on, he asked
Stovall's father to join him as the firm's operations manager, to run
the back-office. This was long before people ever heard about computers, so all transactions were recorded by hand. The elder Stovall
accepted the offer. In 1936, he moved his family to Short Hills, New
Jersey, a well-known suburb of New York. Robert Stovall was ten at

the time. "It was quite a change going from a quiet place like Kentucky to the suburbs of New York and Wall Street," he recalls.

AN INTRODUCTION TO WALL STREET

Stovall was immediately intrigued by the brokerage industry, even as an innocent young lad. "It was exciting, as you were sort of in everybody's business at the same time," he says. "I observed that the grown-ups did a lot of talking about this company and that industry. There was a lot of precision required. I didn't pretend to understand what was going on, but I found it interesting. I've always had a feel for history and a broad knowledge of many different subjects. When I was a kid, I used to read the encyclopedia for fun."

That's certainly not a claim most children can make, but Stovall has always been the studious type. His high school, Seton Hall Prep (a prestigious Catholic institution founded in the 1850s), was very demanding academically, yet Stovall still found time to play in the band, sing in the glee club, and join the dramatic society. He also worked for Reynolds and Company in the summer months and during holiday breaks.

For the most part, Stovall was a messenger boy for the brokerage firm. Before his voice changed, he was also allowed to be a relief switchboard operator, filling in for the woman who normally held that job. "Men were not expected to do that sort of thing in the early 1940s," Stovall explains. "But when I still had my soprano voice, everyone on the phone thought I was a woman anyway so it worked out fine." One of his most exciting jobs came at Christmas time, when he was sent to deliver whiskey to the traders around town. "I was so young, I guess they figured I wouldn't steal the whiskey," he surmises. "They couldn't trust the other messengers. They were all older and might have kept some of it for themselves."

A PRESIDENTIAL CLIENT LIST

Reynolds and Company quickly attracted an impressive clientele. "Some of these brokers, sitting at ordinary little desks, had very big accounts," Stovall says. "I knew how substantial they were because

I'd see their statements come through." In addition to celebrities of the theater and industrialists, the firm's roster of major clients included General Dwight D. Eisenhower. When Eisenhower first signed up, he was enjoying a meteoric rise to fame that began as military commander during World War II and culminated with his election as the thirty-fourth president of the United States in 1953. One of the brokerage firm's partners, Cliff Roberts, was a friend of Ike's and played golf with him frequently at the Augusta National Golf Club (which Roberts founded), home of the famous annual Augusta National Tournament.

Back then, a major account had $2 or $3 million. "Today, it seems everybody who's 28 is worth that amount," Stovall quips. But you must keep this figure in the proper context to appreciate how impressive it was. In the 1940s, the minimum wage, which Stovall was paid, was 25 cents an hour. "That may sound like slavery, but you could have a good lunch at the Automat in New York City for very little," he insists. "A beef pie in a casserole dish cost 15 cents, while milk, coffee, and a roll with butter could be had for a nickel each." As a result, for 30 cents you got a hot entree, with a roll to mop it up and a cold glass of milk to wash everything down.

The brokers Stovall worked with, of course, made much more than minimum wage. Still, their compensation was not nearly as stratospheric as those positions command today. "There were no investment analysts or position traders, and underwriting was small change and infrequent," Stovall notes. "There were two kinds of people who made the most money. First were the brokers with large family or individual trading accounts. Second were those brokers whose daddies could direct bank business their way. They were known as 'lounge lizards,' and often didn't even come into work because they knew daddy would automatically route trades to them. These kinds of directed business transactions are thankfully now a thing of the past."

OFF TO COLLEGE . . . AND WAR

After graduating from Seton Hall Prep in 1943, Stovall went to the University of Pennsylvania's Wharton School of Business with dreams of becoming a financial analyst. It was a great time for button-bright lads such as Stovall to get into college, since women often didn't go for specialized training and most men of his generation were being drafted to duty in World War II. He applied to and was accepted by Harvard, Yale, Georgetown, and Penn, a feat he admits is much more difficult to accomplish now. "My father really didn't want to me go to college," Stovall reveals. "He didn't think it was necessary, because nobody in his family had ever been. He did get a bookkeeping certificate from a mail-order educational program called the International School of Accountancy. He figured I could just follow in his footsteps and become a bookkeeper as well. His point of view was that if I just learned how to keep books and manage people I would do all right. But my mother was more aggressive. Her half-brother was a medical doctor in Louisville. The teachers and headmasters at Seton Prep also encouraged me to further my education. So I did. My father said if I were going to enroll in college, I better go to the Wharton School to learn business, as had Richard Reynolds, Jr., and his business partner Charles Babcock (husband of Mary Reynolds, Richard's sister). His point was that Harvard, Yale, and Georgetown were simply extensions of the classical education I got at the prep school. I guess this reasoning was philosophically appropriate in my case."

Wharton was the first business school organized anywhere in the world. It was financed in the mid-1850s by iron and steel industry magnate Joseph Wharton. After just one semester at Penn, Stovall volunteered to serve his country and enlisted in the Army. "In those years, everyone at Seton Hall was encouraged to volunteer for duty to fight the fascists," he says. "It was a very different environment from what we have now. We all volunteered early on to get into those military programs that supposedly would guarantee to let you continue your education for awhile before going on active duty. Most boys went into the Navy or Marines, if they could pass the physical. Unfortunately, I always had weak eyes and didn't qualify, but the Army took me and sent me off to engineering school for two semesters at Alfred University. It was a small college in Alfred, a tiny frozen town in northern New York state. The politicians kept the brightest students in colleges like this to prevent them from collapsing. They needed warm bodies in the classroom because just about everybody coming out of high school had been or was waiting to be drafted. There were few deferments such as those offered to people in the 1960s during the Vietnam War."

In 1943 and 1944, after the military began to take some bad casualties in the war, the Army's specialized training program (ASTP) was eliminated and these troops were sent to fight on the front lines. "Coincidentally or not, three divisions of my ASTP colleagues with very little training and no combat experience were sent to the Ardennes region in Belgium to fight in the Battle of the Bulge. That was in December 1944," Stovall remembers. "The casualties were terrible. For some reason, the Higher Power always seems to watch over me. I got shipped to Italy instead. I might have been the only one in my ASTP college contingent from Alfred University to go there. Everyone else that I knew went to Germany and many of them were casualties."

During Stovall's two-and-a-half-year military tour of duty, he was a foot soldier in the combat medical service. He was later assigned to a motor ambulance company, which transported the wounded around Italy. During this time, he rose to the rank of corporal. After being discharged from the Army, he went back to Penn and continued to study finance and commerce.

FIRST STOCK PURCHASE

It was about this time that Stovall bought his first stock. Even though he had lived around the world of investing all his life, he had never dabbled in the market himself, largely because he didn't have any extra money. "My first stock purchase was about five shares of Budd Company," he reveals. "Budd made modern automated commuter railroad and subway cars. I was familiar with them because I rode the subway around Manhattan and used the commuter train to get back to New Jersey." The investment wasn't very profitable, and Budd eventually merged out of existence. "Mr. Budd, the founder, spent all the money he earned on new devices," Stovall explains. "He was more of an inventor than a businessman. I later bought some tobacco stocks, which did better. I guess I was attracted to that industry because of my southern connection with Reynolds, plus the fact that the people around me were smoking all the time. I invested in Reynolds Tobacco and American Tobacco. But the stock market overall moved slowly at that time."

OFF TO COPENHAGEN

After earning his undergraduate degree from Penn's Wharton School in 1948, Stovall used the GI bill and a scholarship from the Danish government to fund a year of graduate study at the University of Copenhagen. "I studied political economics and Keynesian economic theory," he says. "It was a lot of fun and I met a beautiful girl there named Inger Bagger, whom I courted diligently. She was a student at the Royal Art Academy. We bicycled together all around Denmark. Two years later, she came to the States and became my wife. We're still together."

But it wasn't a cut-and-dry marriage. Inger's parents weren't happy about losing their daughter to an American. The war was still fresh in everyone's mind, and both of her brothers had been killed, one by the Germans and the other in a freak accident. Her father was a prominent physician and didn't want to see his only daughter move so far away. He felt that Americans were barbarians and didn't like the climate on the East Coast. It also didn't help that Stovall was Catholic, while the Baggers were Evangelical Lutherans. This was the same obstacle Stovall's parents had faced several decades earlier. But like his mom and dad, Stovall eventually prevailed, and the two finally tied the knot. "It was a struggle to get married," he admits. "Maybe that's why we've managed to stay together so long."

THE SEARCH FOR WORK

When Stovall returned from Copenhagen in 1949, he dreamed of becoming a securities analyst. Unfortunately, the United States was in the midst of a recession and the brokerage business was suffering. "I tried to find work and couldn't," he says. "Through one of my father's connections, I got a job with National Distillers, which coincidentally was big in my native state of Kentucky. It made whiskey and other beverage products. I had a very boring position as an accounting clerk. Fortunately, after one year the company put me in its first executive program. They sent me down to Louisville. I lived with some of my aunts and had a nice time learning about how to be a distiller and marketer of alcohol. They also taught me how alcohol is produced, how the barrels are built, techniques for testing the grain, and so forth."

Still, Stovall yearned to do something more challenging, specifically in the investment field. He left National Distillers in late 1952 to become a mutual fund wholesaler. In essence, he was a salesperson charged with getting brokers to sell the two funds he represented. "I worked for a couple of older men who had a wholesaling partnership. I was their leg man. The funds I represented no longer exist," he laments. "One was called Commonwealth Investment Company. It was headquartered in San Francisco. The other was known as the Texas Fund. It featured oil and gas companies that were located primarily in the Southwest. I drove my little Hillman Minx auto all around Pennsylvania, New Jersey, and New York state talking to brokers. I would walk into the firms, discuss our funds with them, and try to convince them to put our literature in their sales racks. Most weren't very interested, but it was a great experience in cold calling."

Mutual funds in general weren't too popular back then. The brokerage community was all aflutter peddling individual stocks and bonds. "The institutional equities market hardly existed," Stovall points out. "Back in the 1940s and 1950s, most institutions bought bonds and mortgages. They owned very few stocks. What equities they did buy were local utilities, banks, and the obvious blue chips. There were very few mutual funds around. Commonwealth was one of the first to offer a monthly investment plan. The Wellington Fund was also a powerful seller, particularly in Pennsylvania, where it was exempt from that state's personal property tax." Wellington, incidentally, was the genesis of what is now the Vanguard Group, which specializes in low-cost index funds. "Some other major funds of that period were the Massachusetts Investment Trust, Canadian Fund, Atomic Development Fund, and Chemical Fund," Stovall adds. "A lot of them have since either changed names or liquidated."

The biggest obstacle for mutual funds of that era may have been their lack of a unique sales hook. "What the brokers did like was the meaty 8 percent sales load attached to most of these funds," Stovall says. "This was long before discounted and negotiated rates, when all commissions were posted and fixed."

1953 . . . A Year to Forget

In the summer of 1953, the Commonwealth Investment Company fired Stovall's wholesaling firm, putting it out of business. To make matters worse, his father died suddenly of a heart attack and his wife almost lost her life during childbirth. "After all this bad news, I got a job with E. F. Hutton as a junior research analyst," he says with a sigh of relief. "I just walked in off the street and was hired to write their morning news wire. This was before we had electronic transmission of news. It came and went over the wire in Morse code. This was a major research product for our clients. E. F. Hutton was especially big in California. In fact, Mr. Edward F. Hutton founded the company in 1902 to bring investment services from the East to the West via private wires. He owned the telegraph lines. This was very high tech for that time. When I joined the firm, most of its production was in California, Arizona, and Texas. It also had a few offices in Chicago, Kansas City, and New York. I had to get the wire written and on the desks of the brokers in California before seven o'clock in the morning, West Coast time."

Stovall's reports talked about the market overall and featured investment ideas from the firm's small team of analysts. "To put this report together, I did all kinds of research," he says. "I would collect newspapers and magazines as fast as I could get them. I read everything from *Chemical Week* to *Engineering News Record* and the *Physician's Desk Reference*. Our in-house analysts followed the regulated industries that ordinary brokers had a hard time understanding, like the utilities, oil and gas pipelines, railroads, airlines, and banks. They also had two or three industrial and technical analysts." The research manager was supposed to be the economist, editor, and team leader as well. So Stovall collected writings from noted bank economists, sifted through them, and came up with a summary of what they thought. It was pretty rudimentary, but it worked.

In no time, Stovall was promoted to industrial analyst, this at a time when analysts had little visibility or status on Wall Street. "Securities analysts, as a group, were just starting to organize and it wasn't even considered to be a legitimate profession," Stovall offers. "I think the first meeting of the New York Society of Security Analysts was in somebody's living room in 1939. They were then on hiatus during World War II. Things didn't get rolling again until the late 1940s. The Chartered Financial Analyst program wasn't started until the early 1960s. I got my CFA as fast as I could in 1965. The CFA designation and its programs have helped the profession to gain much more recognition and professionalism."

THE POLIO REPORT

As a junior analyst for E. F. Hutton in early 1955, Stovall scored a major coup after learning from a journalist friend that the Food and Drug Administration was about to approve the first-ever vaccine against the deadly polio virus. Word was that it had been discovered by a team led by Jonas Salk, a researcher at the University of Pittsburgh. The reporter claimed the government was withholding this announcement until the anniversary of President Franklin Delano Roosevelt's death in April 1955. "I decided to write a report on the drug companies that would likely be licensed to market the Salk polio vaccine," Stovall says. "My fellow Wall Street drug analysts either didn't know or didn't care about this discovery. I figured if the government was going to announce the approval anyway, I would beat the herd by recommending Merck, Parke-Davis, American Home Products, and a small California outfit called Cutter Laboratories beforehand." When the announcement was made, Stovall's recommended stocks went up almost instantly. To the brokers who followed his advice, Stovall became a hero. "They thought I was a genius," he exclaims. "But I was really an opportunistic rookie. I followed this up by recommending Syntex, the first company to come out with a birth-control drug."

These stellar recommendations also helped to further his own career. "E. F. Hutton gave me a promotion," Stovall says. "I went from being a wire answerer and newsletter writer to a senior analyst in just three years." He also became a member of the New York Society of Security Analysts. All of this good fortune set the stage for what would become one of the best years of his life.

1957 . . . A YEAR TO REMEMBER

The death of Stovall's father in 1953 came as a devastating shock. The two were very close, and his passing was completely unexpected. "I admired him so much for what he had done," Stovall explains. "He managed to get himself off the farm and onto Wall Street, which was an amazing accomplishment in those days. In his honor, I decided to get an MBA. I figured he would be proud of that. I went to night school at New York University's Graduate School of Business." Stovall began his studies right after his dad's passing in 1953 and graduated in 1957.

"That same year, I was promoted to captain in the Army reserves and made manager of E. F. Hutton's research department," he says. "What's more, my Danish in-laws finally accepted me as their son-in-law. They took Inger and me to an international surgical conference in Mexico. By that time, we had two sons, Sten and Sam. It was quite a year."

This last event may have been the most personally rewarding for Stovall. His in-laws, who had not been happy about seeing their daughter run off and marry an American, remained firm in their opposition, only not in the traditional sense. For more than seven years, they refused to speak to Stovall. That all changed in 1957. They flew to New York for a visit and finally made amends. What's more, 1957 saw Stovall's wife regain her vigorous good health, lost after suffering a medical setback and the death of an infant child.

INVESTMENT STRATEGISTS— THE UNTOLD STORY

The job of research director in the 1950s normally went to the best writer and public speaker among the brokerage firm's team of analysts. This made sense, because the research director was required to constantly communicate with both brokers and the press. "Back then, they chose the research director like kids choose their football teams," Stovall claims. "The best athlete got to be the quarterback and the kid whose mother bought the football got to be the captain. In other words, the sons of the major partners got jobs in management, and if you were the best analyst, idea generator, and writer you were named research director. That's not the case anymore. Nowadays firms spend millions of dollars on research, and they have several editors on staff to edit the reports. I used to handle all of these functions myself. Today's research director is highly compensated and must be a good administrator who knows how to recruit and maintain all-star analysts, while marketing their skills to corporate deal makers." The research director's role became much more prominent and important once institutional interest in equities ballooned in the 1960s and 1970s. These bigwig clients demanded more detailed and thorough research from their brokers, and the major firms responded.

PARTNERSHIP AT HUTTON

Stovall was made a partner at E. F. Hutton in 1960. "I thought that was quite something because there weren't many big brokerage firms to begin with, and those that were around were mainly partnerships," he says. "Becoming a partner required some capital and was more difficult than being made a paper vice president, which is the popular thing today. Now anyone who is a broker or staff specialist of any substance gets to be a vice president."

Not one to rest on his laurels, Stovall continued to search for promising investment opportunities to recommend to his brokers and clients. "I was trying to be ahead of the competition by linking fundamental values in the market with coming events," he explains. "For example, I witnessed the advent of the discount store in the retail industry. This was a major event. You went from traditional retailing to malls, and then along came the discounters. These creatures hadn't existed before. I also witnessed interesting developments in the chemical and aerospace industries. The 'space age' stocks offered many opportunities, from the landing of Sputnik in 1957 through the early 1960s. I was a frequent contributor to *Barron's* then and wrote pieces on rocketry, high-energy fuels, and space-age materials. That's where the action was."

It was Alan Abelson, the then-managing editor of *Barron's,* who first gave Stovall a crack at bylined journalism in the late 1950s. For more than a decade, Stovall wrote a number of stories for that weekly paper, along with a few book reviews. From early 1968 through 1977, he was a regular columnist for *Forbes.* In 1979, he began writing for *Financial World,* and most recently started penning a bimonthly personal finance column for *Sales and Marketing Management* magazine.

THE MOVE TO NUVEEN

After 14 successful years at E. F. Hutton, where he eventually became a corporate stockholder, Stovall left to join the firm John Nuveen. "E. F. Hutton was wearing me out. They sent me from town to town giving talks to our branch managers, brokers, institutional clients, Rotary clubs, and local colleges," he contends. "I was fully extended. The company kept growing, and I figured I would be better off at a smaller, institutionally oriented firm. In January 1967, I was offered a position at John Nuveen." Nuveen specialized in fixed-income instruments, but wanted to expand its reach into equities. In essence, it hoped to transform itself, Stovall claims, into a boutique version of Salomon Brothers. The firm bought a seat on the New York Stock Exchange and recruited Stovall to be its research director for both stocks and bonds. "We made a lot of progress in equities, until management lost most of our capital speculating on the bond desk," Stovall asserts. "Nuveen had to resign from the stock exchange because of inadequate capital. It was high drama. I had to terminate the various people I recruited for the equity operation in the summer of 1969. It was very embarrassing, yet enlightening."

Stovall decided to follow the golden rule he had learned in grammar school, which called for taking care of the now displaced workers he had recruited. "I tried to get them all interviews and jobs," he recalls. "To show interest in somebody other than yourself on Wall Street in the 1960s was so novel that it attracted a lot of favorable attention. I managed to get interviews for all of the analysts. Some are still working at the places where I opened the doors for them."

One of the more prominent analysts Stovall helped out in 1969 was E. Michael Metz. Metz was hired by Oppenheimer and for years served as their high-profile and frequently quoted chief investment strategist. Stovall was also offered a job as research manager at Oppenheimer during this turmoil, but turned it down, since he viewed Oppenheimer as a "very tough" firm to work for. "I figured if I made any mistakes, I'd be thrown to the lions," he says.

Nuveen survived after being rescued by a cash infusion from an outside insurance company, but its equity operation was forced to shut down. Stovall was about to be unemployed himself when executives at Reynolds and Company heard about his predicament. They offered him a partnership and lead role as the firm's research and marketing director. Remember, this is the same firm that once employed Stovall's dad and that he himself worked for as a teenaged messenger boy. "They knew me and admired my father," he says. "That's why they offered me the job. I had nine different partnership opportunities presented to me that summer, but I went with Reynolds. Once again the Higher Power took care of me. Of those offers, the only firms that really survived and did well during the subsequent two decades were Reynolds and Oppenheimer." The other firms became casualties of the paper crunch of the early 1970s and slowdown in business during and following the 1973–1974 bear market.

"I joined Reynolds on the day after Labor Day in 1969 and stayed there until the day after Labor Day in 1985," Stovall points out. "During that time, the company changed from Reynolds and Company, to Dean Witter Reynolds, to Sears Roebuck (although Sears kept the name Dean Witter). Sears owned the firm when I left. It was a very satisfactory 16 years, and I had a good time. I was the chief investment strategist and corporate communicator. I talked regularly with analysts and others interested in our company, supervised the in-house magazine, coordinated the annual and quarterly reports, and dealt with the press. I also wrote a weekly market letter and gave an occasional speech."

ON HIS OWN

By the time Stovall left what was then called Dean Witter Reynolds in 1985, he was better off financially than he had ever been. His Reynolds stock, which had split several times before being converted into shares of Sears, was worth a pretty penny and allowed him to enjoy a more-than-comfortable lifestyle. Ironically, even though watching and recommending equities was his business, Sears was the only stock he owned in large quantity at the time of his departure. "I guess I've always been somewhat of a moralist," he maintains. "I didn't think it was right for me to trade stocks in my portfolio when I was responsible for making recommendations or editing those of the other analysts under me. I know not everyone agrees with me on this." Besides, he didn't have a lot of money left after expenses. He and his wife were raising six children (their own four and two foster children), and had plenty of tuition to pay. They also invested in homes.

After leaving Dean Witter Reynolds, he hooked up with the small arbitrage firm Twenty-First Securities Corporation. Founded by Robert N. Gordon in 1983, the company specializes in low-risk money management for individuals and institutions. It also has a corporate cash-management department, which uses synthetic money market instruments and bona-fide arbitrage strategies to generate returns that are greater than those offered by Treasury bills for a company's excess cash. Stovall is now a board member of the firm and president of his own investment division, called Stovall/Twenty-First Advisers. "When I left Dean Witter Reynolds, some wealthy families I had been helping informally opened accounts with me right away," he says. "Then, through a combination of my media exposure and recommendations from satisfied clients, I built up a pretty good business of prosperous families and individuals." Stovall and Twenty-First Securities currently oversee around $1 billion in assets. Stovall makes all of the investment decisions for those accounts he personally supervises. "The firm has about 35 employees, but most of them are involved with our risk-averse arbitrage operation," he adds. "We have a trading room, operations department, accountants, tax lawyers, and about eight brokers."

Partly because most of his clients are over the age of 50, he invests their money cautiously. "I use a lot of convertible bonds and convertible preferreds for both the income component and the appreciation potential," he says. "I'm more aggressive with these instruments than most. Many managers don't use convertible preferreds and debentures at all because, at least in their minds, they represent a combination of the worst aspects of both stocks and bonds. The quality rating of a convertible is usually less than that of a better-grade fixed-income security. What's more, if you buy the convertible of a company whose stock is hot, the convertible won't go up nearly as much as the common because it has conversion limitations. But my point of view is that if you can find a company that isn't doing too well, yet has an adequate quality rating, you can invest in it and reduce your risk by buying its convertible preferreds and bonds."

THE GREAT COMMUNICATOR

As an investment strategist for most of his career, Stovall has long been in the public eye. Investment strategists are almost always colorful people in charge of formulating, at any given time, a firm's recommended portfolio weightings in stocks, bonds, and cash. Most are also ready to offer opinions about the market on a moment's notice. Some even make specific stock picks. Regardless of their particular duties, almost every chief investment strategist also acts as the firm's primary spokesperson. After all, when reporters need a talking head to fill in a newspaper or on TV, they usually aren't interested in what some broker in Iowa thinks. They want to talk with the head person, the big cheese, the all-knowing seer. In other words, they seek out the hot brokerage or money management firm of the moment's investment strategist. As a result, Stovall has been a radio and television commentator for years and knows scores of journalists.

Sadly, one look at the overall records of these gurus proves their predictions and market calls are spotty at best. As Stovall puts it, there's a bull and a bear in every crowd, and one is ultimately proven right. It's just impossible to know who is on the mark until after the fact. Honest Wall Street practitioners, including Stovall, admit that the market calls and asset allocation decisions made by these strategists are frequently little more than show business. It's a way for firms to comfort clients by letting them know someone is looking out for them.

A few strategists have made some great calls over the years. However, Stovall refers to most of them as entertainers, not serious market pundits. In his mind, they are always prepared with sound bites, but short on useful information. "If you follow the work of these strategists, you'll see they write very well and are worth reading for the entertainment value," he offers. "Nevertheless, some have been wrong for years. A chimpanzee with a dartboard is more effective than many of them. I've never understood how they could keep such great paying jobs by being so wrong. I recently attended a conference that our firm helped to sponsor at the Columbia School of Journalism. It was entitled 'Wall Street and the Press: Mutual Friends or Enemies?' One panel consisted solely of market strategists. One strategist talked at length about how some of her peers were irresponsible. She claimed they were often cited in the press solely because they were quotable and friendly. But she contended their comments did more harm than good."

Stovall admittedly finds himself in the role of media market strategist on occasion as well, including bimonthly as a panelist on the popular PBS television show *Wall $treet Week With Louis Rukeyser.* While he tries to be careful about what he says on the air, like everyone else in this business, Stovall's comments regrettably aren't always on the mark. Even so, he was elected by viewers to the show's Hall of Fame in 1995.

WALL $TREET WEEK: BEHIND THE SCENES

Stovall first appeared on *Wall $treet Week* in 1976, six years after the program's debut. He was a columnist for *Forbes* at the time and was frequently quoted in the press. This exposure eventually caught the eye of *Wall $treet Week*'s creator and then-producer, Anne Truax Darlington. She phoned Stovall and asked him to come on as a one-time guest. "They wanted to talk about some of the stock market theories I had popularized," he explains. "A popular one was the 'General Motors Bellwether' theory. It was based on my belief back then that the action of General Motors stock was a foreshadower of overall market trends. This was a very effective predictive tool for many years."

Stovall's guest spot went well, so much so that Darlington called back a few months later and asked him to become a regular panelist. "I thought about it briefly on the phone and told her no," he says. "It required going to Owings Mills, Maryland, on Friday afternoon and I figured I wouldn't get out of there until the next morning because of lack of transportation. That would have ruined my weekends." But when Stovall got home that night and told his wife about the offer, she immediately suggested he call back and accept. "My wife insisted that it would be good exposure for me," he recalls. "Of course, she was right."

Stovall now appears on the show about six times a year. He used to be on more frequently, before the show added to its number of panelists in recent years. "Louis realized that *Washington Week in Review,* which airs right before us in most markets, was becoming a group of aging leftists, while we were a group of aging rightists," he reveals. "Louis decided to change that." Rukeyser has added a number of minorities, a cadre of females, and several young up-and-coming new analysts to the show's panel.

The routine for regular panelists goes something like this: A few days before the air date, they get a packet of background information to study. It contains a biography on the week's guest, plus a list of that person's most recent portfolio holdings and analyses. This gives panelists more insight into the guest's philosophy and investment style. "For example, if our guest is the world's leading peanut butter analyst, we'll receive a list of the stocks he or she is recommending to the firm's brokers," Stovall notes. "We'll know if he or she likes Peter Pan better than Skippy or Jif, but that's about it. Knowing the guests' areas of expertise, their track records, and what they like helps us to come up with intelligent questions."

This is the only advance preparation the panelists, or guests for that matter, are given. The one exception is with the viewer questions segment, which has been cut back to once a month since the program's running time was clipped by PBS to add more sponsor announcements. When this feature is included, panelists get their question in advance so they can prepare an accurate answer. "The guest doesn't know which questions are going to be asked, and none of us has a clue as to what Louis will talk about," Stovall adds. "He comes up with all of his own ideas and writes his own script. If you're sitting around the panelist table, and you're number one to talk, you have no idea what leading comment he's going to make. He could remark, 'Well, Bob, there was a big snowstorm in northern Pennsylvania today, so give us your favorite snowstorm stocks.' Or he might talk about how the Miami Dolphins are doing. You just never know."

Panelists and the week's guest are supposed to arrive at the studio in Owings Mills by 6:00 P.M. on Friday, to loosen each other up. They share a light meal, served buffet style, make a quick pass through makeup, and prepare for the unrehearsed show. "The program essentially airs live," Stovall says. "We usually do what's called a live tape. This means we tape the show, but it is not edited and airs a few minutes after completion. We start taping around 7:40 P.M. Eastern Standard Time, finish just after 8:00 P.M., and it airs nationwide at 8:30 P.M. About a third of the time the show is done completely live. That's usually because of equipment problems, a complex graphic is incomplete, or Louis hasn't finished with his script in time for the technical staff to tape it. The year-end and midyear shows, which feature only a group of panelists and the host, are always done live."

The person in charge of making sure all the microphones are plugged in and everyone is in his or her proper seat is the woman you see escorting Rukeyser in at the beginning of the show. "We call her Ms. Smythe," Stovall says. "She's really the floor manager, but the audience seems to think of her as our hostess. She's also responsible for replacing faulty mikes and providing cough syrup if somebody starts to choke." "Ms. Smythe's" real name is Natalie Seltz. She's been at the Maryland Center for Public Broadcasting since the 1970s and also produces a couple of other shows for the station.

THE REAL RUKEYSER

What's host Louis Rukeyser, that personable pundit, *really* like? "He's the same off camera as he is on the show," Stovall insists. "He's witty and very quick. He's a wordsmith, phrasemaker, punster, and he likes fast-paced conversations. I've taken nine cruises with him, along with other panelists such as Frank Cappiello, Carter Randall, Bernadette Murphy, and Gail Dudack. When you have meals or party with him, you'll find he's the same way he is on camera. He's a very well-brought-up fellow. His father was a famous print journalist who worked for Hearst. Louis got his start as a print reporter for the *Baltimore Sun.* He then worked for ABC-TV's London bureau and in India. His three brothers are all involved with communications in one way or another as well. They're all highly educated and fiercely competitive with one another."

While Stovall and the other panelists get a small stipend for appearing on the show, he admits the exposure from being associated with Rukeyser has been priceless. "It has made it possible for me to have my own business and become a nationally recognized Wall Street personality," he says. "It has not only helped me, but every other panelist on the show." The biggest negative, he claims, is that some of his colleagues are jealous and occasionally critical of his participation. Then again, they don't get the numerous speaking engagements, media exposure, and new clients that flow Stovall's way as a direct result of being on the program.

Of all the financial shows on television today, and there are many, *Wall $treet Week* is unquestionably the most powerful and influential. It's every portfolio manager's dream to be asked on as a guest. Among other things, an appearance on the show can lead to hundreds of millions of dollars in new assets. Its following is that strong. The impact that other financial programs and cable networks such as CNBC and CNNfn have on viewers doesn't compare. Stovall knows this firsthand. He's been on almost every national investment show around. "People really don't take you seriously unless you're on *Wall $treet Week*," he says. "I think that's because it is a serious show with clear continuity. For example, if you make a mistake in answering a question, people will write in or call. If Louis catches it, he'll make you apologize and correct it on your next appearance. By contrast, I can go on the major networks and say almost anything and no one will even give a darn, since they're so used to inaccuracies. We also reach a much larger audience. CNN's excellent *Moneyline* show gets one million domestic viewers at the most. Louis says *Wall $treet Week*'s viewership is around ten million. It's a very powerful program. The age of our average viewer is around 55. Interestingly enough, about a third of them don't even invest. They just watch the show for its information, camaraderie, and humor."

FAMILY LIFE

Stovall and his wife have four children. Their eldest, Sten (rhymes with Dean), is a London-based political/economic journalist and global financial editor for Reuters. From 1991 to 1997, he was also the European correspondent for the PBS program *Nightly Business Report*. Their next son, Sam, followed in his dad's footsteps by becoming an investment analyst, speaker, and writer for Standard & Poor's in New York. Daughter Benedikte, the only single one of the bunch, works as a speech language therapist in Sarasota, Florida. And their youngest son, Robert, Jr., is an advertising executive based in Fort Lee, New Jersey. The Stovall's kids have collectively given them five grandchildren so far.

The Stovall's also have an extended family of two Cuban political refugees whom they raised for six years until their birth parents could flee their native land. "They were with us from 1962 to 1968, and we still get together for at least one family reunion each year," Stovall says. "I didn't think Fidel Castro would survive, so I talked my wife into taking these two boys in. They were staying at an orphanage in Paterson, New Jersey. Their parents were in jail in Cuba. Apparently Castro locked up people from aristocratic families, like the boys' parents, so he could take their assets and give them to others. That's how he redistributed wealth in his country. The boys, Enrique and Eduardo Del Riego, had originally been placed with an older couple in our Catholic church diocese. They couldn't handle the boys and sent them back to the orphanage. We drove over to pick Enrique and Eduardo up in our station wagon in July 1962. They sat in the back with our dog and were terrified at first, but after a few days, we adjusted to each other and they've been an important part of our family ever since. The boys grew into nice young men. Both are professionals in the Miami area. One's in medicine and the other's in shipping. They now have wonderful families of their own."

Stovall concedes he was wrong about Castro's demise by at least 35 years. "That's about average for an investment strategist, though," he quips.

MEET PROFESSOR STOVALL

Since 1985, Stovall has been an adjunct professor of finance at New York University's Stern Graduate School of Business. "I teach a course in investment strategy that's always a sellout," he says. "I have 65 MBA candidates every semester. I show them how to pick stocks, when to focus on bonds, discuss asset allocation and debate the merits of both value and growth investing. I also give them techniques for spotting potential takeover candidates, and bring in a number of guest lecturers, including my son Sam, whose specialty is 'sector rotation.' About a third of the class is female, and I have a large number of international students. The average age is around 28. I think one reason students like my course is that I have a reputation for being understandable and somewhat humorous. Many professors at graduate schools around the country are not native English speakers. They are difficult to understand, which makes it tough for students to grasp an intensive subject like finance, especially if English is a second or third language for them, too."

WALL STREET'S UNION CARD

Because of his many connections, Stovall is inundated with requests from students to help them land jobs. Since Wall Street has been on an unfettered boom since 1991, entry-level positions other than as sales trainees are increasingly rare. That's why he often suggests they consider other fields, like industrial finance and communications, which appear to offer more opportunities at this stage of the economic cycle. "Right now, close to 40 percent of all MBAs want to work on Wall Street, which is usually a leading indicator of a market top," Stovall says. "I start off every conversation by telling my job-seeking students they are wise to keep their options open by looking at industries that haven't prospered as much in recent years and are poised for a turnaround. I simply can't lead people to openings in finance as easily as I once could."

Still, without an MBA or a strong background in electronic data processing, Stovall claims it is virtually impossible to break into the investment business, unless you get a formal introduction from a connected insider. "An MBA has become sort of a union card," he says. "In the 1920s, all you needed was a high school diploma. That made you special. Then, for my generation, it was an undergraduate degree. A BA or BS was once stylish on Wall Street because you could be a successful trader, broker, or banker by relying heavily on referrals. Not anymore. It's much more competitive now. These days you need an MBA and strong computer skills."

Furthermore, according to Stovall, an advanced degree gives you the educational edge you need to be a successful practitioner. "You must have a good understanding of futures, options, indexing, and tax law, all of which are subjects they teach in graduate school," he insists. "It's also important to be computer-literate. The requirements for working in a trust company, bank, mutual fund, investment banking firm, or just being a professional in general are much more stringent now than when I got started."

BULLISH ON THE FUTURE

Like the other experts I interviewed for this book, the longevity of the 1990s bull market has taken Stovall by complete surprise. It's unlike anything he has ever seen in his 40-plus years in the business. That makes it difficult for him to even guess what will happen as we enter the new millennium. "Several veteran commentators/strategists from the financial press and major investment houses have been loudly negative and wrong for a long time," he observes.

In mid-1997, Stovall prepared a report for his clients detailing more than a dozen reasons why a major bear may be on the horizon. Although he wasn't advising them to sell out, he cited a number of reasons why the bearish pundits might have a point. Among the warning signs: a high price-dividend ratio for stocks, complacent investor psychology, a rash of mergers and stock splits, heavy trading volume on the major exchanges, record-high seat sales on the New York Stock Exchange, and media glamorization of investment managers. In all fairness, Stovall mentioned that these negatives have been present for some time, yet have done little to faze the relentless bull. The market's enormous momentum, which has confounded almost every stock market historian, makes predicting what the early twenty-first century holds for investors all the more difficult.

"Obviously much of the huge inflow of money into retirement plans right now is going into equities," Stovall observes. "Whether that continues is anyone's guess. Much of this money is invested in mutual funds. The growth of the fund industry holds significant implications for the future of the financial markets. Instead of being very narrow, ownership of mutual funds has broadened during the 1990s. Since there are so many equity fund investors (63 million as of 1998), many of whom have never experienced a major bear market, the real question is how they will behave when and if the market corrects. About two-thirds of all shareholders bought their funds after October 1990, when the most recent bull market began. The Dow Jones Industrial Average stood at 2365. Consequently, most people are pretty sanguine about the continuing cash flow into funds, believing that investors won't panic during the next downturn, especially since they are getting older and are long-term investors saving for retirement through 401(k) plans."

In the same breath, however, Stovall cites an August 1996 article in the *Financial Times* noting that at the start of 1990, equity mutual fund assets in Japan were $250 billion, slightly more than the $249 billion held in U.S. funds at the time. "Japan's total today has plunged to about $30 billion, or less than 1 percent of the current U.S. total of $4.3 trillion," Stovall notes. "More than six years of negative compound returns was clearly enough to trigger huge redemptions in Japan, shrinking total assets in yen by more than 91 percent." Could the same thing happen in the United States? Of course, it could. But will it? That's the trillion-dollar question. Personally, Stovall doubts it.

But Stovall doesn't have much time for pondering such unanswerables. Between managing money, teaching, being a TV star, writing magazine columns for various publications and caring for his large family, he has a very full schedule. While his main office is in New York, Stovall and his wife are constantly traveling around from their principal home in Sarasota, Florida, to their New York apartment and their residence near Honesdale, Pennsylvania. The Pennsylvania home is a working farm of some 120 acres. "There's a tenant farmer who grows hay and pastures his cattle on the land, and I work with him to make sure all of the buildings, fences, and flora are OK," Stovall says.

This investment veteran is a serious collector of Scandinavian oil paintings from the nineteenth and early twentieth centuries. In addition, he has amassed a number of unique paperweights over the years. "I get some exercise, too," he adds. "I like to swim, fish, bicycle, and play squash."

The practicing Catholic also looks forward to December, when he gets to write his annual Christmas "speed letter." It goes out to friends and family and is full of one-line "Stovallisms." Among his favorites over the years is a quote borrowed from gossip columnist Liz Smith. "She once wrote, 'See everything, overlook a great deal, correct a little,'" Stovall observes. "Pope John XXIII said it, but it's really what any father of a big family should do. You need to see everything, be aware of what's happening around you, overlook most of it, and try to correct very little." This is also good all-around advice for every investor who, like Stovall, is on the constant prowl for promising new money-making opportunities.

ROBERT H. STOVALL'S

top 10 GROWTH STOCKS

FOR THE 21ST CENTURY

1. General Electric

2. Coca-Cola

3. Royal Dutch

4. Microsoft

5. Intel

6. Merck

7. America Online

8. Procter & Gamble

9. Citigroup

10. Johnson & Johnson

Rule 5

GET TO KNOW YOUR PARTNERS

Although he was born in Philadelphia, Shelby Davis spent most of his early years in Tarrytown, New York. Even as a young lad, he remembers going around with his father, a well-known Wall Street insurance analyst, to visit potential investments. His dad turned $100,000 into $800 million by investing in a portfolio of carefully selected insurance stocks. Before buying shares in a company, Davis's father believed it was essential to meet with management, the people he referred to as his "partners."

"I loved tagging along with him for these inspections," Davis reflects. "The first visit I remember was in June 1950, right after Truman declared war on Korea. My mom, dad, sister, and I were driving to the Midwest for our summer vacation and dad decided to mix business with pleasure by going to visit some insurance companies. We went to places like Springfield, Illinois, home of Franklin Life, and Fort Wayne, Indiana, where Lincoln National was headquartered. Early on, dad taught me that you should do your own research. That means going to visit companies yourself and meeting with top management.

"While we were in the car, we heard that North Korea had invaded South Korea and President Truman's response was to declare war. He made a dramatic speech, and the stock market cracked badly," Davis continues. "My dad had just started his own investment firm about a year earlier. He said, 'Out of crisis comes opportunity if you know what you're doing.' He was right. It turned out to be a great buying opportunity, because once the war got underway, the stock market took off. Dad often pointed out that you make most of your money in a bear market. You just don't realize it at the time. It causes you to make the tough decision of whether to hold or buy more shares."

Davis went along with his father to query executives at both Franklin Life and Lincoln National. "I didn't say much," he says. "But I listened and was awed by the grandeur of these life-insurance buildings. I figured there must be a lot of money stored inside. These were really glamour stocks at the time. They were doubling every six months to a year. It was pretty much an instant gratification group. If my father liked a stock, you were well-advised to buy it, because he knew what he was doing." Franklin Life was the first stock Davis bought at the tender age of 13. "It was terrific," he says. "I think it went up around 1,000 percent. As Peter Lynch would say, 'It was a ten-bagger.' The company was eventually bought out by American Tobacco."

GETTING A BROAD PERSPECTIVE

Davis majored in history, not finance, at Princeton. "My father said you can always pick up the accounting," he shares. "He felt it was important to have a broad perspective and understand how important people are in the history of the world. Whether it's Jesus Christ, Napoleon, Peter the Great, or Winston Churchill, all had a huge impact on society. I have always been interested in people and the human side of history. Not so much in the battles we have faced, but on the human decision process that goes into making things happen and that change the course of events."

PEOPLE ARE EVERYTHING

Davis's first job out of college was working as a stock analyst for the Bank of New York. He found that the bank was much more interested in raw historical numbers than in going out and inspecting companies. This was different from the approach he had learned from his dad, and Davis pushed hard to have more emphasis placed on talking and visiting with management. "I said, 'Sure, we can update the data using public material and research from other Wall Street firms or sources like *Value Line,* Standard & Poor's, or Moody's,'" he reflects. "But since I believed companies were made up of people, I wanted a travel budget so I could go visit the firms I followed. They did give me a little bit of money for that. I recall spending two or three days in Akron, Ohio, visiting every tire and rubber company. Goodyear, Firestone, General Cooper, Uniroyal, they were all there. Then, like now, I didn't ask just basic questions about the near term. I wanted to know things like, What's your strategy? Where do you want to be in three to five years? How are you going to get there? What tactics will you use? What are some of your most important milestones? What are you spending on capital, versus what you're generating in cash flow? What are your financial needs, if any? It's important to meet management because companies are made up of people. Leadership is vital to success. To me, the people who run the company are what make all the difference."

This is in contrast to the conventional thinking on Wall Street, which seems to suggest that only *today's* numbers matter. Momentum players can care less about the background of a company's CEO. Many money managers can't even tell you what products the companies in their portfolios make. They simply own these stocks because quarterly earnings are going up. This kind of short-term thinking has never made much sense to Davis. "To do proper fundamental analysis, you must understand the business you're investing in," he maintains. "Winning companies are made by good people. A stock is a company, not just a piece of paper. So I evaluate the entire business rather than poring over momentum charts. What you're really doing is becoming a partner in the business. That stock you purchase represents fractional ownership in the company. The people running the show are your partners. In any business venture, you are certainly going to want to know who your managing partners are. I grant you that over a three-month or even a year-long period, it probably doesn't make much difference. But over a ten-year period, I think it does. My father used to say, 'You need to meet the management so you can figure out whether they are *doers* or *bluffers.*' That's really the purpose of doing on-site inspections."

DOERS AND BLUFFERS

Separating those who can tell a good story from those who really mean what they say is no easy task. It often takes more than one meeting. "Wall Street is obviously more sophisticated now than it used to be," Davis points out. "In my father's time, it was extremely rare for an investment manager to go out and visit his holdings. Dad did it with the insurance stocks and made a killing. I naturally gravitated to that same thought process. I figured I could better understand the guts of a business, figure out how it operates, and learn about its major problems and opportunities by talking with the people in charge. It's like getting a lecture from a college professor who knows a lot more about a certain subject than you do."

Davis's reporter instincts come from experience. He worked for the Princeton student newspaper and is comfortable asking questions and taking notes. "When I started out, companies were flattered that you took the time to come and see them," he recalls. "Now they are all shielded by investor relations departments and public relations firms. They have conference calls, and information is disseminated in a much quicker fashion. But I still feel the principle remains the same. *People* make companies, so you should get to know them. What do you have to lose? It is a time-consuming process, and there's no guarantee you won't be badly misled by some of these guys. That has happened to me more than once. But there's no substitute for that face-to-face interaction."

An in-depth meeting can also help you come up with a list of good reasons to terminate your partnership with a company. "If managers fail to do something they promise, if they start fooling with the accounting, or if the story keeps changing, you might want to move on," Davis advises. "Or if you see top management selling a lot of their own stock, while at the same time telling you what a great company they have and how wonderful the future looks, it should definitely send up a warning flag.

"Above all, we sit down with the people running the companies to discuss the fundamental dynamics of their business," Davis adds. "Essential to our thinking is that the goal of research is to separate the company managements who are the 'bluffers' from those who are the 'doers.' Bluffers always have an excuse when things don't turn out as they expect."

ACCESS FOR THE SMALL INVESTOR

If you're not a big investor, like Davis, chances are you won't land a personal meeting with the CEO of a major corporation. But there are other ways to find out what kind of people run the show. Start with a call to the investor relations (IR) department. You might be surprised by how much you can learn from talking with these folks. Most are in direct contact with top company brass. Beyond that, look for interviews with company officials in the media. You might even ask the IR folks to send you a stack of articles and analyst reports about the company. (Most keep this stuff on hand to fulfill such requests.) Finally, you can ask the IR department for a list of brokerage analysts who follow the company. Then, call some of these analysts and get their insights on the company. Many have met the CEO personally and might be able to give you a clue as to how trustworthy he or she and his or her counterparts are.

MEETINGS AND MORE

Davis doesn't necessarily need to meet with executives from every company he invests in. However, he's convinced that the smaller a firm is, the more important a personal inspection becomes. By the same token, it's much easier for individual investors to connect with high-level executives at tinier companies, since these executives are more eager to attract shareholder interest. Don't be surprised if a call to the CEO's office of a small-cap company lands you at least a personal phone meeting with him or her.

In addition to personal visits, Davis goes to a lot of analyst meetings and makes frequent follow-up calls to top executives at the companies he follows. "I believe in Peter Lynch's theory that if you call 10 companies, you'll get one idea. If you call 20 companies, you'll get two ideas, and so forth," he shares. "So I spend a lot of time calling companies from wherever I am. It's easier to call when I'm at my home in Maine sometimes, because the CEO feels as if you're interrupting your vacation to talk to him and will take your call. It works like a charm from Wyoming and Florida too."

If you can't reach the CEO yourself, sometimes the IR department can put you in touch with another executive who can provide similar information. Be persistent when you call. Let the company know you are a shareholder, or potential shareholder, to be reckoned with, regardless of how much you have to invest.

Before leaving on a recent trip from New York to Maine, Davis stopped by to see the management at General Re in Stamford, Connecticut. This is the largest property and casualty reinsurer in the United States, and the fourth largest in the world. It was also one of his favorite and biggest holdings, prior to being bought out by Warren Buffett's Berkshire Hathaway in 1998. Davis's visit convinced him to buy more of the stock, even though its share price had been floundering. That was a good move, since shares of General Re shot up in value once word of the Berkshire acquisition was announced.

INTEGRITY COUNTS

When Don Yacktman does research on a potential investment, he is especially interested in checking out the integrity of the people in charge of running the show, although this isn't always something that can be determined right away. "The only way you can get a sense of what kind of people they are is by talking with them and asking a lot of questions," Yacktman maintains. "I want to know what their strategy is for the cash that's being generated. I want to make sure I completely understand the business. One of the things I listen for is how straight they are in answering my questions. Are they willing to share their true inner feelings about the issues that are important to me? Usually I'm not asking about quarterly earnings estimates. I tend to focus on long-range issues, their vision for the future. And I judge them not only on what they say, but more importantly by what they do. That's how they build credibility. I'll give you a good example. One stock I've followed for a long time is Ralston

Purina. I feel very confident in my ability to predict what CEO Bill Stiritz is going to do. He's established a pattern over the years. In most cases, managements become predictable based on what they've actually done in the past. A management that's not straight with its shareholders will eventually get nailed for it."

GOOD MONEY SPENDERS

Beyond that, Yacktman wants a management team that will live up to its promises, while making good use of the company's assets. "All of my businesses are very profitable and tend to generate a lot of excess cash," he says. "I want management to reinvest that cash to earn an even higher return. The way they allocate this money is a good litmus test for how shareholder-oriented they are. Companies basically have five options as to what they can do with excess cash. Listed in order of importance, they can first put it back into the business, through research and development, marketing, and cost reduction. The other four options are making an acquisition, repurchasing shares, repaying debt, or giving cash back to shareholders in the form of a dividend. The more cash they invest at the top end of the list, the more they'll increase the company's private market value over time. Putting excess cash back into the business is the cheapest way to create value. If you enhance the crown jewel, or the original business, unless something goes terribly wrong, you're bound to increase the value of your company."

You can get a lot of this information through reading the financial statements in a company's annual report and SEC filings. Unfortunately, if the people doing the books don't have integrity, the numbers can't always be trusted. This is what happened with Cendant, a high-flying stock through much of the mid-1990s. Once word came out that the company was accused of cooking the books in mid-1998, the stock got creamed and had a hard time climbing back up. Incidents like this, fortunately, are very rare in corporate America today.

Acquisitions, on the other hand, are more tricky. "They're like trading baseball players," Yacktman maintains. "If done synergistically and at the right price, there's no question it can do wonders for a company. But you have to look at it as a 20- to 30-year investment. On the other hand, if you don't get those two crucial elements just right, it can be a disaster. Quaker Oats is a good example. In 1983, the company bought Stokley–Van Camp. Since then, Quaker has sold off enough of the assets it acquired to get all of its money back and then some. What's more, it still has one product left from that acquisition— Gatorade. Today, Gatorade alone is worth some $3 billion dollars. It was a fabulous acquisition. Why? It was synergistic, it fit right in with the company's other businesses, and it was acquired at a good price.

"Now fast-forward to 1995 when Quaker Oats bought the beverage company Snapple right at the peak of its popularity," he continues. "In this case, it did the exact reverse of the Stokley–Van Camp purchase. Quaker Oats overpaid for Snapple, bought it right when the business was beginning to peak, and got a product that wasn't nearly as synergistic as Gatorade. The two pieces obviously didn't fit together as well and it was far too costly. The management team didn't do its due diligence work properly in advance." To show you how bad this deal was, Quaker Oats paid $1.7 billion for Snapple and wound up selling it to Triarc two years later for just $300 million. Quaker Oats CEO William Smithburg ultimately wound up resigning over the fiasco.

The risk of overpaying for a potentially attractive target is yet another reason Yacktman prefers to see companies plow any extra cash back into existing operations, instead of spending it to buy a competitor. "When you go out and purchase another company, you're forced to pay up, because the seller knows what he or she is doing," Yacktman explains. "The most effective acquisitions are those where one company brings some added value to the process. Here's what I mean: If combining the two operations will increase revenue and save in distribution, advertising or production costs, you can do very well. Yes, acquisitions can be a fabulous 25-year investment. But too often managers pay up dearly for them.

"I often prefer to see companies repurchase their own shares, instead of making high-priced acquisitions," he says. "The Quaker Oats acquisition of Snapple is a good case in point. The company would have been far better off using its extra cash to repurchase its own stock, instead of buying Snapple. Unfortunately, it's very difficult for corporate managers to get away from the idea of kingdom building. It's a natural problem many of them face. If abused, it can lead to disaster, especially if they don't pay the right price."

Yacktman doesn't force himself to meet personally with management before investing in a company. In fact, although he does at least try to talk with them by phone, if he thinks he understands the company well enough without such a meeting he may still purchase a big block of shares. In addition, the more stock top managers own, the more impressed and interested Yacktman becomes. You can get this information from the company or through various research services. "I believe shareholder-oriented managers do a better job of allocating investment capital, particularly excess cash, than do corporate kingdom builders. They will often improve their company's mix of businesses over time," he maintains. "I remember sitting across the table from a CEO who didn't have a lot of personal assets but what he did have was all tied up in his company. He even had a mortgage on his home to help support the stock he owned. I was very impressed. He obviously knew what was going on in the company and would do everything in his power to make it succeed."

GETTING INVOLVED

Once he has invested in a company, Yacktman's not afraid to get involved with top management, even offering suggestions when he thinks they're going in the wrong direction. Most of the time, he's in there telling them what he views as the best way to spend free cash. "I'm trying to indicate how I feel they can build their private market value the fastest and therefore get the highest return for investors," he says. "Sometimes, if there's a lack of objectivity on their part, my suggestion may have to be given in a stronger tone. I'm really not trying to be antagonistic or condescending. I'm genuinely trying to help out. Usually I'll talk to the chief financial officer or CEO directly."

Yacktman enjoys this kind of access because he takes substantial positions in the companies he owns. It's more of a challenge for individual investors to make their feelings known. Nevertheless, there's nothing to stop you from firing off a letter to a company president, expressing your suggestions. If nothing else, it's bound to get a fair reading by someone in the investor relations department.

I asked Yacktman if he felt company managements would rather he simply remained a silent shareholder. He contends if he provides input in a diplomatic way, they are usually pretty receptive to what he has to say. Of course, sometimes corporate executives don't immediately see eye-to-eye with him. "When Franklin Quest prepared to acquire The Covey Institute in 1997, they wanted to do it using a pooling of interests," he reflects. "The problem was that accounting method would have required them to resell about 1.5 million shares of stock to the public. I didn't think this route made any sense, because they had purchased those shares on the open market for a great price. I suggested they restructure the deal and make it more of a win-win arrangement. I told them I'd rather have them give the Covey people some cash and fewer shares of stock so they wouldn't have as much dilution. I think cash earnings, which add goodwill back into earnings per share, are a much better measure of earnings than reported earnings anyway. They ultimately agreed with me, especially after they talked with some other large shareholders who saw things in the same way I did."

Another time, Yacktman questioned lawn-care provider Barefoot about why it wasn't spending all the free cash it had built up to buy back more shares. Executives kept offering one excuse after another, which was frustrating. "It turned out they couldn't say anything because they were being acquired by another company," he says. "They couldn't give me insider information, and I wouldn't want them to. But it wasn't until after the announcement was made that their decision to hold onto the cash made sense. Several of the companies I've invested in have been bought out. They're good businesses and are attractive to others. If they are having problems, that usually makes management more willing to sell out. It happened to Tambrands in 1997. The company was temporarily struggling so it allowed Procter & Gamble to acquire it."

THE DOWNSIDE OF MEETING MANAGEMENT

When Robert Stovall first started in the investment business more than 40 years ago, he, too, spent a lot of time visiting companies in person before committing any of his cash for purchase. In many cases, he met with management and got to know them face-to-face. Occasionally he even put in his own two cents about what direction he thought the company ought to be heading. However, Stovall has since changed his attitude about the benefit of forging such close relationships. "I found it doesn't always necessarily pay to get tightly involved with management, because when they make a mistake, you are sometimes left saying, 'He's such a great guy, I'm sure he'll straighten this out' when the problems are really beyond easy repair," he explains. "I guess you could say I'm an agnostic when it comes to the value of becoming intimate with management. I don't restrict myself to buying stock only in companies where I have met the people in charge. I think that's too confining. Sometimes waiting to meet them costs you an opportunity to get in or out at an attractive price. Besides, I've been lied to by some of the finest names in north America over the years. I know you can be misled or blindsided by what you think are close connections, but really turn out to be no connections at all, or even short circuits."

That's not to say Stovall completely ignores the track records of executives in the companies he invests in. Quite the opposite. He pays close attention to what they've done and to what they say they're going to do in the future. He just isn't convinced that it's necessary to meet them face-to-face in order to make an informed decision about whether to become an investment partner.

Neither does Elizabeth Bramwell. She utilizes conference calls extensively and finds analyst meetings with managements to be very helpful. This is one reason she decided to locate her firm in New York's shopping district, instead of on Wall Street. "Our location is great because analyst meetings are held nearby and we can walk back and forth to them throughout the day," she says. "I often go to road shows across the street at the Plaza Hotel. It's a misperception that all money managers are on Wall Street. They've been moving uptown for a long time. They started coming here because they found it was easier to get in and out of the city. They didn't like commuting out of Grand Central, getting on a subway, and going back and forth to downtown. Once the independent managers started relocating here some ten years ago, many of the major brokerage firms followed. Morgan Stanley is nearby and so is Smith Barney. It's easy for people visiting the city to come here, and you're closer to your clients. It's an upbeat part of town." While you probably won't get invited to a road show, unless you've got millions of dollars to invest, an increasing number of companies now allow individual investors to listen in on analyst conference calls. Some will also send you a transcript of these events.

Don't Believe Everything You Hear

Given that analyst meetings and conferences are such formally organized and orchestrated events, I asked Bramwell whether they were a reliable source of objective investment information. "There's no question they are a great way to get up to speed on a company quickly," she replied, "but I try to listen between the lines and pay close attention to what is *not* said. The question-and-answer sessions are also quite helpful."

In addition to holding meetings with company analysts in New York City, company managements frequently stop by Bramwell's office during their trips to the East Coast. As a result, she rarely has to conduct on-site inspections these days. What's more, with conference calls, fax machines, CNBC, and the Internet, the flow of information about virtually any business is continuous and easily accessible. Being away from the office might even cause her to miss some of this breaking news. Keep in mind that much of this information is also available online to individual investors at the exact same time the professionals get it.

The Bottom Line

Whether you visit your potential investments in person, or just make a call to the investor relations department, always find out about top management before buying shares in a company. These people are your partners, and how they act will determine whether you make or lose money in both the long and the short term. Make sure they have integrity and are "doers," not "bluffers."

After becoming a shareholder, don't be afraid to contact the people in charge if you fear the company is moving in the wrong direction. Of course, if you don't own many shares, you may not get through to the CEO. But, at the very least, an investor relations executive should be willing to talk with you.

Rule 6

AVOID
UNNECESSARY
RISK

This may sound ironic and seemingly goes against the conventional thinking on Wall Street, but reducing your investment risk can actually help to increase your overall performance results. Sure, it's sometimes thrilling to buy a "high-flyer" of the moment, with dreams of seeing it double or triple in a matter of months. Unfortunately, more times than not, bets like this backfire. Highly volatile stocks often fall faster much more than they rise, especially if every broker in town is hyping them. And big losers can take a long time to come back.

A COOL TRIO TURNS COLD

Shelby Davis knows this from experience. When he first started managing the New York Venture Fund in 1969, he loaded up on the classic "go-go" stocks of that era. It worked, at least for awhile. New York Venture was the number-one fund in the nation during its rookie year, up 25.3 percent. This performance brought Davis and his two partners much media attention, including a feature article in *Business Week.* "I'll never forget the headline above the photo. It read 'Cool Trio Runs Hot Fund,' referring to the three of us (Davis, Guy Palmer, and Jeremy Biggs) who managed the fund," Davis recalls. "Let me tell you, that was like the kiss of death. When the article came out, it all but marked the end of our hot streak. We were number one in 1969, then in the bottom 10 percent of all funds in 1970. Our stocks got creamed. The United States went into a tight money environment. Interest rates were raised, many of our companies were highly leveraged, and expectations were sky-high. That's one difference between then and now. Today's small-cap companies aren't as leveraged as they used to be. In those days, leverage was the name of the game. Many computer companies had to lease their equipment, because that was the way the game was played. They had to borrow heavily to finance those leases."

New York Venture continued to act like a tennis ball for several years, up 22 percent one year, then down 24 percent the next. In the end, it basically went nowhere. "If you invested $10,000 at the start in 1969, you were still even at best in 1975," Shelby laments. "Granted, the overall market had gone through a bad cycle. But we made no progress after the first year." Still, the fund had around $50 million in assets and Davis was developing an audited public track record, which eventually helped to attract new cash. "The good news is that after a bad period, you usually have a good period," he says. "The market had been really strong from 1949 to 1969, then it got choppy just as we started our fund on February 17, 1969. The Dow literally made no headway for 12 years. In 1982, you could have bought the Dow at the exact same level as when we opened for business. But after that first five- or six-year period where we went up and down, from 1975 on we finally started to make money."

What Goes Down Doesn't Always Come Back Up

Davis wasn't alone in playing this risky game. The pervasive feeling among investors in the late 1960s was that the market would keep going higher, no matter what. Davis personally felt invincible. "My attitude was I had been in the business for ten years and had seen it all," he reveals. "We had a few corrections that were pretty steep, including one in 1962 and another in 1966. But I felt the most I could lose in a stock was 50 percent. If it was a total dud, it would probably bounce back and I'd get out at a 25 percent loss. If it was a winner, I'd be making money again in six months. But in 1973–1974, stocks didn't bounce back. The glamour stocks went down 40 to 50 percent in year one, then another 40 to 50 percent in year two. It was a humbling experience to see the leadership of that day—Avon, Polaroid, and Xerox—drop 70 to 80 percent. When you lose even 50 percent, you have to double your money from that level just to get even. That's one thing I learned. It's no good having a growth company that goes up 50 percent and then drops 50 percent. You're behind on the math. Let's say that, over a three-year period, you have a stock that goes from $100 to $150, and then drops 50 percent down to $75. You've lost 25 percent of your money. That's a lousy way to compound your wealth. Many people find this truth hard to comprehend. It's just math, though. Investors will often say, 'I've got a stock that's going to go up 50 percent, but it might drop 50 percent. If it does, that's all right because I'll break even.' However, that's not the case. You would be down 25 percent. You see, if a stock is up 50 percent, it can drop only 33 percent from that level for you to break even. Likewise, a stock with a PE ratio of 50 has a lot farther to fall when things go bad than one with a PE of 15."

Buying Sustainable Growth

By 1982, New York Venture was ahead of the game, even though the market averages were going nowhere. By then, Davis had changed the fund's investment focus. "As I got more experience and gray hair, it turned into much more of a combination growth and value fund," he says. "I was never that comfortable buying popular stocks at any price after 1970. In 1973–1974, unlike a lot of growth funds, we didn't do any worse than the market, because we had sold most of our high-multiple stocks. It was still a horrible time, but I got rid of companies such as Avon, Polaroid, and Xerox, which were selling for 50 times earnings. I concluded that I was only getting a 2 percent earnings yield on my money in an environment where interest rates were going up. I didn't need that."

This experience caused Davis to combine the best traits of growth and value investing at the hip. "I now ask two questions before buying any stock: 'How much can I make, and how much can I lose?' I guess it goes back to my roots, but I'm much more comfortable with the insurance-type stocks that are growing between 7 and 15 percent a year," he says. "That's my sweet spot. I love the 7 to 15 percent growers. There are a broad array of industries and companies that meet these criteria. I also think the growth rates in that range are more sustainable and plenty good enough to make your money go up eight- or tenfold in a generation."

DAVIS DOUBLE PLAY

The most important thing, in Davis's assessment, is to reduce the risk of what his father referred to as a "Davis double play" on the downside. When prices are going up, it's great. You want to look for companies with sustainable earnings growth that are capable of expanding their multiples even further, since that can generate a double compounding of your money. "However, it also works in reverse," Davis warns. "If you start out with a high multiple, and the earnings growth rate is reduced, even if it's still a good number, the lowered expectation will cause you to get a compression in the multiple. That's detrimental to your wealth."

ASSESSING RISK

One thing every equity investor must figure out is how much pain he or she is willing to suffer during periods when the market is getting slammed. "I discovered in the 1970s that a lot of bad things can happen to you in a bear market," Davis shares. "If a company has a weak balance sheet, it will turn into a disaster, since interest rates usually go up during market declines. As a result, the cost of operating the business rises and the company needs more money to keep going. Yet the banks won't make any new loans, feeling the business is already inundated with high-priced debt. Therefore, it's next to impossible to raise equity. Nothing can kill a company faster than losing access to money."

The other thing he realized is that if you own a growth company for which Wall Street has high expectations, and those expectations are not met during a bear market, look out below. "You can get a wicked multiple contraction and see a tremendous exit from the company when that happens, because there's not a natural buyer for the stock," he says. "You'll have a stock at 40 times earnings that falls to 25 times earnings and still isn't a bargain. That's because your natural constituency has moved on to another hot growth company and there's no value buyer there to sop it up 'even' at 25 times earnings. Some of these small-cap high-growth companies can languish for years once a bear market breaks their charm."

Still, size has never been a big factor in Shelby's decision-making process. "I don't mind large or small, as long as the growth is relatively predictable, the multiple isn't too high, and management is doing its job to build the business in a sensible way," he contends. "Having said that, the technology sector is tough because change, in a way, is your enemy. These companies are spending between 10 and 20 percent of sales on research and development. Guess what that's for? To bring out new products. I own some of those companies right now, but I tend to gravitate toward the larger ones because they can suffer a setback in any one product and still remain intact. For the smaller ones, if someone beats them to the punch, they're dead."

DODGE THE FADS

Internet start-ups; toy companies with the hot product of the season; a restaurant chain that people can't seem to eat at often enough—all are good examples of "fad businesses," which Davis won't touch. "I hate them because obviously this amazing growth isn't going to last," he concludes. "I'm usually not into the new-issue game either, especially if it's a start-up company, since it hasn't stood the test of time. I'm looking for time-tested warriors that are, I hope, going to be well managed throughout a generation. The problem is that management, industry conditions, and companies change. I'm not worried about quarter-to-quarter issues that much, but I am concerned about the three-to-five-year view, which is about as far as I think any company can project. You don't have to be a rocket scientist to know that when you look all over the world, the steel industry doesn't get a very high multiple, whereas media and pharmaceutical companies do. Newspapers, broadcasters, and drug makers all enjoy high valuations. Financial companies don't, although a lot of them usually don't get the lowest multiples either."

SOME ADDITIONAL CAVEATS

Because most financial companies are highly leveraged, Davis asserts it's crucial for potential investors to perform extra due diligence before establishing a position. Assets for a financial institution usually amount to about ten times equity, so there is a lot of inherent leverage on the equity base. If some of these assets start to go bad, or management makes poor decisions about how they should be allocated, it will have a leveraged effect on the equity. That's another reason you need to make sure the company is run by competent management. "The other risk in buying insurance companies is that a lot of the earnings are, in a sense, educated estimates of earnings power, because you're basically setting up reserves for events that haven't occurred yet," Davis points out. "If you're writing life insurance policies, you don't know when somebody's going to die. You have actuary tables, but you could get adverse selection. When it comes to property-casualty claims, you often don't know about the claim when you're settling your books. Even if an auto accident takes place, or a home burns down, chances are it won't show up in your books, even though it happened in the current quarter. It can sometimes take weeks for this information to get to you."

But, for the most part, these types of claims are peanuts. The real threats to insurers are the unknown liabilities you never planned on or anticipated. One chilling example of this is the liability exposure many companies began to face in the 1980s after it was learned that asbestos could cause cancer. "Asbestos was a legal product being sold and promoted by the government," Davis says. "It was used as insulation in submarines and warships, and the government told us to use it on pipes in our homes. Fifty years later, they find out asbestos dust causes lung diseases such as cancer and emphysema. Lawyers began to claim the asbestos companies were liable, even though they were producing a fully legal product. Nobody could have anticipated this. One asbestos manufacturer, Johns Manville, which was a blue chip in good standing and formerly one of 30 stocks in the Dow Jones Industrial Average, went bankrupt over this."

This same reasoning once led Davis to believe that tobacco giant Philip Morris would go bankrupt. He figured if it happened to Johns Manville, it could certainly happen to Big Mo. "I figured if it lost a couple of the smoking cases, it would have a giant class-action lawsuit on its hands with millions of people suing for trillions of dollars," he explains. "To settle that kind of claim, the company would have to go bankrupt and declare Chapter 11." Interestingly enough, it appears that a final settlement being worked out with states across the country will actually reduce, if not eliminate, this risk.

Incidentally, Roy Papp categorically avoids tobacco stocks to this day. At first it was a personal thing. He smoked a pipe for years before quitting in 1981. His wife is also a former smoker, though she kicked the habit almost two decades before he did. Realizing his clients weren't paying him to be judgmental, Papp eventually bought Philip Morris in the late 1980s, though now he won't touch it. His reasoning is that the tobacco companies still face too much potential political and legal exposure, even with the settlement.

An investment Davis made in a tiny company in the 1970s further drove home the lesson about what unforeseen liability can do to a business, especially in the insurance industry. "I purchased this relatively new issue of a small regional property and casualty insurer," he reveals. "Arthur Andersen and Price Waterhouse had audited the books. The stock came out on Veterans' Day for $6 a share. I remember this, because the bank was closed but I came in to work just so I could go to lunch and hear management talk. My impression was that it was a pretty low quality company, but it was a new issue that was cheap on reported earnings, so I thought why not take a chance and buy it. Boy, did I learn a lesson! Everything was fine at first, and the stock made new highs by February. Within three months, it had jumped almost 30 percent and was trading at $8. I felt pretty good. Then an item came across the Dow Jones news wire. It read: 'Security America of Chicago, or whatever this thing was called, has announced that trading in the stock has been suspended.' The company had uncovered some reserve deficiencies from a discontinued line of business that wiped out its equity.

Trading in the stock never resumed and the company eventually declared bankruptcy. So this stock went from hitting a new high to bankruptcy almost instantly. That's the ultimate risk with an insurance company."

There's a modern-day sequel to this story. In the 1960s, Chubb acquired California insurer Pacific Indemnity, which had written a general liability policy for Fiberboard. "It wrote the policy for only two years in the 1950s, but Fiberboard had an asbestos plant," Davis notes. "Remember, Chubb didn't even write this. It was Pacific Indemnity. I think they collected all of $30,000 in premiums for it. Then Fiberboard got sued, and between Chubb and CNA, they have paid out some $1 billion in damages during the 1990s. All of this for a $30,000 premium on a policy that had been discontinued for more than 35 years. Yet Chubb was still found liable and had to pay the claim. The difference between the first example and the second is that Chubb had a conservative balance sheet. The company had grown dramatically and successfully and was able to pay that claim without really missing a heartbeat."

SAFETY IN NUMBERS

Even getting to know management couldn't have alerted you to unforeseen liabilities such as these. "That's one of the reasons I think financial companies tend to get lower multiples," Davis surmises. "Another reason is that there are a lot of them to choose from. There's only one Coca-Cola and one Procter & Gamble. Sure, there are maybe 50 great consumer-product companies around the world. But there are many more financial companies than that."

Financial companies, other than undercapitalized insurers, also come with less valuation and product obsolescence risk. For one thing, they tend to trade at low price/earnings multiples to begin with. These multiples can go lower, but a solid financial-services stock almost never trades at a P/E below 6 or 7 times earnings. "If they're at 14, 12, or 10 to begin with, you've got a maximum 50 percent risk if everything goes bad," Davis says. Financial-services companies also face relatively low potential product liability. "It's possible someone may eventually prove that drinking 500 Coca-Cola's a day gives you cancer," Davis suggests. "By contrast, in financial companies, it's hard to prove that money is a disaster, so the problems are usually man-made, having to do with poor management decisions. Even then, the business will continue to go on in some shape or form. Maybe that's why I've always felt so strongly about managements, because they are absolutely critical to the success of financial companies.

"I would also say the entry price at which you invest and the longevity of the businesses a company is in have a lot to do with reducing risk," he adds. "Take insurers such as Travelers (now part of Citigroup), Aetna, and Cigna. They've all been around since the 1800s. Until recently, they haven't been very well managed, yet they're still in business. They've survived wars, depressions, periods of inflation and deflation, and so on. This proves financial companies will stay around unless they go bankrupt. On the other hand, many technology companies eventually disappear once their current lineup of products becomes obsolete." Don't be misled. Davis isn't recommending that you avoid financial services and insurance stocks. In fact, those are his favorite areas of the market. He just wants you to know what to look out for as you do your homework before investing.

AVOID CYCLICALITY

Davis must feel confident that a company he's considering for purchase is in an industry that is making money and has growth potential, even if that potential is modest. "In cyclical businesses, you have to make two right decisions," he observes. "You have to get in and out at the right time, because if the business keeps going up and down, you'll never get ahead. I've gravitated more and more away from cyclical companies because you have to be correct twice and pay taxes along the way. I try to find companies that have the kind of cyclical movement I can stomach, if they're cyclical at all. I don't mind variability in earnings. I call that volatility. What I don't want is a purely cyclical business that goes up and down to the same point. I want a rising sequence of bottoms and tops."

The auto industry is an interesting case in point. Davis has tried to make money in that business several times with little success. "The way you've made money with the auto companies in recent years is to say if you broke them up, they'd be worth more in pieces than they are whole," he concludes. "I tried that with General Motors, but later sold it and bought something else. One reason is that fundamentally it's a one-shot play, and I don't think the automobile business is a good growth business. Let's compare the auto industry to the investment-banking brokerage industry. Both are very volatile businesses, with varied quarterly earnings. But there's an underlying growth trend with investment bankers that you don't see with the automakers, at least there has been for my entire investment career."

Davis offers an example to prove that. "I went to Princeton with Dick Fisher, who eventually became the head of Morgan Stanley," he says. "When he went to work at Morgan, it was located at 23 Wall Street, employed about 60 people, and had stated equity capital of less than $20 million. One generation later, forgetting about the merger with Dean Witter, Morgan Stanley is operating on five continents, has revenues in the billions, and earnings of around $1 billion. So if it started with $20 million of capital in 1962, and now earns $1 billion, I would say that's a good growth business. But it's very volatile. I don't mind volatility. I obviously grew up with it. My father never cared to predict the earnings of property-casualty companies by quarters. In fact, they didn't even used to report by quarter because you can't plan for hurricanes, earthquakes, wicked storms, or any number of calamities that come along out of the blue. So quarterly earnings have always been somewhat irrelevant to me. They're useful as checkpoints and maybe to take advantage of short-term disappointments. That's why I've never been that enamored of building earnings models by quarter and trying to develop every statistic on a company."

COMPANIES TO SHY AWAY FROM

There are certain kinds of companies Davis categorically avoids. "In insurance, I stay away from those without regular underwriting profits, because they're not really generating free cash flow and may be underreserving," he says. "I try to steer clear of financial companies at the high end of the risk spectrum. In the lending world, I really don't like subprime auto lenders that are making loans on used cars to people on hourly wages or college kids with no credit ratings.

"I don't usually buy small oil and gas companies that have plays going in only one particular field, because if it doesn't work out, they're out of business," he shares. "I've seen reserves disappear in insurance and oil in the same way—by the stroke of somebody's pen. They decide the oil and gas they thought was underground isn't really there. That's why I like to own bigger companies. One of the things that's generally unrecognized about big companies is they have much more staying power and diversification. You give something up in that they often aren't growing as rapidly, but you also gain something in return. If you're trying to compound money, avoiding substantial losses is just as important as making huge hits. I think a big company gives you more of a chance to avoid the significant losses, especially if you're not buying at a high price."

What's more, if you're a buy-and-hold investor, like Davis, you're more likely to be able to safely stick with a large company for the long term. "That invariably makes your portfolio more tax efficient, because chances are those big companies can live through the inevitable bear markets, interest-rate squeezes, and recessions," he reasons. "Big companies have more staying power on their balance sheets. From my point of view, owning something for a long time is wonderful, and not just for tax efficiency. It also fits into my system of getting to know management. Most mutual funds have turnover of 200 or 300 percent a year. What's the point of talking to management if you're going to turn the portfolio over three times a year? What are you saying by doing that much trading? Are you trying to find out what management is doing for the next three or six months? What they're eating for breakfast? It makes no sense. If you're doing your research in anticipation of holding on for three to five years, like I am, then getting to know management is very valuable."

It's Not How Much You Make, But How Little You Lose

As you might have guessed, Davis's first rule of making money is having the sense not to lose it in the first place. "At the heart of my approach to money management is my view about risk," he emphasizes. "I now ask, 'How much can I lose?' before I even dream about 'How much can I make?' Every decision is formed by my belief that continuous risk management is the key to delivering superior long-term investment results. For me there are two fundamental investment risks. The first is what kind of businesses I own. The second is whether I pay too much for a company's stock. I evaluate risk on a company-by-company basis. Experience has taught me that good companies can prosper in lagging sectors, while badly managed companies often perform poorly in sectors that are doing well.

"Before I invest a penny, I ask myself such questions as, 'If I had unlimited funds, would I want to own the whole company at the price I am paying for this fractional interest? Or, can I make 50 percent over a three-year period?'" he says. "More important, I also ask myself, 'If this stock goes down by 15 to 20 percent, would I still want to own it? And how much can I lose?' These are very important questions to ask when you're trying to manage an all-weather portfolio that you want to do well in both up and down markets."

BE SELECTIVE

One way Don Yacktman and his team of analysts reduce risk is by focusing their efforts on following only a select group of stocks, most of which have reported earnings in excess of $100 million. "These are financially strong companies," he says. "This is a good starting point for reducing risk. I liken companies on a solid financial foundation to homeowners who have paid off their mortgages. When you get into a comfortable situation like that, it's pretty hard for creditors to take anything away from you. You know that these companies aren't going to close down overnight because they have the money to survive almost anything that comes their way."

That doesn't mean Yacktman won't touch a tinier name. He just believes the level of safety increases dramatically when investing in bigger businesses. "The trade-off is as companies grow larger, managements sometimes invest free cash flow in such a way that the return on assets starts to fall," he admits. "So we almost always have a higher hurdle that we make smaller companies jump over."

WATCH OUT FOR DEBT

Low debt is another risk-reducing sign in Yacktman's book. Admittedly, most of the time capital-intensive companies must borrow money to achieve a high return on assets. Yacktman contends that if a business he owns takes out a loan, it's usually because it's looking for a way to enhance overall returns. "The company doesn't need the money to get an adequate return on assets," he insists. "This isn't to say a business shouldn't have any debt, because I think it should. It keeps the cost of capital down. The ideal capital-structure strategy for a business is to run it with single A credit, but not to pay a dividend. Reebok is a good example. The company made a marvelous move when it repurchased stock in a Dutch tender and eliminated its dividend. This charge allowed all of the cash flow to be applied to debt repayment. It also meant if the stock came down, management was in a position to buy back more shares. This is how I would run the financial side of a company. I wouldn't pay a dividend, and I'd try to operate it with a single A credit rating, because I think that's the best combination of financial engineering you can hope for."

Furthermore, even if it is a good, low-debt business, Yacktman, like Davis, normally avoids companies that are cyclical in nature, especially since he wants to be a long-term holder. "Lindsay Manufacturing is a company I recently passed on," he reveals. "This is a tiny but good operation. It makes those wide lawn sprinkler systems on wheels that are used in farming, which is a very profitable business. But how long can you keep getting a steady stream of orders? This industry is very cyclical. If farmers have a bad period, they're going to slow down their purchases of sprinklers. The company might be doing well now, because the farming industry is strong, but that won't last forever. Once more, it is a capital-goods-oriented business, which means there is a continuous swing in volume."

Yacktman also tries to avoid such cyclical industries as the airlines, railroads, utilities, steel manufacturers, and chemical companies. Does that mean you can't make any money in these businesses? Absolutely not. They just don't fit in with his criteria. "If you bought Chrysler at $10, you made a lot of money; if you bought IBM below $50, you're happy as well. In both cases, I did not buy, not because I didn't think I could make money, but because I was concentrating on better businesses. By staying focused, I can hit my goal of having the highest returns with the least amount of risk. My overall strategy is first, protect the capital of my investors, and second, grow it. I conceptually refer to this strategy as buying beach balls that are being pushed under the water as the water level is rising. Continued pressure can keep the beach balls under water, but eventually the pressure comes off, and the beach balls, or share prices, rise rather quickly."

Roy Papp agrees that high leverage should usually be taken as a warning sign. "I normally prefer to see less than 25 percent debt," he says. "When it gets up to 50 percent, I'm scared. Companies with a lot of debt sometimes go bankrupt. Beyond that, suppose we get hit with a recession, which we will. You don't even need a full-fledged recession, just a slowdown in business. Companies with a lot of debt still have to pay interest on it, even though they're bringing in less money. If you've got a company whose earnings grow at 13 or 14 percent a year with 50 percent debt, it's not worth as much as a similar company growing by the same 13 or 14 percent but with no debt. There are some exceptions. I'm happy to live with funeral-homeowner Service Corporation even though half of its balance sheet is made up of debt. What's different is that this company's business is relatively stable. If we have a recession, I can guarantee you nobody will postpone burying their loved ones, even if they have to borrow money to do it." Service Corporation, one of Papp's major holdings, has been plowing much of that borrowed money into acquisitions, both in the United States and abroad, to strengthen its growing dominant position in the industry.

Papp can also stomach 50 percent debt in utility companies as well, since their business is little impacted by changes in the economy. "I love to own monopolies in lead positions within their industry," he says. "I like to own franchises and patent companies, too. I'm very keen on predictability. I can't tell you what a steel or chemical company is going to earn tomorrow. Neither can anyone else. But I think I can come much closer predicting earnings for a couple of drug companies or something like Service Corporation, where the business is quite stable." If earnings are more predictable, so is the expected growth rate, which is a number you must have a handle on in order to properly evaluate the price you're willing to pay for the stock, especially using Papp's formula.

One should never forget, however, that monopolies don't always last forever. It's a lesson Papp learned all too well during the 1972–1974 "Nifty 50" era. "A lot of companies sold at very high prices of up to 50 times earnings," he recalls. "Among the most expensive [as Davis pointed out] were Xerox, Polaroid, and Avon. Every magazine said they were the best and most brilliant companies in the world. They always made the right acquisitions, and earnings kept going up. Suddenly, this perfect world began to crumble in late 1975. Polaroid lost its patent protection on the instant camera. Xerox lost its patent protection on some of its copiers. New competitors began to encroach on Avon's territory, while at the same time more women went back to work. These companies suddenly saw their businesses being destroyed, and their stocks have been sick ever since."

What the media and Papp didn't realize at the time was that the monopolies these corporations enjoyed were temporary. "Now we always look closely at whether a company's monopolistic position is permanent or endangered," he says. "One must never become complacent."

BEWARE OF THE UNKNOWN

Papp further warns that individual investors should tread lightly into tiny unknown firms. "If you work in a particular field and know a lot about an industry or company, it's fine to put a little bit of money in a small stock," he offers. "In fact, I have found that if you have your own company, you are almost always best to put as much of your money in it is as you feel comfortable with, especially if it will help you to grow. After all, you're going to earn a better return in your own company than by giving it to some stranger out in the field. If a doctor has a chance to invest money in his office to improve his equipment, he should do it. He'll make more money on that than anything else."

YIELDING TO THE BOND DEBATE

Keeping risk to a minimum is just as important to Robert Stovall. He does this by sticking with highly liquid, dividend-paying companies. "I don't like stocks whose prices scoot up and down like a roller shade," he says. "That scares me." As a result, this timid investor stays with the best and usually the biggest in whatever industry he's investing in. "For example, in the computer-manufacturing area, there are two large companies, Applied Materials and KLA-Tencor, and a much smaller one called Brook's Automation," he observes. "The performance of Applied and KLA-Tencor is volatile enough. But look at Brook's Automation. This stock had a price range of $9 to $41 in the preceding 52 weeks. This kind of performance makes me and my older clients nervous. While the upside of Brook's might be greater, and I emphasize the word *might,* I can explain the volatility of KLA-Tencor and Applied Materials to them better than I can the violent price swings of Brook's."

As an added risk buffer, Stovall pads his portfolios with bonds. These instruments are more stable, provide reliable income, and also have a bit of appreciation potential. "I further use convertible securities, which many people avoid," he says. "Still, I frequently outperform both the S&P 500 and the Dow 30, which is pretty good in my business. Granted, it's rare for me to come out number one or two in any stock picking contest, because I do want to keep risk under control. However, to use a baseball analogy, my goal is to get on base a lot. I'd rather have a good batting average than hit a lot of home runs. That's how you survive in this business."

Papp, on the other hand, doesn't think much of bonds. Although he owns a few Treasuries in his personal portfolio, he's clearly a man of the stock market. Papp views bonds as inferior investments that are expensive compared to stocks. "As we speak, you are being forced to pay 16.5 times earnings for a five-year Treasury," he concludes. "I get that number by taking the price of a bond ($1,000) and dividing it by the amount of interest it pays each year ($64). I'd rather pay 20 times earnings for a stock. I know that historically the return on stocks has been approximately four times the return on bonds. Bonds to me are appropriate only as a short-term parking place."

While some investors feel bonds are a "safer" investment, Papp turns to yet another baseball analogy to show why he disagrees. "If you're playing in a game, the only place you're completely safe is at home plate," he explains. "If you're on first, second, or third, you might not get back home to score. The only place you're 100 percent safe is at home. Most people in this world think of cash as home plate in the game of investing. If they hold stocks or other investments, they never feel they are completely safe until they have turned their money back into cash. My feeling is that the only time I feel comfortable is when I'm in stocks. Cash is the unsafe place to be. Stocks are the permanent place. That's where the returns are. For many people, this thinking is turned around. I admit I'm guilty of thinking outside the box. But if you stop and think about it logically, you realize that over the long term, stocks have been the best investment you could ever make. They are your home plate."

Davis has a similar view of bonds. He always starts out with the premise that any investor can take his or her cash and put it in a zero-coupon bond that will compound free of interest rate or default risk through maturity. "That, in a sense, is the bogey of an equity investor," he maintains. "Stocks, in my view, also print a coupon, just not on a certificate. It is a mystery coupon. Equities are just another form of investment that compete with the risk-free rate of return you can get in a zero-coupon bond. My job is to analyze companies and figure out ahead of time what kind of coupon they're going to print, not this quarter or this year, but one, five, ten, or twenty years down the road, just like a bond."

Given that scenario, Davis is still much more optimistic about stocks than bonds. The reason? Over the years, stocks have outperformed bonds by about two to one. Granted, in certain decades, such as the 1970s, even ultrasafe bank certificates of deposit outperform both stocks and bonds. In the mid-1980s to early 1990s, bonds did as well as, if not better than, stocks. But over long periods of time, stocks have historically made investors the most money. "Part of the problem with comparing the performance of most bonds and CDs is that you face reinvestment risk," Davis adds. "That's why I use zero coupons. You lock in the coupon rate, as long as you hold on until maturity. Obviously, that risk-free rate is always changing with interest rates. That's why multiples can expand and contract with the level of interest rates, because you're competing, at least theoretically, with this risk-free rate."

The growth investor's job is to figure out what that "phantom" risk-free coupon rate is on a stock. They don't print it there for you to read, so you have to do research, understand management, know the business, and buy the stock at a price that will give you a rate of return in excess of what you would earn on a safer investment.

Therefore, although bonds can serve to temper the fluctuations in your portfolio (assuming you're talking about high-quality, short-term instruments) if history continues to repeat itself, they will also serve to severely reduce your overall returns.

THE BOTTOM LINE

Never fail to evaluate the risks involved with every security you buy. With short-term bonds and cash, your greatest risk is that you'll earn an inferior return that might not keep up even with the rate of inflation. This is yet another reason why equity investing makes so much sense.

Without question, stocks are inherently volatile. One way to reduce your risk is by concentrating on large corporations with proven staying power, low debt, and a diverse product line. Also pay attention to the price you pay for your shares. The cheaper your entry point, the less downside exposure you face.

SHELBY DAVIS

$\mathcal{I}$f true investment genius is an inherited trait, the requisite genes for such brilliance clearly run deep within the Davis family bloodline. Shelby Davis is a legend in the mutual fund business. Over a 28-year period, he achieved one of the best and most consistent performance records in the industry as skipper of the Davis New York Venture Fund. In 1997, he turned the reins of this fund over to son Christopher, although he remains actively involved with it. But there is more to the story. Another Shelby Davis walked onto the investment scene decades earlier, in the late 1940s to be exact. He's Shelby's dad, a man who turned $100,000 into a fortune now valued at more than $800 million. He did it primarily by investing in insurance stocks.

SHELBY, SR.

Shelby Cullom Davis Senior was born in Peoria, Illinois, back in 1909. He was a private person, whose dress and demeanor remained understated even after he amassed his enormous wealth. He earned an undergraduate degree at Princeton, his master's at Columbia, and a Ph.D. at the University of Geneva, all in political science. At Columbia, he fell in love with another graduate student, Kathryn, a beautiful, petite blonde woman of German descent from Philadelphia. Although the two attended the same school in the United States, they actually met on a train bound from Paris to Geneva during a spring break trip to Russia. They later studied together at the University of Geneva, where both earned doctorate degrees. They were married in January of 1932.

Davis and his wife graduated in the midst of the Great Depression, when jobs in the United States were hard to come by. He took a job in Europe working as a radio correspondent for CBS. Davis always had an affection for good journalism and, as an undergraduate, had been managing editor of the Princeton University campus newspaper. He wrote four books during those early years, including *America Faces the Forties,* which detailed his predictions about what lay ahead politically and economically for the United States. Among those who read the book was Thomas E. Dewey, then governor of New York. Dewey was thinking of running for president of the United States at the time and hired Davis to be his speech writer and quasi-economist, since Davis had so many ideas about what was going to happen over the next decade.

GOVERNMENT SERVICE

Dewey staged two aggressive campaigns but never made it to the White House, losing to Franklin Roosevelt in 1944 and unexpectedly to Harry Truman in 1948. When Davis returned from serving on the War Production Board during World War II, he was appointed by Dewey as Deputy Insurance Commissioner for the State of New York. Before taking this job, Davis worked for a short time at a Philadelphia brokerage firm, so he knew a little about stocks. He also had a shrewd mind for finance. As Insurance Commissioner, he began to notice that insurance stocks in the late 1940s were selling for extremely low multiples. Eventually, he quit his government job and bought control of a small New York brokerage firm. He renamed it Shelby Cullom Davis and Company. Davis started with $100,000. Some was his own money, the rest he borrowed from his wife. This was a tidy sum for that time. He opened his doors in 1947, right when insurance stocks began a decade-long run as the darlings of Wall Street. They were like the biotech or Internet stocks of the 1990s.

INSURANCE EXPLOSION

Between 1949 and 1956, the great life insurance companies benefited from rising interest rates and a burgeoning new market created by soldiers coming back from war and starting families. The first thing you worried about after having children in those days was life insurance. With their growing offspring, the GIs became easy targets for life insurance salesmen. Stocks such as Lincoln National Life and Franklin Life experienced tremendous growth.

The media further helped to fuel this interest. An article in the July 1948 issue of *Kiplinger's Magazine—The Changing Times* was headlined, "What a Young Man Should Do With His Money." It offered the following advice: "The young man should start by buying at least $20,000 of life insurance, half in convertible term and half in ordinary life. Twenty thousand dollars may sound like a lot, but it won't provide much of an income."

Davis was a late bloomer when it came to Wall Street. He didn't begin his investment career until he was in his late thirties, but his timing couldn't have been more perfect. Within eight years of starting his brokerage firm, Davis's net worth went from $100,000 to around $50 million. He got into the market at the low and rode one of the leading sectors all the way up.

THE INSURANCE EXPERT

In addition to managing his own personal fortune, Davis positioned himself as an expert in insurance stocks and promoted them to various financial institutions. The U.S. Steel Pension Fund, Putnam Funds, and Fidelity Funds were all clients. He became known as the dean of insurance stocks at a time when they were glamorous and underowned. At about this time, he was named president of the New York Society of Security Analysts. To add to his good fortune, Davis went to Japan in 1951, where he discovered that insurance stocks there were also undervalued. What's more, they represented an incredibly attractive opportunity. Davis bought some Japanese insurance stocks, and saw many of his investments go up a thousandfold in a few short years.

THE TREND COOLS

Insurance stocks began to lose favor in the 1960s. By then, they were no longer undiscovered; in fact, most had become overpriced. Some life insurance companies were selling for as much as 30 times estimated earnings. Like all high-multiple stocks that are unable to sustain this kind of giddy growth, the life insurance companies got hammered and underwent a significant correction. That's when people began to focus on property and casualty insurers. It became evident that all of those returning GIs were building or buying new homes, which meant they needed to purchase property and casualty insurance both for their dwellings and their cars. Once traders realized this, property and casualty insurance stock prices began to go through the roof. As usual, Davis was among the first to recognize this trend, and he profited handsomely from it.

Davis didn't really have an investment management arm at his brokerage firm. Instead, he earned a commission each time a client bought stocks (based on his uncanny recommendations). But he didn't become a multimillionaire from the commissions he generated. His real money was made by picking winners for himself. The commissions were just icing on the cake.

SERVICE IN SWITZERLAND

Once more, timing was everything. In 1968, President Nixon tapped the elder Davis to become U.S. ambassador to Switzerland. It was a post for which he was well qualified because of his long history and connection with Switzerland. He went to school there and had made many connections both as a student and a reporter. He and his wife moved to Bern, where they lived for six years.

As ambassador, Davis left his fortune behind in New York and no longer followed the stock market very closely. But some of the biggest insurers in the world are in Switzerland, including Swiss Re and Zurich Insurance. Of course he monitored their progress. Nevertheless, investing had become little more than a sideline. When he returned to the United States in 1974, he discovered his net worth had dramatically fallen, due in large part to the stock market crash of 1973–1974. He decided to focus on rebuilding his personal fortune. For the next 15 years, he worked harder than ever, analyzing stocks, closely monitoring his holdings, and making sure always to keep his eye on the ball. Although he served as chairman of the Heritage Foundation, a conservative Washington think tank, investing was once again the passion that ruled his life. This hard work paid off. He continued to build his fortune, which grew from about $20 million in 1974 to some $400 million by 1990, at which time he became ill and began funneling money into son Shelby, Jr.'s mutual funds.

THE RUSSIAN EXPERT

Shelby Cullom Davis and Company, the firm, still exists today. Kathryn Davis continues as its only partner and, at 92, is the oldest female member of the New York Stock Exchange. Kathryn has never been an active investor herself. She was so intrigued by Russia during her trip there as a college student, she made studying the country a lifelong career. She has traveled there 25 times and is an accomplished speaker and author on both Russia and China. Her Ph.D. thesis, entitled "The Soviets at Geneva," chronicled Russian behavior at the League of Nations. It received renewed interest following World War II, when the United Nations was formed. Today, Kathryn is as busy as ever. She lives in Florida and continues to lecture on the history and sights of Russia to audiences around the nation. (Ironically, the Davis family has never invested in Russia.) She is a trustee of Wellesley College, her undergraduate alma mater, still likes to travel, and is always up for a swim and good game of tennis.

MEET SHELBY, JR.

The senior Shelby Cullom Davis didn't want his son to be known merely as "junior." So he gave him an extended version of his own name: Shelby Moore Cullom Davis. The Moore was a logical addition; both men were named after a Republican politician from Illinois: Shelby Moore Cullom. Cullom spent 50 years in public office during the late 1800s and early 1900s. He served two terms as governor of Illinois, two terms in the House of Representatives, and 30 years as a U.S. senator. Senator Cullom was credited with founding the Interstate Commerce Commission, which was set up to regulate the railroads. He established the Commission after becoming convinced that farmers in his state were being victimized by the railroad companies. It cost them more in freight charges to send grain from Springfield, Illinois, to Chicago by rail than from Chicago to Liverpool, England, by ship. In other words, the railroads were gouging farmers on short hauls, and the Interstate Commerce Commission was put in place to stop that. (Fifty years later, most of the railroad companies were nearly bankrupt, and the Commission was finally repealed by President Ronald Reagan.) When Theodore Roosevelt was president, Senator Cullom was also chairman of the Foreign Relations Committee, which helped to pass legislation for financing the construction of the Panama Canal. The younger Shelby Davis still has a painting of Senator Cullom in his office, as does son Chris, who now occupies his grandfather's old office on Fifth Avenue in New York.

From now on, when I refer to "Davis," I'll be talking about Shelby Moore Cullom Davis, the offspring of the great insurance-stock investor who has become a mutual fund superstar. Davis always hated having such a long name. As a youngster, he shortened it to just Shelby M.C. Davis. "Frankly, most people have always called me Junior anyway, because when your dad has the same name, it's hard to get away from that," he admits. But Davis has long been fascinated by his namesake Senator Cullom, so much so that he traveled to Springfield, Illinois, in college to do a research paper on him. "I found people who knew the man, even though it had been 40 years since he died," he says. "I also dug around in the Springfield library, going through a lot of older papers. I worked on this project for a good couple of weeks." The paper became his senior history thesis at Princeton.

Davis, who has one younger sister, was about ten years old when his father decided to make the transition to Wall Street. "The first thing I remember was that he was a very hard worker," Davis recalls. "When he finally agreed to let us build a swimming pool at our house in Tarrytown, a small suburb north of New York City, he made me, my sister, and my mom help him dig the hole. We eventually had to hire a professional, because we ran into boulders. But that's the kind of guy he was. We also had planted a Victory Garden and raised chickens and pigs, like a lot of other people during World War II. People planted their own vegetables to save money and grow their own food so the more commercial goods could go to the troops."

Davis has fond memories of going into the campaign head-quarters of Governor Dewey on the night he lost the presidential race to Harry Truman in 1948. "He was supposed to win that one, but managed to snatch defeat from the jaws of victory," Davis says. "My father was working for Dewey when I was born in 1937, and Dewey was my godfather. I met him a few times and got to know his sons very well. One of them went to Princeton with me, and another married one of my best friends from Tarrytown."

LEARNING FROM A FATHER'S LEGEND

Davis started working with his dad at an early age. He accompanied his father on visits with management at the various insurance companies whose stocks he owned. One summer, the Davis family rented a home in Madison, Connecticut, for a month. Davis tagged along with his father each morning for the long commute to his New York office at 110 William Street, in the heart of Wall Street's insurance district. "We'd get up at 5 A.M. and arrive at the office around 9 A.M. Then we'd leave around 3:30 P.M. and return to Madison around 7:30 P.M.," he reflects. "I would run the mimeograph machine, which was operated with a hand crank. I helped address envelopes to my dad's clients; then I stamped and sealed them. There were no computers back then. My father would write out some of the trade confirmations by hand on the train and dump them in the mailbox during one of the stops along the way."

Davis's father wrote a weekly newsletter about the insurance industry and his favorite stocks. He worked many fall and winter weekends at the office. "Wall Street was empty, but he wanted to get an early jump on the week ahead," Davis explains. "He printed up the weekly letter Sunday afternoon and mailed it that night. I helped him stuff and seal the envelopes." Davis was rewarded with dinner at one of the nearby restaurants. A few years later, his dad moved the office to 70 Pine Street, about a block away. That's where it remained until he died in May 1994. The firm was then moved to Fifth Avenue in Manhattan, where it is today.

Davis always knew he wanted to work on Wall Street, just like his dad. "For one thing, it played into all the things I enjoyed, like doing research and meeting new people," he says. "I also liked the fact that you weren't tied down to just one company or industry. You could use your brain to find out about a lot of different things. It was an extension of the research work I enjoyed in college. I wrote a

200-page thesis that concluded companies were nothing more than a collection of people working together to move a company forward. You could measure their progress by either earnings or the stock price. When you think about it, the history of a country is basically made by a collection of people. Leaders of countries can make a big difference if they do a good job."

BANKING ON HIS FUTURE

Right out of Princeton, Davis was recruited to go into the training program at the Bank of New York. He discussed working with his father, but both felt it was important for him to get experience somewhere else. "Besides, Dad was difficult to work for and probably wouldn't have paid me," he quips. "Many times he would say, 'Come work for me and we'll see how it goes,' but I wanted to get a job on my own."

The Bank of New York was the oldest financial institution in the state. It was known for being research-oriented, with a strong trust and money management department. "What I liked most about it was it didn't have a long training program, where you had to spend time being a teller or dealing with a lot of back-office issues in order to move up in the ranks," Davis says. "I immediately went to work in the equity research department. I was an assistant to a research analyst, hoping to one day become an analyst myself." Bank of New York analysts prepared regular industry reports, which were widely respected. They were mailed out to institutions around the country, including insurance companies and other banks that wanted help in running their own trust departments. They would compensate the bank for these reports either with cash or by establishing an account. There were 15 to 20 analysts on staff, all of whom enjoyed a national reputation. "The bank was also willing to move you along in your investment career quickly, because it didn't care if you knew how the rest of the bank operated," Davis adds. "If you wanted to be on the research side, that's where you started on day one."

Because he already had some investing experience from working for his dad, Davis wanted to step right into the firing line of picking stocks. It was a great time to be in the market. The 1950s were glorious years for equities, similar to the 1980s. "It was a wonderful era, and I was lucky because a lot of the analysts I worked with at the bank got better job offers after I arrived," he recalls. "That meant I was quickly promoted to senior analyst. I covered many industries, including aluminum, copper, nickel, machinery, cement, automobiles, steel, oil, and rubber. Some very good men trained me. I did industry comparisons, looking at sales, profit margins, and earnings, and evaluating each company to see how it stacked up against the competition. I wanted those stocks that were outperforming in terms of profit margins and returns on capital. I also factored in price. Once a year, I put out a report on each of the industries I was in charge of. They were distributed to all of our important clients."

A YOUNG PRODIGY

Davis didn't get to cover insurance stocks at the Bank of New York, though he continued to watch them on the side. "When I was promoted, I began following the oil industry," he says. "That was one of the bank's biggest groups for its trust accounts. Everybody owned a lot of oil stocks in those days. The Seven Sisters experienced phenomenal growth. I also did work with chemical companies, plus the wood products and building industry, and a few banks as well." After seven years, at the age of 28, he became the bank's youngest vice president since its founder Alexander Hamilton, who had served as U.S. treasury secretary under George Washington. Davis was later named head of equity research.

After this coveted promotion, Davis was told that if he stuck around for another 30 years, he would probably become president of the bank. "I started to look closer at what the president did and decided I didn't want his job," Davis reveals. "I didn't like what he did. He went to a lot of official functions, luncheons, and dinners. He visited the bank's current clients and was always prospecting for new ones. His job was vital, but it wasn't the same as visiting companies and trying to make money in stocks. He was 'Mr. Outside.' I liked making investment decisions on the inside. I'd rather visit companies than clients."

ON HIS OWN

One of the portfolio managers Davis worked with at the bank was Guy Palmer. In 1967, after Davis decided he had gone as far as he wanted to at the bank, he teamed up with Palmer to start an investment firm. They named it Davis, Palmer and Company. Two years later, they enticed Jeremy Biggs, a manager of the $1 billion U.S. Steel pension fund, to join them. Davis had worked for Biggs's father, whom he considered his mentor, at the Bank of New York. "His dad, William R. Biggs, was vice chairman and chief investment officer of the Bank of New York," Davis notes. "That's how Jeremy and I met. When Jeremy came aboard in 1969, the Dow stood at 800 and our firm was renamed Davis, Palmer and Biggs."

That same year, the partners were hired by the investment firm Calvin Bullock Limited to act as subadviser to a new mutual fund it planned to launch called New York Venture. "It was supposed to be comparable to a small-cap or emerging-growth fund of today," Davis says. "The people at Calvin Bullock didn't want to run it in-house, so they decided to retain us. Since the fund had only about $1 million to start, they couldn't pay us anything. So they agreed to give us 45 percent ownership of the new management company that was being set up to run the fund. If the venture was successful, we knew that 45 percent would be worth something."

Calvin Bullock was owned by Sir Hugh Bullock, a grand old gentleman and Anglophile who was also chairman of the Pilgrim's Society. He inherited the firm from his father and eventually sold it to the Equitable Companies. In 1969, Bullock's executive vice president in charge of marketing, Martin Proyect, convinced Bullock that the whole world was moving toward offering aggressive growth funds, yet the firm didn't have one. Bullock didn't want to put his name on a hot growth fund. However, he told Proyect if it was necessary to keep the firm's broker-dealers happy, he could start one, but only if he found someone else to run it. That's when they struck a deal with Davis, Palmer and Biggs.

As it turned out, New York Venture was the number-one fund in its rookie year, up 25.3 percent. "We were focused on the speculative, high-growth stocks," Davis says. "We owned companies that made peripheral equipment for computers, such as Memorex and Mohawk Data, and some nursing homes, such as the predecessor to Humana. They were the classic go-go stocks of the time." The following years were much more shaky. Davis's high-flying stocks were clipped by the ensuing bear market, and it took several years for his original shareholders to break even.

SELLING OUT

By 1978, Davis, Palmer and Biggs had around $400 million under management. The fund represented only around 15 percent of that. "We had some very prestigious institutional accounts, such as the Boy Scouts of America, American Red Cross, Smithsonian Institution, Dun and Bradstreet, and Rohm and Haas," he says. "Fiduciary Trust Company liked our client list and that we were relatively young. They offered to buy the firm." It was an offer Davis couldn't refuse. After all, he had been through 12 tough years in the market and was flattered that someone was willing to pay him so much cash to pick stocks. Each partner was also offered a five-year employment contract with the bank.

"Fiduciary Trust couldn't buy New York Venture (the mutual fund company) because of the Glass-Steagall regulation," he says. "So they let us keep it. It was very small at the time. They said as long as we cleared our orders through their trading desk, allowing them to monitor everything to make sure there were no conflicts of interest, they didn't mind us keeping the fund." Davis and his partners made several million dollars on the deal, which turned out to be a huge bargain for Fiduciary Trust. The bank eliminated the name Davis, Palmer and Biggs and integrated the investment firm into its existing operations. Guy Palmer left a short time later, despite his five-year contract, to become head of the General Motors pension plan. Davis and Biggs stayed on. New York Venture was subsequently renamed Davis New York Venture.

"At the end of the five-year contract period, I told Jeremy I wanted to focus my efforts on the mutual fund," Davis says. "I had bought out Guy Palmer's interest when he quit and had 30 percent ownership of the management company. Jeremy sold me part of his interest too. The bank was helpful and let me stay on as a consultant. Jeremy went on to become vice-chairman and chief investment officer of Fiduciary Trust, just as his father was at the Bank of New York. His brother, Barton Biggs, is now the chief investment strategist at Morgan Stanley, so he came from an investment family too. Jeremy and I have been working together and sitting in the same partners' office since 1969."

Davis had been the firm's research heavyweight. He did all of the in-depth analysis on almost every company. Biggs was also focused on research, but had a more broad interest in economics. In addition, he set the investment strategy. "He offered wisdom and judgment," says Davis. "Thankfully, he shot down some of my worst ideas." Biggs had gone to Yale University and had done post-graduate work at the London School of Economics. He was the overall portfolio strategist. Davis was the stock picker. Palmer's main focus, before he left, was generating new business and making client contacts. After Davis's contract was up, the bank had no problem letting him stay on as a consultant, since it could benefit from his research.

GROWING HIS FIRM

When Davis decided to leave the bank to focus on the mutual fund business in 1983, the first thing he realized was that in order to make his company grow, he had to have more than just one fund. That's when the old Lincoln National came back into his life. "It controlled a company called Chicago Title and Trust," he says. "Chicago Title owned a group of mutual funds called the Retirement Planning Funds of America. They weren't making any money for the company, so I was able to buy them for a very good price." Davis acquired three funds in the deal and transformed them into the Davis Growth Opportunity Fund, the Davis High Income Fund, and the Davis Tax-Free High Income Fund, all of which are run by other managers.

Several years later, Davis won the management agreement to run the Selected Funds, following the departure of Don Yacktman and Ron Ball, who, as we now know, went on to form their own investment firm. Davis says he had tried to get the management contract before, but had lost out to Yacktman's old firm, Prescott Ball and Turben. After Yacktman's highly publicized departure from Kemper Financial, the company wanted to add a load to the Selected funds so they could be sold by Kemper's team of brokers. However, Selected's independent board of directors refused to go along with the plan. The funds had been around since the 1930s and historically had been no-loads. "The board's attitude was we've had several people run our funds in the past, but we have always dictated who was going to manage them and how they would be sold," Davis says. "They didn't want the funds to have a sales load. So they decided to search for another money manager, and we were lucky enough to win the search."

As part of the deal, Davis agreed to change the name of his firm to Davis Selected Advisers. The Selected Funds board wanted to maintain its independence, so Davis obliged them by listing the Selected and Davis funds separately in the newspaper. Davis inherited and initially managed both Selected American, a growth and income fund, and Selected Special, which is more oriented toward small companies. Later, he hired Elizabeth Bramwell to take over Special in 1994, after she left the Gabelli Growth fund to go out on her own. "I saw that she was leaving, and, since I no longer wanted to run the Special fund because I was focused on following different kinds of stocks, I called her. She saw it as a great opportunity as well," he says.

KEEPING YOUR FOCUS

Maintaining your focus, in both life and investing, is something Davis has always taken very seriously. It's also a lesson he has passed on to his six kids. He has three children from his first marriage, Andrew, Christopher, and Victoria. Like his father, Davis let them work for him during the summer. Unlike his dad, however, he offered them a real incentive to perform. "They were all given a chance to go out with me on many of the company meetings held in New York," he explains. "It's like going to a lecture and hearing management tell its story. After that, they would have to write up a one-page report, based on a format I gave them. It was to include a few statistics, a description of the company, a discussion of current operations, and its outlook for the future. If they did the report, they would get $100. That way, they could make as little or as much as they chose. I didn't pay them until they produced a report."

VICTORIA DAVIS

Victoria really broke the bank. "She was writing five or six reports a week," Davis says. "Chris and Andrew did only two or three. But it was a good introduction for them on how I go about looking at a company. You hear their story and keep track of what happens. I remember Victoria heard the president of MCI when the stock was trading for around $3 or $4 a share. She told me to buy it. I eventually did, but she got the first double. A lot of my kids bought stock with the money they earned, and sometimes I would even match it."

Ironically, Victoria, 31, is the only one of Davis' three eldest children not to enter the investment business. She's a Harvard graduate who is now attending Stanford Medical School. She plans to become a general practitioner. His other two elder children, Andrew and Chris, initially took different routes, but now have high-profile jobs at Davis's firm. "It was a big surprise that any of them came to work for me," he says. "I never really pushed it. When they were younger, I used to tell them that it didn't matter if they chose a different vocation in life; it would still be valuable for them to know how to pick stocks, since it could make them a lot of money. At the least, they would know how to respond to a money manager who was trying to advise them on their stock portfolio."

ANDREW DAVIS

Andrew, 36, is president of Davis Selected Advisers and manages the company's real estate and convertible securities funds. "Andrew came out of Colby College and got a job at Shawmut Bank, which was in the mutual fund business," Davis says. "He moved to New York a year later and became an analyst at Paine Webber. He worked under Peter Marcus, who has been around a long time and was the dean of steel and metal analysts on Wall Street. Peter used to hire apprentices to do his spreadsheets. He was very analytical. He had reams of data on each mill. I knew Peter would be a very quantitative and traditional analyst, so Andrew would really get to learn about a company and understand that earnings don't just magically appear. Peter taught Andrew to pay attention to details such as: What are the gross margins? How do you come to that gross margin? What are the variables? What are the fuel costs? What are the labor costs? What's the transportation advantage or disadvantage the company has versus its competitors? What does it cost per dollar of sales in capital to build new plants? Sure enough, within a year, Andrew was promoted to analyst of a full-fledged group that followed closed-end bond funds."

Andrew was promoted again to head of the convertible-bond research department. "When an analyst liked a company, if it had a convertible, Andrew would see if that was an intriguing way to own the common, with less upside, but also less downside," Davis adds. "Andrew gravitated toward this risk-reward trade-off idea right away. He developed a whole computer system to rank convertible bonds, which Paine Webber still uses. When I wanted to start a convertible bond fund in 1992, I enticed him to come work for me, since I felt he was the ideal person to run it."

Davis also liked Andrew's brokerage experience, since his Davis family of funds are load offerings sold through broker-dealers. "I knew our president Martin Proyect was going to retire, and Andrew spoke the broker language," he says. "Brokers are our primary sales outlet. I eventually named Andrew president of the company after Martin retired in December 1995."

Andrew Davis lives in Santa Fe, New Mexico, which is where Davis Selected Advisers is headquartered. How it wound up there is a story in itself. When Martin Proyect left Calvin Bullock Limited, he acquired Sir Hugh Bullock's 51 percent ownership interest in Venture Fund's management company. He then decided to relocate from New York to Santa Fe. Proyect and his wife were both in their midforties, and his wife wanted to move to a smaller town to start a furniture store. He realized he could market the funds from anywhere, as long as he had a phone and access to an airport.

Proyect also has a legal background and was instrumental in convincing the Selected board to let Davis take over management of the funds. "I have always been the money manager," Davis says. "Martin was able to answer all of the legal questions. When he retired a few years ago, I bought out his interest and made Andrew president." In 1995, Davis named his longtime associate and former business partner Jeremy Biggs chairman of the Davis Funds. Davis Selected Advisers, the management company, is now almost entirely owned by the Davis family and the firm's senior managers, although Biggs maintains a minority interest.

CHRISTOPHER DAVIS

Chris studied philosophy and theology at St. Andrew's University in Scotland and originally thought of becoming a priest. After concluding that the family investment bug was too strong to resist, he went to work after graduation for State Street Bank as an accountant for international funds. Following some basic training there, he joined

Graham Tanaka at Tanaka Capital Management, the subadviser to the Davis Growth Opportunity Fund. "Tanaka's a traditional analyst trained by J. P. Morgan and Fiduciary Trust. He taught Chris the tools of the trade," Davis says. "About two years later, my father's health started to fail. Dad asked if someone from the family could come work for him, and Chris took up the opportunity with the understanding that he would really be working with me, since I was helping my father, too. We also saw the day coming when we would merge the two firms and put the money my father had made into the mutual funds. It was really more of a transition that Chris was brought in to look over. He also wrote the weekly insurance letter for my father for almost three years and learned the discipline of getting things down on paper, meeting deadlines, and focusing on companies rather than on big trends." Later, when Davis started the Davis Financial Fund, Chris became its manager.

Chris was named co-portfolio manager of Davis New York Venture and Selected American in 1995, before being promoted to portfolio manager two years later at the age of 32. "I was 32 when I started the fund," Shelby points out. "I figured if he was going to generate a 28-year record as I had done, it was time for him to take charge. He earned this promotion with great performance. He had been sole portfolio manager of the Davis Financial Fund for three years and received a five-star rating from Morningstar. Besides, we're really alter egos." When Davis promoted Chris, he also promoted himself to chief investment officer, although he has never liked official titles. "I like to say I'm now the coach, developing the game plan and calling in some plays, while Chris is the quarterback," he adds. "It's like having a 60-year-old brain running with 30-year-old legs." The transition allows Shelby to focus on strategy and in-depth company research, instead of spending time attending committee meetings.

"Andrew and Chris are slightly different," he notes. "Andrew's a year older and more quantitative, while Chris is more qualitative. Both are great at communicating ideas and have learned each other's skills. Andrew likes to meet with the managements of his real estate holdings. Chris has a broader canvas in managing our growth and income funds, but he also loves talking to managements. I've brought in a team of analysts to help them out. And I'm still in there coaching and calling companies, too. After all, picking stocks is my favorite sport."

SHELBY'S SECOND FAMILY

Shelby was divorced from his first wife after 18 years of marriage, probably because he spent so much time building the business. Two years later, he tied the knot with one of his firm's portfolio assistants, Gale Lansing. They have been married for more than two decades and have three children, Lansing, 19, Alida, 17, and Edith, 12, all of whom spend much of the year in boarding schools. Lansing works at his father's office during summer vacations and writes those $100 research reports just as his older brothers and sister had done before him.

A FORTUNE IN THE FUNDS

After Davis Senior passed away, the $800 million fortune he amassed was put into a charitable remainder trust, which is now primarily invested in Davis's many mutual funds, including New York Venture. Any income the trust generates goes to Davis's mom, Kathryn. Upon her death, it reverts to the family's charitable foundation.

The trust was set up like this because the Davis family has long been against leaving large inheritances to family members. "We want our kids to be comfortable," Davis explains. "But we think the biggest disservice you can do for somebody is to cut off their sense of accomplishment. If I had a son or daughter who was going to get a great sense of accomplishment by going into the ministry, for example, that wouldn't bother me. I would make sure he or she were well enough taken care of to live a good life, just not with a jet airplane. I'm not going to leave kids money to become idle rich. I want them to pursue whatever career they want and do it extraordinarily well, just as I believe in having focus and staying within your circle of competence in investing. You should look in the mirror and be able to feel proud of what you do in life, whether you're an artist, minister, doctor, investor, politician, or anything else. The reason I'm against giving kids money is because I think it corrupts those instincts to achieve. My father did leave me money, in the sense that he gave me the opportunity to manage it. But he was willing to do that because I proved I could manage it well. If I don't, the independent board of directors at our mutual funds has the power to fire me. So it's not as if I was left an income stream that I don't have to work for. I feel the same way about my kids. I want them to do well on their own, and I think they will."

WORKING FROM HOME

When Davis turned over day-to-day management of New York Venture and Selected American to Chris, he had no intention of retiring. Far from it. He now works harder than ever. But he spends little time inside his New York office at the World Trade Center, which overlooks the Statue of Liberty. Instead, he and wife Gale are on the road most of the year, working from one of their three other homes in Northeast Harbor, Maine, Jackson Hole, Wyoming, and Jupiter Island, Florida. All have fully equipped offices, with computers, fax machines, and Bloomberg stock market information terminals. Davis has access to First Call earnings estimates, his electronic calendar, and is increasingly communicating with his associates by E-mail. This way he can keep a constant pulse on the market and stay in regular contact with Chris, Andrew, and his other analysts and fund managers. Davis is greeted by the FedEx delivery driver each morning, who shows up at his door with a package containing brokerage reports and other research material. When Davis has free time, he spends it skiing, hiking, fishing, swimming, or sailing in his Hinckley sailboat.

"On a typical day, I'm on the phone with Chris at least five times," he says. "I also talk to Andrew once or twice a day, because he more or less runs his own show, picking the convertibles and researching real estate. I also have discussions with our five analysts in New York, to see what they think about the various ideas I throw out to them. For example, today I was watching my quote machine and noticed IBM opened down two points. I called and said, 'Shouldn't we be buying more IBM in here? The group's strong, so let's pick up more.'"

Now that the next generation is in place, Davis insists he has no plans ever to sell his firm, even though there are plenty of would-be acquirers out there. "I manage $7 billion," he points out. "If my performance continues at just half the rate it has over the next 30 years, that number will grow to $140 billion from the magic of compounding alone. Why should I sell out if this next generation can look forward to that kind of asset base? I know it sounds preposterous to have these kinds of expectations, but I have a vision. I was around when T. Rowe Price was at $1 billion and Fidelity only had $3 billion." Today, Price manages $56 billion and Fidelity more than $270 billion in mutual funds alone.

THE BULLISH SURPRISE

The strength of the 1990s bull market admittedly caught Davis off guard. When you look back on some of his past writings, you'll notice he wasn't expecting anything even resembling the incredible performance investors have enjoyed in recent years. In July 1994, he told shareholders he felt the market would trade in the 3,000 to 5,000 range through the rest of the decade. "Clearly, I was wrong," he now concedes. "I based that prediction on the facts, though. The average price-earnings multiple for stocks in the Standard & Poor's 500 over the last 50 years is around 15 times earnings. As we speak, that number is above 20. This worries me. I think we'll revert to the mean at some point. But I must admit I've never seen financial conditions quite as favorable as they are right now. We have low interest rates, low inflation curves, high productivity, and a real focus on the bottom line. American companies are more competitive than ever, and they have an entire world to go out and conquer. The sun is shining, and it's a blue-sky day. I'm just saying that eventually we will have some clouds."

While investors overall seem to be exuberant, despite the severe market correction in mid-1998, Davis is a little scared that many fail to realize the risks you face when buying equities. "Investors today don't know what a serious bear market is," he contends. "What happened in 1973–1974 was a real nightmare. When you buy a stock at 12 times earnings and the earnings do OK, yet the stock goes down to 9 times earnings, you've lost 33 percent of your money. That's what happens in a full-fledged bear. We're in a wonderful environment right now. I'm not knocking it. But I'm nervous. I think the market has been relatively well-behaved, considering how high it is."

ON BECOMING A GSP

Unlike many of today's most successful mutual fund managers, Davis and his sons are not CFAs, or certified financial analysts. This designation is awarded by the Institute of Chartered Financial Analysts to those who have passed a series of three rigorous, numbers-based exams on securities analysis. When he was at the Bank of New York, Davis actually taught refresher courses for the CFA and took two of the three exams required for the certificate. But he lost interest when he started his own firm. "I said to myself in 1969 that I'd rather be known as a GSP than a CFA, and that's a 'good stock picker,'" he maintains. "I told my kids the same thing. Some books and professors try to make this business so complicated. What we're doing is about as old-fashioned and uncomplicated as it gets. You just need to understand what makes companies run, and that's people. Find good people and bet on them, but try not to pay an unreasonably high price. It's just like buying a house. You look for a good location and then try to strike a good deal. Who needs to be a CFA to buy a house? I like to always keep this house mentality at the forefront of my thinking. As a matter of fact, the only thing I own, besides stocks, is homes."

THE ATTRACTION OF INSURANCE STOCKS

Financial companies have been attractive to Davis for years. Owning them is one reason his funds performed so well during the 1990s. "A good financial company to me is an outstanding investment because you aren't paying a lot for it in relation to most of the industrials," he maintains. "A financial company can compound assets and earnings because its product is one that allows it to make a spread on money. It takes in money from customers, be it banks, insurance companies, or brokerage firms, then invests or manages it on the other side and makes a spread in between. Money doesn't become obsolete. Everybody needs it, and making a spread on money is the second-oldest business in the world. Money grows with the economies of the world and compounds itself. We view financial companies as 'growth stocks in disguise' because of their potential for growth and relatively low price/earnings multiples. These companies are beneficiaries of two long-term trends: the aging of America's baby boomers and the expansion of financial services around the world."

Like his dad, Davis is especially enamored of insurance companies in the financial sector. The ultimate modern-day insurance company CEO, in his opinion, is none other than fellow growth stock investor Warren Buffett. "He owns several great insurance companies, including Geico," Davis notes. "Operationally, they underwrite at a profit. Then he takes that extra cash flow and invests it. Because Buffett is so overcapitalized, he can invest most of it in equities and in equity-type investments, whereas most insurance companies stick with fixed-coupon instruments or have only part of their free cash flow in stocks.

"I also like the compounding effect you get from investment income in the insurance business in general, especially with companies that underwrite well," Davis adds. "Those that have underwritten at more or less break-even or at a profit have free cash flow that can be put to work in other income-producing instruments. Think about it. When you're running an insurance company and make an investment, you're not buying a steel mill or an auto plant, nor are you doing a lot of research and development on a drug that may never see the light of day. You aren't hunting for oil or producing a depleting asset. What are you doing with your money? You're investing it, mostly in mortgages and bonds. Sometimes these companies stray into tanker loans, Third World debt, leveraged buyout loans, and such. Sometimes they lose their shirts on these deals. But successful insurance companies have the fundamentals right. They've managed the investment side of the house as well as the operating side, and when both work in harmony, you make a lot of money. If the insurer's investment department has any brains at all, it has positive cash flow and is, in effect, compounding money on money."

LOOKING AHEAD

Looking to the next century, Davis predicts that the drug companies, especially those involved in gene and cell-based research, will be among the major beneficiaries of an aging population. "These biotechnology folks are searching for genes and cells that work in the body to alter disease development," he says. "It involves understanding which genes and cells fight off certain diseases and then introducing those cells into the body to multiply. It's like the good-guy Pac Man's eating the bad guys. This is a whole new dimension to finding cures and preventing problems. I think it's a long-term theme that will make many investors rich."

He's also excited about the opportunities equity investors are being presented with as we enter the twenty-first century. "I believe investing is the most exciting business in the world because it doesn't limit you to one industry," he says. "I have great faith in this country, in the fundamental soundness of our economy, and in our people who have come here from all over the globe to start businesses and make their fortunes. This is what makes great companies and great investment opportunities."

SHELBY DAVIS'S
top 10 GROWTH STOCKS

1. Citigroup

2. Schlumberger Ltd.

3. Texas Instruments

4. American Express

5. McDonald's

6. Hewlett-Packard

7. Morgan Stanley, Dean Witter, Discover and Co.

8. Bristol-Myers Squibb

9. Wells Fargo & Company

10. Berkshire Hathaway

Rule 7

TRAVEL AROUND THE GLOBE, BUT STAY AT HOME

Roy Papp has visited almost every country in the world at least once. He also lived in Manila for two years as U.S. representative to the Asian Development Bank under President Ford in the mid-1970s. During the first half of 1997 alone, he and his wife jetted to Italy, Switzerland, France, England, Norway, Sweden, Finland, Russia, Hong Kong, Singapore, Bali, Indonesia, and Tokyo. He sits behind a desk in an office the size of a large one-bedroom apartment adorned by two silk Persian-design rugs from Shanghai. A console behind his guest chairs sports treasures he has collected from his travels, including a globe from China and figurines of several past and present Soviet leaders. It's easy to see he has an affinity for the entire world, and, as a red-blooded investor, he wants to profit from that interest. That's why he likes to buy companies with significant overseas operations.

Don't Pack Your Bags Just Yet

But wait. There's a catch. The well-traveled Papp stays away from foreign-domiciled corporations and advises investors to avoid international mutual funds. Instead, he recommends that you exploit global opportunities by purchasing shares in American corporations that do a significant amount of business abroad.

His reasoning is straightforward: Overseas stocks are too dangerous. Who would know this better than a man who has been to the far reaches of the world, in some cases several times? "Almost every other country is in serious trouble compared to our lack of problems in the United States," he observes. "By comparison, most foreign economic environments offer varying degrees of exceedingly high unemployment, inflated stock prices, the threat of small wars getting bigger, financial instability, political unrest, terrorism, drugs, AIDS, untried financial systems, inefficient small-sized production, and, for most of us, language barriers. I go to bed saying, 'Thank God I live and invest in America.' Obviously, we also have some of these problems. But when did you last wake up worried that we would be attacked, faced with runaway inflation, a political coup, or just a neighbor dropping some bombs on us?"

The Risks of Investing in Foreign Equities

After pointing out that many of today's international fund managers, who are supposed to be experts on the entire world, are under 40 and haven't even been to many of the countries they're investing in, he lists some of the risks Americans take on when dabbling in stocks domiciled on foreign soil.

"First is the currency risk, because you can encounter some enormous swings," he begins. "Second, the accounting in many foreign countries is different from our own. I call it funny accounting. Third is the fact that most of the world's markets are rigged and dishonest. People get caught doing things you simply can't get away with in the United States. Fourth, the cost of transactions and maintaining custody of securities abroad is high. Fifth, you have political and socioeconomic risks in foreign countries." To back up his thesis, he offers the following illustration: "I went to Switzerland thinking that was the safest place to invest. What happens? In early 1997 word breaks out that Switzerland was sympathetic to the Nazis during the war and cheated the Jews and Germans. That adverse publicity hurt the financial markets. Now let's talk about Thailand, Malaysia, the Philippines, Turkey, or even Japan. These markets have all been through the wringer. Yes, the U.S. market can get hurt too, but not in the same way."

Furthermore, in the process of turning dollars into foreign currency to buy overseas stocks, you get hit with currency risk from both sides. "When you buy shares in U.S. companies that do business internationally, it's true their earnings are also impacted by currency swings," Papp points out. "Let's say the value of the dollar increases by 7 percent. Instead of earnings being up 14 or 15 percent, they may increase by only 11 or 12 percent. But suppose you bought a foreign stock and had a 7 percent change. You wouldn't lose 7 percent of your earnings. You'd lose 7 percent of your principal. The magnitude of the damage is 20 times greater."

What's more, as soon as you purchase a stock in a foreign market, you forgo what Papp considers to be a treasured perk: SEC protection. "You also lose the maximum benefit of U.S. research and development, which is feeding the technology growth in our country," he maintains. "You lose the benefit of having 70 percent of the world's entrepreneurs here in the United States. While other countries experience a tremendous brain drain, we in the United States benefit from tremendous brain gain. A good illustration of that can be found by looking at the Indian Institute of Technology, which is India's equivalent of MIT. It gets 100,000 qualified applicants each year, of which 2,000 are accepted. When those folks graduate four years later, 65 percent of them come to the United States for advanced education. Most of them stay here to work."

U.S. ECONOMIC DOMINANCE AND FOREIGN INVESTING

There is also the matter of U.S. economic superiority compared to the rest of the world. "In the eighteenth and nineteenth centuries England and Europe were at the center of the economic stage; in the twentieth century this economic power shifted to the United States and North America," Papp claims, "The twenty-first century will see China and its satellites plus Japan representing Asia as the center of the world's economic power for a short time. However, that power will clearly be shared with the United States. We may not have as many people to produce a larger gross national product, but the per-capita income and true economic power will remain here. It is also fortunate that most of the world's truly global companies, along with the center of entrepreneurship, productive research, best advanced educational facilities, and strongest true military power will all be centered in America." For this reason, when buying global, Papp purchases U.S. corporations that are making a significant amount of money overseas.

INVESTING GLOBAL BY BUYING AMERICAN STOCKS

Although this globalization test is now applied to every stock he buys, Papp didn't think about venturing overseas until some clients began pressuring him to buy foreign stocks in the late 1980s. It was all the rage in the media, and his clients wanted a piece of the action. "Every time I looked for potential candidates, I held my breath because I knew the risks," he reveals. "Finally, I decided I had to give in and buy some foreign stocks. I first looked at the Swiss company Nestlé and was shocked to find out that 4 percent of its sales came from Switzerland and 40 percent from the United States. I started to think that if 40 percent of Nestlé's sales came from the United States, why not build a fund full of American multinationals that did a majority of their business overseas. I did some research and developed a list of U.S. corporations that did about 55 percent of their business overseas. Then, I looked at the international benchmark Morgan Stanley World Index. I discovered that some 59 percent of the earnings in those [non-U.S.] companies came from outside the United States, which is almost identical to the American stocks I found." Following this logic, Papp invests overseas by buying stock in American companies doing a large percentage of their business outside our borders.

In Papp's estimation, this trend of companies earning an overwhelming amount of their income overseas is likely to grow even stronger. "You're seeing more and more U.S. companies take their operations abroad," he says. "As one example, I own State Street Bank. It now has physical plants in 16 countries and does business in more than 70. Another of my companies, Manpower, has bigger operations abroad every year. These are just two of the many companies building an increasing overseas presence."

NO REASON TO LEAVE HOME

While some argue that going overseas and buying stocks in foreign countries helps to diversify your portfolio and therefore reduce risk, Papp disagrees. He feels it's nonsense to believe that an overseas investment will cushion you from a potential fall in the United States. "Today we have a consolidated world where we are all tied in to each other," he claims. "It's naive to say you're investing in a foreign country. When you put money overseas, you're investing in America once removed. You can have only one real market, and it's here. The other countries are all copying us. It's different if you want to gamble on some underdeveloped nation. That's almost the same as going to Las Vegas. The world markets are getting more and more coupled each day. The reality is if our market heads down, the whole world follows us. We're the leader. When America gets a cold, everybody else gets pneumonia. Look at what happened during the 1998 global stock market correction. Excluding the small underdeveloped countries, there was a high correlation between the U.S. and foreign markets. In my mind, it makes less sense than ever to lose SEC protection and buy overseas stocks. I truly cannot understand the wisdom of taking your money into uncertain parts of the world." By investing in multinationals, you also enjoy some degree of protection in the event the domestic economy fares worse than some of our trading partners.

Papp points to the Asian debacle of 1997, which drove stocks in some overseas markets down more than 30 percent in just a few weeks. During this same period, the Dow Jones Industrial Average fell by only 10 percent. Despite the recent turmoil, Papp remains exceedingly optimistic about Asia's future. "In the year 2000, this world will have three great economic powers, and the United States will be the only one outside of Asia," he predicts. "Japan already has a stock market equal to almost twice the value of, not the largest

European country, but all of Europe combined. Migration in the United States and Canada to the west is likely to accelerate as the world increasingly discovers Asia and the United States discovers the West Coast."

Still, Papp emphasizes you're better off tapping into this potential with American multinationals. Yet another reason Papp prefers to stay at home with his investments is because there's no reason for him to leave. "*Fortune* magazine does a study every August on the 500 largest companies in the world," he points out. "In 1997, 24 of the biggest were U.S. companies, yet they accounted for half of the earnings of the top 100 companies. In other words, 24 percent of the companies made 50 percent of the earnings, and they're all American. Thus, American companies earn three times as much as their foreign competitors. They are also much better run and more efficient. We have so many advantages in the United States, it's unbelievable. Why would I want to leave the best, strongest growth stocks in the universe to go buy a bunch of junk around the world and take all those risks? I feel you should buy the best companies in the world rather than second-rate companies just because they are foreign. The origin of a multinational company is less important than its quality and ability to grow."

AMERICA: THE WAL-MART OF THE WORLD

Interestingly, Papp notes that we're not seeing the reverse take place, namely foreign companies infiltrating the U.S. market. He has a simple explanation for this: "They can't compete effectively on a level playing field. Look at Wal-Mart, which has been a roaring success for many years. It grew by going into small towns and wiping out the mom-and-pop stores down the street. Unfortunately, it has run out of small towns to conquer and has been forced to move into the big cities. The company is still successful, but doesn't do nearly as well competing with the likes of K-mart and Sears. Similarly, when U.S. companies go into these small countries, they mop them up, like Wal-Mart in the small towns. The foreign companies can't compete. But when they come here, it's like Wal-Mart competing with its equals. There's probably business for everyone, but the outsiders aren't going to do fantastically well.

"Another thing I'll tell you, and this has never been in print before, is that we've had periods where one country was stronger than another, but we've never had anything comparable to the Gulf War," he adds. "America took on the fifth largest military army in the world that had been supplied and trained by the Russians and we wiped them out in about a day. This shook everybody up, especially the Chinese. They panicked because they realized for the first time that even with a large population, there was no way to win a technological war. They decided they had to modernize in a hurry, threw communism out the door, and quickly started free enterprise in an effort to catch up. The Gulf War clearly etched U.S. superiority into the annals of history. If you go back to the 1960s, you'll find that over half of the world lived under some form of communism, which was believed to be the clear winner. Then Russia was dominant, with Sputnik and other such events. Now you have a situation where communism is gone and no one country can threaten the United States. In this environment, American stocks are even more valuable."

Robert Stovall agrees that it makes sense to find U.S.-based companies that can make money overseas instead of looking for creative ways to invest directly in foreign countries. "Rather than buying a Brazilian or Hong Kong company, I think it's better to purchase shares in an American business with investments in those areas," he says. "The emerging markets often turn out to be submerging markets. That doesn't stop them from duping many investors, though. I feel that if you want to participate in the growth of the Pacific Rim or another fast-growing region, you are better off buying American multinationals, instead of local companies. I would much rather own Coca-Cola over a hot-shot bottling company in Malaysia. Sure, investing directly in stocks domiciled in these foreign lands can give you a much bigger short-run bang for your buck, but too often they wind up seriously collapsing or even disappearing."

There are very few international names in Stovall's portfolio, except for the American Depositary Receipts (foreign stocks traded on a U.S. exchange) of a select handful of companies based in Canada, the United Kingdom, and northern Europe. "At least I can read and understand the language that their annual reports are written in," he notes. "In addition, given the differences in accounting among the various countries, I will buy stocks only in areas where the financials are fairly straightforward."

GLOBAL-GROWTH GUIDELINES

On the globalization front, Papp prefers American companies that get 50 percent of their business abroad, although that number is somewhat flexible as long as it's above the average of 10 to 15 percent. "In addition, I prefer to buy companies with real volume growth," he adds. "A company that has made a lot of money and saved even more by cost reduction and restructuring is a one-shot deal. I want the growth to be from volume and pricing growth."

Although Papp's acumen for reducing risk often leads him to large, established companies, he's always willing to look at promising smaller candidates as well. "I don't have a requirement to buy large stocks," he says. "It just so happens that many global companies tend to be larger. But I'm not buying them because they're large. I'm buying them because they're global and in the right industry. If they happen to be large, that's fine. But that's not my goal." It amuses Papp that many reporters refer to him as a large-cap manager. When I posed the size question to him, he almost angrily pulled out his list of top holdings in the America Abroad fund to prove that five of his biggest names were smaller companies.

GLOBALIZATION: THE WAVE OF THE NEW MILLENNIUM

Papp feels this globalization of the world will continue to be a major investment theme throughout the twenty-first century, and investors who ignore the enormous opportunities overseas do so at their own peril. "It's the engine that's likely to drive our economy for the next 20 years," he predicts. "The rate of globalization is accelerating and becoming more important to us and the rest of the world." He wants to exploit this potential by staying in U.S. businesses. "In the early 1990s, the United States had a $300 billion annual deficit," he points out. "We were hooked on a drug. We were hyped. How do you get off that without collapsing the economy? Nobody thought you could. Now we have close to a break-even deficit problem. Where did the additional business come from? I think a large part of it was globalization."

Elizabeth Bramwell concurs. She's convinced that one reason the market has done so well in the 1980s and 1990s is because free-market economies have evolved globally, thus facilitating trade, economic growth, and rising standards of living around the world. "Interest rates are low worldwide, and investment bankers are everywhere," she notes. "They're putting money all over the place, including China and Latin America. Growth begets growth. Because of all the changes that have taken place, I'm much more aware of international events. I used to ignore events such as elections in India. I don't anymore."

A GREAT TIME FOR INVESTORS

Papp maintains there's never been a better time in the history of the world to be an investor. "I challenge you to tell me when in your lifetime there was a better time to be living," Papp offers. "In the depression thirties? World War II in the forties? The Sputnik Cold War in the fifties? Vietnam in the sixties? The oil crisis of the seventies? Or the culmination of the Cold War in the late eighties? Never has anybody had the expectation of a healthier, longer life than today. During a recent vacation, I noticed that EPCOT Center had an exhibition on the quality of life that has resulted from our use of electricity. They picked out five periods, starting with the late 1800s. The exhibit was particularly impressive to me when I compared the quality of life 100 years ago with today. In addition, we have almost eliminated the threat of nuclear war. We have a much smaller chance of a serious, large war than ever before in history. I believe that well-managed, growth-oriented U.S. companies are uniquely suited to successfully compete in this worldwide marketplace. Some are household names no matter where you happen to live. Others are technological powerhouses whose leadership in various areas of expertise is unquestioned. As the standard of living continues to rise in nations such as China, Indonesia, and Malaysia, so will the demand for American goods, services, and technology."

Papp's conviction was heightened by a trip to Asia in November 1998. "I went to Hong Kong and Japan to review the economic situation there," he shares. "The economy in Hong Kong is still declining modestly. On the positive side, the people are hardworking, intelligent, and well disciplined. The Japanese economy started having problems about eight years ago. I expect a continuation of this at least through the new millennium. The hotels and restaurants in Japan were quite sparse. How fortunate the U.S. has been to have enjoyed eight wonderful years while Japan has suffered. I see this trend continuing. My fundamental problem with Japan is its unwillingness to accept a free market and price competition, which results in almost all goods and services costing more there than in the United States. While I still believe the twenty-first century will be the Asian century, this trip reinforced my belief that the safest, most profitable way to participate in this growth is by owning the American multinational companies that do business there."

PEACE PROPELS PROFITS

The current peaceful environment, and opening up of international markets to U.S. companies, are powerful developments that Shelby Davis also feels could lead to years of financial prosperity for both America and its equity investors. "We've had a gigantic peace dividend that's been rightly recognized by the market," he says. "The other thing that's happened is we've seen a tremendous focus on the evolving American business model, which calls for concentrating on your core business, keeping an eye on the bottom line, and giving workers incentives to build on it. Companies are getting rid of low-return businesses and are being run under a new form of management called EVA, which stands for Economic Value Added. Under EVA, you try to raise returns on capital and equity. This concept is sweeping around the world, along with shareholder capitalism. Furthermore, companies are trying to grow business and the bottom line without raising prices. America has become leaner and more efficient, and that's a huge plus for stockholders. And Japan, which used to be our major competitor, is now much weaker and not nearly as influential."

As a result, Davis also looks to fill his portfolios with companies boasting successful international operations. He believes corporations that expand overseas reduce the risk of being tied too closely to our economic and business cycles in the United States. He is further convinced that such companies merit higher valuations in the market. "They deserve a premium, especially the bigger companies, because they have staying power combined with global opportunities that didn't exist in the early 1970s," he insists. "Capitalism and free enterprise have won out over socialism. Just look at Procter & Gamble. It might have been a mature company if it were selling just to Western Europe and the United States. But now it can move into Eastern Europe, Russia, China, and South America. That's also true of Coke, McDonald's, Colgate, and a bunch of other consumer products companies. It further applies to Hewlett-Packard, IBM, Intel, and many more technology companies."

THE ONE EXCEPTION TO THE "BUY-AMERICAN" RULE

There is one exception to Papp's America-only rule. He'll buy a stock directly overseas if he can't legally exploit the opportunity some other way in the United States. "Let's say you were convinced diamonds were going through the roof," he offers. "You'd buy DeBeers in South Africa because that's the only real option you have. It's not an American company, so you must purchase it abroad. Overall, there are very few occasions where you get a benefit from buying into a developed market abroad. In most instances, you can find a pretty darn good substitute in the United States that's going to perform better for you over a long period of time. You're not going to find the French, German, or Japanese economy growing a lot faster than ours. You might find a developing country where that can happen. But the accompanying risk goes through the roof."

THE BOTTOM LINE

Wise investors look to profit from the prosperity being enjoyed by countries around the world, not just the United States. However, instead of buying stocks on foreign soil, seek out American companies that derive a good portion of their earnings from overseas sales.

U.S. companies are more stable, closely regulated, easier to follow, and governed by strict accounting and regulatory standards. They also tend to be better run and are often fiercer competitors than their foreign counterparts.

Rule 8

BE WILLING TO CHANGE

Roy Papp is clearly one of the oldest active portfolio managers in the investment business today, even though he's only in his early seventies. By contrast, the average mutual fund manager is around 40. Unlike many of his generation, Papp is continually altering his investment process to keep up with the times and changing market conditions. "A lot of older investors don't accept the new world, and they've been wrong for years," he says. "Benjamin Graham was really the first stock analyst in the 1930s. He's the father of the CFA and was everyone's hero. If you followed his advice, you would have had trouble buying stocks after 1949. Things change. His teachings are now somewhat outdated."

KEEPING UP WITH THE TIMES

As an investor, you must always be willing to alter and refine your investment process and beliefs, since the world is constantly evolving. In a letter dated January 1, 1977, head-lined "Views from Beautiful Downtown Manila," Papp told his clients, "Being halfway around the world, I am completely out of touch with the thinking of the professional investment community and thus have reconsidered my own criteria. I believe stocks should be bought for their total return, which consists of dividends and appreciation. The less dependable the appreciation becomes, the more important the dividends should become. I think this shift has begun and will con-tinue." At the bottom of the letter, he lists the 11 characteristics he seeks in every stock he buys, among them, being established 20 years or more, a price/earnings ratio of around six or seven times earnings, a yield of 6 percent, and a market price below book value. Like Graham, if Papp followed his own teachings from back then, he'd be sitting in cash, and avoiding stocks like the plague. That's why today he adheres to very few of these original 11 rules.

For one thing, back then the average stock's price/earnings ratio was around 8. Today, it's above 20. Equity yields have accordingly plummeted. "Remember, when I wrote this we had just come out of the 1968–1974 recession," he says. "The median decline in the New York Stock Exchange was 60 percent, while it was around 80 percent on both the American Exchange and the over-the-counter market. Cash dividends are now much less important because corporations and investment firms aren't as interested in them. If you get a cash dividend, you have to pay up to 40 percent of it in taxes. Companies have learned that buying back stock, instead of paying dividends, puts everyone ahead of the game. If you take your appreciation in the form of a capital gain instead, your tax load is cut in half."

Papp further argues that Graham's favorite yardstick, book value, has no real value today. "Restructuring, inflation, and the accounting rules have destroyed it," he maintains. "Most important, our society has moved from steel to silicon. In silicon companies, book value walks out the door every night. There isn't any. Microsoft has no book value. Most of the electronics companies trade based on intelligence, not book value. Brick and mortar don't count as much any more. Things really have changed. I love to say the four most dangerous words in the English language are not 'this time it's different,' but rather 'history always repeats itself.' There are general trends that you learn from history, and you better know them. But they're different every time."

For this reason, Papp thinks people who do relentless back-testing and look at what worked on Wall Street in the past are wasting their time. "You can go back and do something that worked in hindsight and find it doesn't work now because things change so fast," he insists. "Among other things, our economy is fundamentally different. Yes, we will still have recessions, but they won't occur as often. Why do I say that? Just look at what caused recessions over the last 200 years. Almost every time, inventory problems were to blame. Now you have computers telling you how large your inventory is. Surprise inventories are what caused the problem. You don't get them anymore. The restructuring of our society over the last decade has worked because the computer has made it possible. Years ago, my peers and I lived in a society where the chairman of a company had to wait until his middle managers accumulated all the sales figures they got from going out in the field before he would react. Today, that chairman can look at yesterday's sales on a specific product in a particular store. He doesn't have to wait. It's instantaneous. If you've got too much of a product, you simply stop producing it for a week. There is now no reason for inventories to get six months out of control."

EXPERIENCE COUNTS . . . IF YOU'RE WILLING TO CHANGE

Born in 1927, Papp has decades of experience under his belt. He confesses to being somewhat prejudiced against all of the recent college graduates who are being allowed to manage billions of mutual fund dollars these days. "I think the really young ones will continue to underperform the market," he predicts. "For one thing, I believe experience is worth something. It's not going to make a difference between a star and a bum, but it should let you perform a couple of percentage points better than average, provided that it doesn't drag you down to the point where you're unwilling to do new things and accept change. I think I've proven I'm willing to change and look at the future. That's rare for someone my age. I'm different. But then I've spent my whole life being different."

Many investors of Papp's generation have been bearish for years. Most of them missed out on the bull market of the 1980s and 1990s, and, as a result, have significantly underperformed their benchmark averages. Papp thinks he knows why. "They don't realize we've gone from a steel to a silicon society," he surmises. "Two thousand years ago, there were only a few things that were regarded as storehouses of value. One was real estate. The others were coins, precious metals (gold and silver), and artifacts (soft durable goods). Then along came the industrial revolution in the 1700s, and the invention of stocks, bonds, and paper money. We moved away from the hard stuff to softer instruments. We became an industrial society. Now, we are an information society. The storehouses of value are much different. In today's world, one storehouse of value is having a special talent or skill. Another is knowledge and education. A third is smarts. As an example, baseball players, movie stars, and singers never earned a fantastic amount of money before. Today, they make fortunes.

"Let's take this another step," he continues. "Corporations used to be owned by wealthy families and were handed down from generation to generation. Now, they are owned by institutions, and top managers can get both options and enormous salaries, enabling them to become rich in less than three years. Additionally, you have special talents in the business world. Bill Gates has made more money than anyone in the United States, and he started with nothing, not even a college degree. All kinds of people in California have made fortunes in five years or less in technology. Smarts are now as much of an asset as soft paper and stock certificates were relative to hard money decades ago. It's hard for people to equate this asset to real money. A bond that matures in 30 years is not cash, although one maturing in a month is. The same thing's true here. These storehouses of value I just mentioned are not cash today, but they will be. When you look at the first *Forbes* 400 list in 1984, you find that most of the top ten people on the list had inherited their wealth. Today, that's true of only one of the top ten. The rest are self-made. We live in a different society. Those who don't adjust to that will be left in the dust."

SOME THINGS STAY THE SAME

That's not to say that certain aspects of history won't ever be repeated. To the contrary, Papp is convinced that we will have more bear markets, though he doubts we'll have more crashes, or "financial accidents" as he calls them, like the one in 1987. "I think one of the major ingredients that caused that event was Congress passing a bill in late July eliminating the investment tax credit. They went back and instituted it retroactive to January first," he offers. "Consequently, earnings were revised way down, meaning the stock market was trading at 23 times earnings. That was unheard of. People panicked, not realizing that tax rates for corporations would go down significantly the following year to compensate for this. You also had the media out scaring people. They were on the tube the day of the crash telling people it's 1929 all over again. The media accidentally messed people up badly. They have become much more conscientious since then. When the Gulf War started, they discussed why the market dropped and that it was just a short-term event. For the most part, the same thing happened during the 1998 correction. They have also taught everybody that stocks aren't a dirty word, while informing the public that buying bonds is not as safe as they might believe."

SHATTERING OLD MYTHS

A changing world also caused Robert Stovall to throw out the theory that originally got him a guest spot on *Wall $treet Week With Louis Rukeyser* back in 1976. At the time, he wrote a column for *Forbes* and popularized what he termed the "General Motors Bellwether" theory. It stated that the price action of GM stock was a leading foreshadower of coming trends for the entire market. He no longer believes that to be true. "I am continually altering the way I think," Stovall says. "I have to. I don't even like to talk about the old times or people I used to deal with because that's boring to the younger generation and usually not too relevant either."

There are many myths about the market that have been around for decades. Stovall admittedly once bought into a number of them. Now he claims they are pretty much useless. "One of my favorite mantras was that you should always avoid stocks when the yield of the S&P 500 index falls below 3 percent," he offers. "That wasn't a bad rule of thumb when companies were paying out 50 percent of their income in the form of dividends. Unfortunately, you're lucky now if they pass out 35 percent. With today's tax-law changes and the various incentives available to corporations, many prefer to spend earned cash on new capital investment or for buying back their own stock. In most cases, companies can find more shareholder-pleasing uses for this money than paying it out to investors. Shareholders also seem to like that, since they pay less in taxes for capital gains than they do for dividend income."

Another myth that has been shattered by time is, "Don't buy a stock if its price/earnings ratio is greater than its growth rate." That may have worked when bull markets were dominated by fluctuating economic cycles, but not anymore. "It used to be that companies would do well for a year or two and then burn out with the changing cycles, which used to last about four years apiece. Their fortunes were also based mainly on domestic events," Stovall says. "When that was the case, this rule made sense. Today, however, the bull market is fueled by great multinational growth companies with dominant brand names. These globally diverse producers can enjoy long-lived boom cycles, especially with the enormous markets now open to them overseas. The stocks of many of these companies sell at up to twice their growth rates. However, I would argue they are worth it, since there is convincing evidence to suggest this international brand acceptance merits a premium. What's more, they enjoy a steady stream of new business from markets around the world. Besides, it's difficult to find companies selling for PEs less than their growth rates today. If that were your steadfast rule, you might not find anything to buy."

Two other myths that have gone out the door in recent years: Don't purchase a stock if its price exceeds book value by four times, and do the opposite of small investors, since they are always wrong. "In terms of the first one (as Papp also pointed out), book value was a useful gauge years ago when we were mainly an industrial society, with manufacturing and extractive industries dominating the scene," Stovall surmises. "Now we are in a service and information economy. Book value means more to an oil conglomerate than it does to a Hewlett-Packard, Intel, or Microsoft. These companies have most of their assets tied up in techniques, people, and patents. In addition, we've had 17 new tax bills in the past 21 years. Many of them have resulted in companies taking write-offs, which reduces book value, but not necessarily the underlying worth of the company's income stream. As for ignoring small investors, that is a myth that once permeated the floor of the New York Stock Exchange.

Most professionals felt this way. Has that ever changed! Small investors now have better information and instant access to much of the same data as that enjoyed by the professionals. Small investors have shown an amazing ability to be on the right side of trades for several years now. They buy steadily on weakness and hold on during downturns, which is the smart thing to do."

MEETING WITH THE FATHER OF VALUE

As an up-and-coming analyst and fund manager in the late 1960s, Shelby Davis thought he could do no wrong. The market was in a clear bull trend and he was riding high buying the "go-go" stocks of the moment. The price he paid for these companies was of little concern, since he reasoned they would keep going up no matter what. But this belief was shattered by the 1973–1974 bear, which virtually wiped out all of the gains he had achieved investing in these stocks in the preceding years. Humbled and in need of guidance, Davis sought advice from a man who is one of the most admired value investors the world has ever known, Benjamin Graham. As we know, today Papp considers many of Graham's teachings to be outdated, but some of the lessons Davis learned continue to serve him well today.

"I was out in California in 1974 and called Graham, the father of value investing, at his home in La Jolla," Davis reflects. "He was gracious enough to see me, and we had tea together. Graham was the dean of security analysis. I studied his work while preparing for the CFA exam. It was sort of the bible for analysts. In the late 1960s, when the market went straight up, people said he was too old-fashioned, since he didn't crank growth rates into stock valuations. He just looked at net asset values or intrinsic value. His detractors argued that market pricing was based on supply and demand, and if there were more buyers than sellers, prices would go up. They got away from the fundamentals. What he told me changed my life. He said, 'Don't be discouraged. Just keep doing your work. There are plenty of bargains out there.' By then, he was becoming bullish. He was pretty old, but full of wisdom."

Graham revealed to Davis that his best investment ever was Geico, the insurer later bought out by Warren Buffett's holding com-

pany Berkshire Hathaway. (Buffett has long admitted to being a dis-
ciple of Graham's as well.) Geico was a terrific growth company
without a lot of assets. "What I learned is that a high return on equity
is a wonderful thing for a company to have," Davis says. "If you pay
50 times earnings for a stock, you're only getting a 2 percent return
on your equity, because you're not buying it at book value. That
may be justified if a company is young and growing dynamically, or
even if it has start-up problems that are expected to go away
quickly. Otherwise, you're playing with fire. From then on, that kind
of high-multiple investing became the exception for me, rather than
the rule. I still always have an open mind. I'm not one of these guys
who will never buy a small-cap or a mid-cap stock. I'll buy anything.
I'm a little like Peter Lynch in that respect. But over the years, I have
developed mental screens that keep me out of a lot of stocks. I don't
have to hear more than a minute's worth of a story before I know
I'm never going to buy it."

THE BOTTOM LINE

You must be willing to alter your investment process to keep up
with the changing times. Stock market techniques and theories that
worked decades ago may no longer be relevant. Failing to adapt to
current conditions can cause you to invest in companies and industries that are no longer growing, while preventing you from buying
more promising prospects.

Rule 9

NEVER UNDERESTIMATE THE POWER OF TECHNOLOGY

Although today Roy Papp preaches the merits of technology, taking the plunge to buy computer stocks was initially the hardest thing he ever had to do. Papp used to hate them. He credits daughter Tori with changing his mind. Although she's primarily involved in managing accounts and creating brochures for his firm, in 1994 she began pushing her dad to start investing in the post-industrial society. "She was the force driving me to throw my prejudice against technology out the door," he says. "She kept telling me it was the right thing to do. I just didn't buy computer stocks. I saw them take a bath in 1983 and 1984. They were a disaster and went to hell in a hand basket. I had seen the high-techs fade out many times before as well. For example, in 1970 everybody was convinced that lasers would create an enormous market, and the companies involved with that technology were selling at 50 to 60 times earnings. These expectations never panned out, although they are starting to now. Next, everybody said solar energy was going to be the hot thing, and those stocks went wild. It never happened. I have seen more technologies that were supposed to be wonderful but never worked out than I can count. That's why I've always been concerned about buying this year's fashions. But Tori convinced me that the electronics industry truly was different this time. It was the future. When she got that concept over to me, I reeducated everybody at the firm. At the time, we all believed we should stay away from these high-tech stocks. I finally came down here and told everyone that even though they didn't agree with me, we were going to buy tech stocks."

Still concerned about risk, Papp decided to stick with the biggest and best technology stocks in their respective fields. Motorola for wireless telephones, Microsoft for software, Intel for the chip business, and Hewlett-Packard for computers and printers. He also owns a few smaller high-tech firms, but all have been in business for decades.

"What changed to make me want to buy them?" Papp asks. "The major thing is that their degree of cyclicality went way down. That's because electrical products and electronic components are now the biggest segment of our manufacturing society. You can't have a society that's booming while electronics are going down, because they are the dominant factor. The economy moves with them. They've become that important."

STICK WITH THE STRONGEST AND BEST

Shelby Davis has a similar discipline for buying technology shares. Although he doesn't invest heavily in this sector, when he does, he, too, buys the most diversified behemoths, including Motorola, Intel, IBM, Texas Instruments, and Hewlett-Packard. "That way, I'm not betting on a pure-play product," he explains. "These companies all have other businesses to fall back on if one product loses market share because someone beats them to the punch or they fall asleep at the switch. The smaller high-tech firms can go up like rocket ships, but they can also flame out. Memorex was a rocket. You could say nothing but wonderful things about Memorex's products and the growing markets it served. The company made tapes and floppy disks for computers. What could be better? Yet it's been a very tough business because supply exceeded demand and price cutting was lethal to the company's ability to sustain compounded earnings, which have since been nil."

THE KEY ECONOMIC DRIVER

Robert Stovall agrees that, since technology is now our biggest industry, investors must take it super-seriously. "When I started out, automobile manufacturers, construction companies, and natural-resource extractors were the most important businesses for an investor to follow," he recalls. "We then moved along to computer hardware. Now it's computer software, along with telecommunications of all sorts. It doesn't matter whether you're talking about wireless, fiber optics, or whatever. All of these communications technologies will be increasingly important throughout the twenty-first century, and you can't afford to ignore them."

Like Papp, Stovall was slow to grab on to this concept, partly because he noticed that his colleagues who invested in some of the upstart technology concerns had most of their gains wiped out by offsetting losses. "That was when technology was evolving out of its infancy and there were a lot of fly-by-night companies out there," he shares. "Now that technology is unquestionably the biggest and most important business in the world, you can't help but take it seriously. Some older investment professionals don't see it that way. They sit back and say, 'I don't understand technology so I'll invest in something else.' I suppose there's nothing fundamentally wrong with that, but, as for me, I can't just sit here and let 30 percent of the economy blow right by me without getting involved."

In accordance with his philosophy of keeping risk to a minimum, Stovall prefers to own the large blue-chip technology operations, as opposed to some of the recent start-ups. "However, when I get more confidence in myself and the industry in general, whichever comes first, I'm sure I will branch out into several of the smaller names as well," he says. Stovall is growing increasingly more accustomed to the sector, especially since he now uses computers regularly to manage his own investment practice.

A CHANGE IN PHILOSOPHY

Globalization and technology now form the primary foundation of Roy Papp's entire investment philosophy and process. "Because the rate of change is so much faster than it has been historically, I think the impact of these two factors on our society will be greater than electricity was in 1900 or the railroads were in the late 1800s," he predicts. "Our changes today are faster and more dramatic. They're the two driving forces of everything. Keeping with the globalization theme, when you go back to the beginning of western civilization, we went through Egypt, Crete, Greece, and Rome. But when Marco Polo finally got to China, he realized it was miles ahead in everything, from printing to gun powder. In the 1700s, the center of civilization and most productive economic returns moved from China to Holland, then back to England in the eighteenth and nineteenth centuries. In the twentieth century, it came to the North Americas. In the twenty-first century, I believe it's going back over to China. I think we better accept that fact and learn from it. The only threat we have in this country over the next 15 to 25 years is getting along with China." Papp has even started a mutual fund that invests solely in U.S. multinationals that get a large part of their overseas earnings from the Pacific Rim.

"I believe the computer, new telecommunications, fax machines, and other to-be-announced improvements in technology will cause dramatic population shifts and changes in industry that few people appreciate today," Papp predicts. "I expect the size of many of our big cities to decline, more people to work at home, and more firms to have two or three people share an office as many accounting firms are doing today. These innovations will allow people to avoid crowded cities, pollution, high-tax states, and high-crime areas. As we rush into the post-industrial, or informational society, we will begin to realize that the electronic and medical-technology industries are more important in today's worlds than the railroads or electricity were to their ages."

TECHNOLOGY INVESTING FOR NERVOUS NELLIES

Don Yacktman is a little more nervous about investing in technology. You won't find many high-tech names in his portfolio, if any.

The reason: He believes the potential risks in this area are greater than the rewards. "There are two main problems with technology companies that normally keep me out of them," he argues. "One is pricing. Most of the time, they are overpriced. I'm looking for stocks priced below their private-market value. Technology stocks customarily sell at a high premium to actual value based on optimistic investor expectations." While some contend that technology stocks should be valued differently because of their strong growth prospects, Yacktman disagrees, especially since there's no assurance this upward rise will continue into the next quarter, let alone next year. Another reason for Yacktman's wariness of technology stocks is that many of these businesses are early-stage capital goods providers. "In the early stages, when they're making money, the stocks are extremely expensive," he insists. "When they come down in price, they start to look more like cyclical businesses. By then, the return on assets has dropped to a level where you wouldn't want to own them anyway. In either case, you're out of the stock. There's no question Microsoft is a terrific business. I think it's much better than Intel, because Intel has an enormous number of plants, which takes away from free cash. Microsoft, on the other hand, is a people business. I must admit that if Microsoft came down to an attractive valuation, I might be interested in it, but not in the small technology companies that just have one product. If that product fizzles out, the business goes broke."

REDUCING RISK WITH DIVERSIFICATION

Just because Yacktman's not a big fan of technology stocks doesn't mean they don't belong in your portfolio. As he pointed out, it's not that he thinks there's anything inherently wrong with them. They just fail to meet his price criteria most of the time. Shelby Davis shares Yacktman's concerns, but notes that high-tech stocks can still make a nice addition to almost every investor's portfolio. "The way I look at it, there's more than one way to paint a beautiful painting," he offers. "The brush strokes are totally different between Picasso and Rembrandt. They don't even have the same feel. Yet both produced wonderful masterpieces. You can see that by going to any museum. I feel the same way about an investment portfolio. There's no one style or sector that's always right when it comes to stock selection. You better find out what your style is, though, before you get started. I don't think Rembrandt could have painted like Picasso, and Picasso couldn't have painted like Rembrandt. They each had their own style. That's the key. If there are investors who know technology well, they can probably make much more money in those stocks than I can. They could put more in their portfolio as well. One reason I'm relatively light in technology is that I have long held that one way for a business not to make money is to lose a lot by getting into a big hole, which is exactly what happens to many technology companies, especially the upstarts. That's why I tend to be leery of them. But that doesn't negate the fact that technology will remain one of the biggest areas of growth in our economy for the foreseeable future."

A Back-door Approach
to Technology Investing

One way to gain exposure to this area without investing directly in high-tech stocks is by buying shares in companies that are heavy users of technology. "Financial services is an example of an industry where economies of scale encourage the use of technology," notes Elizabeth Bramwell. "On the revenue side, an expanding middle class has increased the demand for financial products worldwide, including insurance, credit cards, and mortgages. At the same time, technology has reduced the processing costs and enhanced the revenue potential of these companies. Product upgrades are driving demand for richer and faster forms of computing, and new methods of communicating, such as the Internet, are creating new operating procedures, distribution channels, and businesses. Updating databases for the year 2000 is stimulating job creation as well as improved information systems. We live in an age of accelerating change, which should provide numerous investment opportunities. For this reason, I expect many large-capitalization stocks will continue to outperform the averages as a result of globalization, critical mass, brand identity, and the economies of scale enjoyed by using technology to reduce expenses and increase revenues. In addition, new technologies, such as advanced satellites, digital electronics, the

Internet, and genetic engineering are creating their own markets and transcending traditional economic cycles."

THE BOTTOM LINE

Technology stocks should be a part of every twenty-first-century investment portfolio. Since high-tech companies are inherently volatile, you can reduce your risk by sticking with some of the established names with diversified product lines, such as Intel, Motorola, Hewlett-Packard, Lucent Technologies, and Microsoft. Furthermore, be on the lookout for companies in other industries that use technology well to reduce costs and increase profitability.

ONE-ON-ONE

L. ROY PAPP

$\mathscr{W}$hen I told L. Roy Papp I was flying out to spend the day with him in Phoenix, he immediately replied, "What time does your plane arrive? I'll come pick you up at the airport." I told him I could easily take a cab or shuttle bus into town. "I know you can, but I'm offering, and I'm going to pick you up. And if you can spend the night, my wife and I would love to take you out for dinner." It was clear Papp would be a most hospitable host.

Sure enough, there he was when I stepped into the terminal. As we drove to his office, he explained that he grew accustomed to picking people up at the airport while working for the U.S. government in Manila during the 1970s. Many of the representatives he was to meet with would arrive on red-eye flights that touched down early in the morning. They were tired and weary and in a place they knew nothing about. The best way to put them at ease was to have someone greet them personally at the terminal, instead of making them go through the hassle of finding ground transportation to their hotel. It became regular protocol, one Papp continues to practice more than 20 years later. As I think he quickly realized, I was most grateful.

While pointing out his city's finest landmarks, Papp shared that Phoenix isn't a very good place to be an investment manager, since most folks here park their money in real estate, not stocks. Papp was one of the first investment advisers to set up shop here almost two decades ago. Until a large mutual fund company relocated its head-quarters to Phoenix in 1997, he was by far the largest player in town. He clearly has a lot to show for his success. After having lunch at the Phoenix Country Club, where he works out several times a week, Papp took me a couple of blocks down to what he describes as "one of the best apartments in Phoenix." His nineteenth-floor con-dominium rests atop the city's largest residential building. It looks like a museum inside, boasting beautiful paintings from around the world in every room. The place has a decidedly Asian theme, com-plete with two real-life Siamese cats roaming around from room to room. Papp has also amassed one of the world's largest private art collections from China's Ming and Qing dynasties. If you desire something else to look at, you need merely gaze out one of the apartment's many windows, which offer a 360-degree view of Phoenix, from the airport and downtown to Camelback mountain and the surrounding hillside.

MOVING ON UP

This boy from New Jersey has clearly come a long way. He readily admits, "God has been good to me." When Papp graduated from Trenton Central High School in June 1945, he was supposed to attend the Massachusetts Institute of Technology to pursue a degree in engi-neering. That was a little more than a month before the end of World War II, and the Army decided it needed him even more. When Papp finished his 18-month tour of duty, he decided to go to Brown University instead of MIT. "After two years of undergraduate work, I took my first real course in engineering," he recalls. "I found out a third of the class got an A, B, or C. A third of the class got a D. The rest got an E (the equivalent of an F). I got a D. The school didn't have enough facilities for all of those who wanted to study engi-neering, so they encouraged people like me to change their majors."

He opted to go into economics instead and loved it. After completing his studies, Papp went on to the Wharton Graduate School at the University of Pennsylvania. By then he was married to his wife, Marilyn, whom he met during summer school at the University of Wisconsin in Madison. The head of Wharton's finance department encouraged Papp to accept a job at the investment firm Stein Roe & Farnham in Chicago, and he agreed. While Papp wasn't specifically preparing for a career in money management when he first went to college, his love affair with stocks actually began in high school.

Papp's parents, who were both immigrants from Hungary, knew little about Wall Street. His dad, who died when Papp was 18, had several different businesses, including a golf bag manufacturing company and a restaurant. He started them during the Depression, and none were very successful. Papp's mom, a housewife, was much more scholarly. She encouraged both Papp and his older sister to get a good education. By the time Papp was a teenager, he figured out that if he wanted to enjoy the highest chance for success and a good income, the best thing he could do was prepare for a career in finance. "When I graduated from college, advertising was the big thing," he says. "That's where people were making premium dollars. But I figured that wasn't going to last permanently. Ten years later, everybody wanted to be a doctor, feeling that was the sure path to success. Engineering was also very important then, because the war was ending and we were going to rebuild the world. But I was always interested in math and science. That's why this was a very logical business for me."

STARTING AT STEIN ROE

Stein Roe & Farnham was founded in 1932 by partners Sydney Stein, Frederick Roe, and Wells Farnham. "Farnham and Stein were the two bright ones who understood stocks better than anybody else," Papp claims. "Roe ran the research department." When Papp joined the firm in 1955, he worked closely with Farnham as part of the money management team. "I was a clerk to begin with," he remembers. "I had a unique opportunity to see Farnham working and learned a lot. I also learned from Stein, although we seemed to have constant problems with each other. I wasn't there very long before we started having some differences of opinion. The attitude of the firm was they really didn't want new recruits to have an opinion on anything for a couple of years. They wanted you to just sit back and listen. They weren't in a hurry for you to be dollar-productive. You were in school."

The three main partners were occasionally at odds with each other as well, according to Papp. "I remember Farnham disliked cigarette stocks because he thought there would be a law passed banning them after we had the original scare in the early 1950s. He was on vacation once and Stein's committee put a cigarette company on the buy list. Farnham came back and said, 'I see that we've decided to purchase cigarettes.' He didn't say 'while I was gone.' He was much more subtle than that. Instead he said, 'I see we bought them for this and that reason. That's a perfect description of the kinds of stocks we want in our fund, so we should definitely put that in.' He then bought the stock for our funds, even though he hated cigarettes. He knew that doing so would make Stein furious, since he was expecting the opposite reaction. Then, once Farnham got his point across, the stock was out."

PAPP'S POLITICAL MACHINE

Papp and Stein were often at odds with each other away from the office as well, particularly on the political front. The trouble began in 1962, when a young stockbroker friend of Papp's called and said he was going to run for Congress. "He wanted my wife and me to run his campaign in Evanston, which was 25 percent of the district," Papp shares. "He was a stockbroker named Don Rumsfeld. I said, 'Don we'll help you, but I don't know anything about politics.' He told me, 'That's all right. I'll teach you.' He was only 28 years old, but he won." Two years later, Rumsfeld asked Papp to help out fellow Republican Chuck Percy, who was running for governor. He agreed and did so on weekends and evenings, as he had done for Rumsfeld in his bid for Congress before.

A few years later, he served as Richard Nixon's local presidential campaign chairman in Cook County. At the same time, Stein and his wife were staunch supporters and close friends of the opposing liberal candidates in almost every campaign Papp was involved in.

The Steins were friends of Hubert Humphrey and were financial contributors to the Kennedys. Fortunately for Papp, Roe and Farnham were Republicans and supported his political endeavors. Papp kept a very low profile in the campaign, yet enjoyed enormous success. "I guess I was lucky," he surmises. "For one thing, the timing was right and the candidates I helped were going to do well regardless of whether I got involved or not. The reason I did well personally is because I tried to hide and stay out of the public eye. Hardly anybody knew I was even involved. The more people knew, the madder Stein got."

The tension between these two came to a head in 1969, when Papp was tapped to serve on a board charged with transforming Fannie Mae into a private company. There were nine slots available. Among those also being considered was Ferd Kramer, Stein's brother-in-law, who was already on the board. When Papp was chosen to replace Kramer, he claims Stein went ballistic. "For one thing, Stein thought he would get to go to Washington with Kennedy, and that never happened," Papp says. "Then I was chosen for Fannie Mae over his relative. By then, he had pretty much retired from the firm, but he called me in and said if I gave up my spot on Fannie Mae, he could help me move up faster at the firm. I told him I was happy with the way my career was progressing. I had been selected to manage $100 million for the state of Ohio teachers' retirement system. That account led to another one worth $100 million from the Virginia retirement system. I had the second-highest billings at Stein Roe and knew Stein couldn't get rid of me. However, I admit I wasn't so happy at the firm in those early years when he was all over me. On the other hand, I felt a warm spot toward Stein because he was smart and taught me a lot. I couldn't blame him for being mad."

In 1972, the GOP came back to Papp and asked him to direct Nixon's reelection campaign for the state of Illinois. "I said, 'No, I can't do that because I like investing.' That's what I want to do," he reflects. "The politics were fun, and I was an idealist, particularly when I was younger. If you're not a liberal when you're 20, you have no heart. If you're not a conservative when you're 40, you have no head. So I was more idealistic then. I enjoyed it and had a good time. But I didn't want to make a career out of it. It was just a hobby." Nixon won without Papp's help.

Because of his involvement with Fannie Mae and his knowledge of the inner workings of government, Papp was put on the five-member investment policy committee at Stein Roe. This group was charged with setting out the firm's investment strategy and philosophy during the late 1960s. About that time, Larry Hickey became the firm's new managing partner. "Larry wanted to be totally in charge," Papp alleges. "You either did everything he wanted, or he didn't trust you. I was not one of his fair-haired boys, but I wasn't the enemy either. He would tolerate my being a little independent because I had a lot of accounts."

THE EARLY YEARS AT STEIN ROE

During Papp's years at Stein Roe, the firm didn't play the same earnings-momentum game it ventured into in the 1980s. "Momentum was not in the ballpark," Papp says. "Actually, it was the exact opposite. If a stock went down, they liked it better. They were very research-oriented." In fact, a third of the firm was devoted to research, which Papp always considered to be ironic since Stein and Farnham made all of the real decisions anyway. Years after he left, Papp had lunch with Stein and asked him why that was so. "I said, 'Why did you keep that whole research department when you didn't need it?' He replied, 'We kept it so that if we got an idea, we could check it with them to avoid looking foolish. It also kept us from making mistakes.'"

Papp tried to prevent the firm from making what turned out to be a big mistake in 1973, but to no avail. "In 1972, I was bullish on the market," he says. "Then in March 1973, we had some questions about credit in this country and called a policy meeting. The votes at these meetings were almost always unanimous. I told them that even though I had been bullish, I had changed my mind. I said, 'The market's down 7 percent. I would vote now to sell stocks.' Hickey, the head of the firm, was on vacation. I realized that if the market went down badly, he would hang it on me, because I was bullish in 1972. So I went to the secretary of the committee and said, 'Here's a summary of what I said at the meeting, stating that I voted to sell stocks. I know you won't print it, but I want you to see this and write on here if you disagree.' He refused, but that didn't matter. I passed out a copy of my statement to all of the committee members, to make sure I was on the record. I felt that strongly. I was scared of the market. I also felt that Hickey would pin the blame on me. It's not that I was afraid of blame. I was more than willing to stick my neck out. But I had changed my mind. Every so often something happens where you do change your mind. I was also protecting myself."

As it turned out, Papp was right. His prediction that the market had farther to fall came true, and the firm suffered. "I remember one three-month period in the summer of 1974 where our holdings were down some 35 percent for the quarter," he says. "That was horrendous."

SHORT-TERM FOCUS

When Papp was there, Stein Roe tended to be a somewhat cyclical and short-term-oriented operation. "I questioned Stein about that," Papp says. "He told me, 'T. Rowe Price and I, Jim Stein (his name was Sydney but he called himself Jim), had the same idea. We both felt that buying quality growth stocks was the right way to invest. The difference is Price went all the way and really did it. We hedged, because we weren't sure. So we bought the cyclicals as well as the growth stocks. Price did it right; we didn't. We followed chemical, steel, and cement companies.' You see, if you have all those research people, you have to expect that they will push you to buy their stocks. Otherwise they don't have anything to do. Therefore, you get forced into purchasing things you're not attracted to. I contend that you don't want too many researchers on staff. That's one of the troubles with Wall Street research, and why I don't use it. I think Stein Roe did a good job, particularly in the environment they lived in, but the environment changed so much. I think they were looking for some magic elixir that would work at all times. Hickey started pouring $250,000 a year into computer research. By the time I left, they were using computers to play the momentum game. It was a disaster. It just doesn't work because in this industry, making an evaluation on the future value of a company is inherently impossible to do using science. As long as people are making the final judgments, emotions will always interfere. You either have a sixth sense or you don't. That's why you must be willing to change when conditions change. A machine can't do that."

MANILA BOUND

By 1975, the young stockbroker Papp helped get elected to Congress had moved up the political ranks and become President Gerald Ford's chief of staff. Don Rumsfeld was charged with filling a vacancy on the Asian Development Bank board and felt Papp would be perfect for the job. "The Asian Development Bank is almost a carbon copy of the World Bank, except it's in Manila," Papp explains. "It loans money to foreign governments to help them out with specific projects. There were 43 member countries at the time, with approximately 300 professionals working at the Bank. It made 15-year loans at rates in the range of 1 or 2 percent, well below the market. This was at a time when inflation was around 7 percent. I talked to my wife about the opening and she said, 'Let's do it.' So we sold our house and I resigned from Stein Roe."

This all took place shortly after Nixon's resignation. The White House was super-sensitive about potential scandals and conflicts of interest. "So in order to be appointed to the post, I had to agree I would take no profits out of Stein Roe when I left," Papp reveals. "I had put in $20,000 of equity as a partner. When I left, I took out $20,000 and no profits. I walked out with my original capital back and nothing else."

Why would Papp leave an extremely high-paying partnership in the investment business to go work for a much more modest salary in another country? "Maybe money was less important to me," he concludes. "Half of the partners in the firm, including Stein, were jealous as hell. The other half thought I was crazy. I was making a lot of money. Anybody who has been in my business for 20 years and is good at it is financially well-off, assuming they haven't had a disastrous divorce. You don't even have to be a genius, just good. The White House warned me that although this was a great job, it would be very difficult to reenter the U.S. workforce from Manila. They said that leaving my field for two years would hurt my career. I decided to do it anyway."

SERVING TWO MASTERS

There were 12 directors in all on the Asian Development Bank board. Most represented more than one country, although the United States and Japan were large enough to have seats of their own. The board of directors reviewed all applications and decided who got money. As the U.S. representative, Papp had two jobs. One was to see that American companies got a fair shake at getting some business from the countries that received money. The other was to make sure the Bank was run as efficiently as possible. "It was a funny job because you were paid by the Bank, and your responsibility as a director was to do what was right for the Bank," he says. "But you were also appointed by the United States government to take their seat and vote their share. There was an automatic conflict. Occasionally, you had to do something you weren't sure was right. It was always very interesting."

In hindsight, Papp feels his time on the board made two significant contributions, both to America and the Bank. "I went there with one bit of instruction from the congressional committee," he reflects. "They wanted me to make sure no loans were made to Vietnam. We had just left Vietnam and were embarrassed and mad. I saw to it that they didn't get any money. One way I did this was by helping out the Japanese president. In return, his director voted with me. I learned after about two months that if we voted with the Japanese, we had 33 percent of the vote between us, and the Japanese president could strong-arm a couple of its borrowers to make sure we always had 50 percent of the vote. As long as the two of us could control the board together, the Japanese wouldn't do anything to upset us, such as making loans to Vietnam. Whenever it came up, and it did, the board would push for a Vietnam loan. The Japanese president would then decide he'd have to send a mission to Vietnam to see how things were going there. That would take six months. Then he had to put out a report three months later. By then it was too late.

"I did another thing to help the Bank," Papp continues. "The Bank borrowed money largely from the United States at that time in the free market. The investment bankers would take the World Bank price of money and make us pay a quarter of a point more. The rationale was they were bigger and older, and we were out there in Asia. I told the Japanese president I didn't understand why we were paying more, since he was running this Bank better than the World Bank. I felt we should pay *less,* not more. He agreed. But he said the availability of money was more important to him than the rate. I assured him we could still get the money, but should press for a lower rate. The next time the investment bankers came to Manila to tell us what the price should be, I told the Japanese president to object to it. He did and asked for the lower rate. The investment bankers promptly shouted, 'We're insulted you would ask us that.' I told the president to tell them he was being pushed by his board to go to competitive bidding for future loans, to see how they would react. The bankers almost panicked. They countered by claiming that the market sets the rate, and whatever World Bank bonds sell for, ours sell for a quarter point higher. I told the president to take a chance, cut the rate, and see if our bonds would sell anyway. Of course, they did. What happened is the secondary market immediately cut the spread from a quarter of a point to 15 basis points (0.15 percent), because as long as every investor knew the next offering would be 25 basis points more, the secondary market wasn't going to flinch. But if we changed the offering, suddenly the secondary market would reflect that. I figure I saved the Asian Development Bank 10 or 15 basis points on every bond issue that came after that. They borrow in the billions, so that's a lot of money."

COMING TO AMERICA

Papp's service on the Asian Development Bank board ended when he turned 50. He assumed he and wife Marilyn would return to Chicago and start over. Their eldest son, Harry, was a student at Brown University. Daughter Victoria, whom they call Tori, was in a New England boarding school. All of their friends were in Illinois. But after spending two years in the tropics, Marilyn wanted to live in a warmer climate. "I like Chicago and the people there, but the weather is awful," Papp admits. "So we came back to the States and considered San Diego, Phoenix, and Dallas. San Diego was scratched, because Marilyn has an arthritis problem, and humid weather makes it worse. I had been to Dallas a number of times and liked it, but wasn't sure I would want to live in the middle of the rah-rah Texas spirit. So we chose Phoenix." At that point, he had no job, didn't know what he was going to do, and was without a single friend in the Grand Canyon State. He had never even been to Phoenix. Still, he had all of his possessions shipped from Manila to a Phoenix warehouse. "I guess you could say we were a little adventurous," he adds.

Papp and his wife did fly back to Chicago, but only to buy a car and leave their cats with Harry. They then drove to Phoenix, sneaking in a scenic cross-country vacation along the way. Marilyn's first reaction was, "They do have some skyscrapers here." She had been worried that Arizona had only single-story buildings. The Papps wound up buying their first condo a day and a half later. "Marilyn then booked us on a trip to Egypt," he recalls. "I came back early, and I figured I better get settled. I started looking around at the town and learned something very quickly. In 1973–1974, the Arizona bank stocks lost 75 to 80 percent of their value. I started buying United Bank of Arizona, which was the third-largest bank in the state. I paid about four times earnings for it. It sold for right around book value, a measurement that had some meaning back then. I then bought stock in Arizona Bank and Continental Bank, and held on until 1985, when they all were acquired by some out-of-town banks. I made eight to ten times on my money. It worked out very well. In the meantime, I registered with the SEC and started working as an investment adviser from my home." He also joined the board of directors of four corporations. "My idea when I came back from Manila was to spend a third of my time taking care of my own money, a third of my time on boards of directors, and a third of my time managing accounts for some friends and clients."

Papp quickly talked his way onto the boards of several companies, including Scott Foresman, Booth Financial, Del Webb, and Sullair. "When I went on the board of Fannie Mae, I was pretty young and found it to be interesting," he explains. "I was sitting there looking at the whole business and making judgments. Being on corporate boards helps you to better understand what makes a company work and why one is good while another isn't."

BACK IN THE INVESTMENT BUSINESS

Papp's small investment firm was up and running in 1978. His first clients were attorneys and bankers from Illinois that he had worked with when he was at Stein Roe. His results were good, and the business quickly grew. "In 1981, I told my wife, 'I've got a problem,'" he remembers. "'I've either got to hire someone to work with me or I've got to stop taking all new business.' I learned from Stein Roe that when you turn down new clients, nobody's going to recommend you and suddenly you have no additional business. Either I had to decide not ever to get bigger or I had to get help. I was out visiting my son, Harry, in Chicago and told him I had gotten busy enough to hire someone." At that point, Harry had an MBA and worked in the treasurer's office at pharmaceutical giant G. D. Searle & Co. He was responsible for overseas financing and acquisitions, and he managed the company's domestic real estate holdings. Harry's wife, Rose, also worked there as an analyst, supervising the corporation's financial planning process. "Harry told me if I was serious about expanding my firm, he would like to come down and work with me. I agreed, but told him I had a couple of requirements. First, I have a problem with nepotism. So even though he had two master's degrees, I pushed him to get his CFA. That would be an outside credential indicating he really knew the business we're in. He agreed. Second, I told him he would have to take a pay cut. I didn't want him to come join me just because he got more money. He had to really want it."

Then Papp started to think about his daughter-in-law, Rose. Phoenix, at the time, did not have the same financial opportunities that were available in Chicago. He knew it would be tough for Rose to find a job with comparable status in Phoenix. "It dawned on me that if they moved down here and she wasn't happy, it wouldn't be long before they'd want to leave," Papp says. "I decided to do what a lot of people warned me against. I hired Rose as well as Harry. I figured they were either going to make it together, or not at all. I asked her to become a CFA too. It turned out to be both brilliant and inspired, because she has taken to stock research with a real love and vengeance and is really good at it. She's been my research director since day one."

Rose has worked her way up to becoming Papp's equal in the stock-picking department. "During our first year together, I made all of the final judgments," he notes. "After two or three years, we made the decisions together, with my desires getting about 80 percent of the weighting. After she had been here for about eight years, we moved toward the two of us having a unanimous decision. That meant one would have to cave in to the other's desires. Now we honestly have an equal say in what we buy, and we really do agree most of the time."

Harry is in charge of overseeing all client accounts. "When he came down here, he got me to become more systematized and to do things in an orderly fashion," Papp says. "I was working with about 28 clients and could run the business out of my coat pocket. It was real easy. I had been doing this all my life. Harry made me get a routine. Of course, as the firm grew, that was a blessing. Coming from a big company, he understood the way things had to be done. I had never worked for a big company, other than as a director."

ALL IN THE FAMILY

The business has turned into a real family affair. Papp's daughter, Tori, also works for the company in account management and marketing. He made her get an MBA and CFA as well before hiring her. She's highly allergic to the carpet glue in Papp's building and is forced to work with clients from home or in restaurants. "If you ever see pictures of our family together, they are always taken in our apartment," Papp says. "We can't even bring her into this building."

Today, L. Roy Papp Investment Counsel has ten partners and manages some $1.2 billion in assets. The "L" in his name stands for Lessel, which goes way back in the Papp family. "Nobody's ever heard of it so I dropped it," he says. "I never used it except on government records. But when I was at Stein Roe, I always felt that signing the name Roy Papp was too short. So I started using L. Roy Papp to lengthen it a little. Maybe I'm nuts, but I think it sits better than just Roy Papp."

GROWING FUNDS

For the first several years after moving from his home into a full-fledged office, Papp didn't list his number in the Yellow Pages. He had all the business he could handle, overseeing mostly private accounts. But his clients kept begging him to manage money for friends with smaller sums than his normal minimum of $500,000. That's when he got the idea to start the L. Roy Papp Stock Fund, which debuted in December 1989. Papp figured it would be a way for local residents and friends with modest portfolios to tap into his stock-picking expertise. Two years later, he decided to launch the Papp America-Abroad fund. "I invented the concept of investing in the globalization of the world by buying U.S. stocks," he claims. "I had an awful job getting the prospectus through the SEC. They were cooperative and wanted me to do it. The problem was it didn't fit their formula. They had a rule that said in order to put the name of a country on a fund, you must place 65 percent of your investments in that country. In order to call it global, international, abroad, or anything that suggests you're worldwide, you had to have at least 10 percent of your investments in five different countries. I didn't qualify under either scenario. After about two months of going back and forth, they finally allowed me to call it America-Abroad."

Papp's fund operation is as down-home and hospitable as he is. The prospectuses, annual reports, and sales brochures are prepared in-house on a typewriter or computer. Until recently, they were duplicated on the company copying machine and stapled by hand. The firm's only logo is a 1980 sketch of Papp smoking a pipe that was drawn by one of his favorite American artists, Leroy Neiman. The most elaborate artwork you'll find are pictures of some of Papp's favorite paintings, which grace the covers of single-page glossy brochures put together on daughter Tori's computer.

Judging from the fund material alone, you might assume Papp were running these funds from his kitchen table. But there's something nice about that in this day of mutual fund behemoths. It almost gives you the sense that Papp is personally writing these letters to you. You get the feeling you could pick up the phone and say, "Roy, why did you buy this stock or that stock?" and he would kindly give you a detailed explanation. Changes are being made, however, as the amount of money and number of fund shareholders explodes. What a difference a few years can make, especially after you've garnered a good amount of national media attention. In a letter to shareholders of the America-Abroad Fund in January 1992, Papp boasted about how the fund's net assets for the year had risen to $1.37 million. Now it's not unusual for the fund to get close to $8 million in new assets in one day.

LOVE OF WORK

When you look at Papp's home, car, and lifestyle, it's clear this man doesn't need to work for a living. He lives in a gorgeous penthouse, complete with a great art collection and prints by artists from

Rembrandt to Renoir, drives around in a brand-new Lexus, and is a regular at Phoenix's premier country club. So why come into the office everyday? Why not just stay at home and tend to his own substantial personal portfolio? "Because I love the business I'm in," he quickly replies. "That's why I didn't get into politics when I had the opportunity to do so. I like the challenge, and frankly I enjoy helping people. I've been very lucky and feel I owe something to society. More important, I have always worked with older people. I learned that once folks retire and start playing golf, they stop at the nineteenth hole for a drink. After awhile, many of them drink more often. Then they die. I've decided to try and live longer. I stopped smoking my pipe. I exercise three times a week. I'm happy with life. I find that by working, I get more ambition and, I hope, will live longer."

Papp has limited his outside activities somewhat. He's no longer on any corporate boards. He's restricted his civic involvement to two organizations, the Phoenix Art Museum and the prestigious Thunderbird Graduate Business School, the only business school in the world with campuses on three continents. He and his wife continue to collect artwork from around the world, some of which is on display in their home. The rest is loaned out to museums and shown around the world. They have personally visited more than 250 museums around the globe. Papp also enjoys traveling and playing bridge. "I have no plans to retire until my mental and physical health give out," he says. At that point, he plans to turn the business over to his kids, with Rose continuing as the firm's prime stock picker and Harry as CEO.

Despite the ever-present "bad-news bears" out there, always forecasting doom and gloom for the market, Papp remains optimistic as we enter the new millennium. "Since I started in this business, I have annually heard or read the statement that the last year was a very difficult one in which to invest money. I expect to hear this every year for the rest of my life," he says. "The stock market has benefited from its own structural change caused by the enormous amount of money going into retirement programs such as 401(k)s. Along with this, corporate America has shifted potential dividend increases to buyback programs, thus shrinking or reducing the amount of stock available to the public. In my opinion, this trend will continue, benefiting the equity markets in the process."

L. ROY PAPP'S
top 10 GROWTH STOCKS
FOR THE 21ST CENTURY

1. State Street

2. Microsoft

3. Intel

4. General Electric

5. Merck

6. Medtronic

7. American Power Conversion

8. Service Corp International

9. Interpublic Group

10. T. Rowe Price

Rule 10

READ THE FINE PRINT

Now that you know what fundamental characteristics to look for when selecting growth stocks, let's talk about the steps you should follow once you've identified a specific company you want to buy. The first thing you should do is call the company's investor relations department to order a copy of the latest annual and quarterly reports, along with any other research material they can provide you. These documents will tell you more about the company's past, present, and future. They also contain all of the pertinent balance sheets and other financial information you need to determine how fiscally strong the business is. Other items you should get your hands on include the latest proxy statement, along with forms 10-Q and 10-K, formal documents that must be filed by every public company annually with the Securities and Exchange Commission.

ANALYZING ANNUAL REPORTS

Each publicly traded company is required to send out an annual report to shareholders and anyone else who asks for one. Sometimes these are rich, glossy, colorful productions, which cost several dollars apiece to produce. Other times, they are stripped-down, black-and-white briefings that consist mostly of the form 10-K filing and little else. In either case, they are usually prepared by investor relations experts, who live to put a positive spin on the companies they represent. Given this obvious bias, how should you, as an investor, use annual reports, and what must you look for? To begin with, Shelby Davis says, you must keep an eye out for two things that will let you know whether a company is a good investment: the quality of its business and what price you are being asked to pay for it.

"If you determine it is a good investment, what you should do is turn to the back of the report and pore over the financials," he suggests. "Look at the return on assets and equity over a 10- or 20-year period, along with what management has done with cash flow and whether that money is being spent correctly for the future. If it's a drug company, you'll want to check on spending for research and development and whether it has a history of bringing out new products. If it's an insurance company, find out if it is keeping up with technology and whether it's focused on the new distribution paradigms that are being created through channels such as the Internet. I also like to look at the footnotes to make sure I don't see anything that strikes me as novel in the accounting, or whether the company is faced with any threatening lawsuits. I really don't like the special charges that are constantly being coughed up by companies these days. They are often referred to as 'restructuring charges.' I feel this gives companies an awful lot of latitude to restructure today and report good earnings tomorrow, then come out and restructure two years from now and report good earnings even farther down the line."

Having said that, Davis concedes he's been wrong about his dislike for restructuring charges when it comes to consumer product companies such as Colgate. "This company has had several restructuring charges, and it doesn't seem to matter because investors realize it was a valid step to take," he says. "I mean, if you're going to consolidate 50 toothpaste plants down to five, maybe you need to have a special charge to give away severance packages, close the buildings, and sell off machines. Coca-Cola hardly ever has a restructuring charge. PepsiCo has had dozens of them, and it's been a relatively poor stock compared to Coke. Sometimes new management comes in and keeps taking restructuring charges to make it look as if they have a turnaround going, when maybe they don't. On the other hand, Colgate has been brilliant. The president, Ruben Mark, is using EVA. (EVA stands for Economic Value Added. Under this structure, managers are forced to act like owners by putting their own capital at risk. EVA provides a strategy for creating corporate and shareholder wealth. It also gives investors a better measurement of a company's true profitability.) Mark is driving up returns, and the ongoing earnings power is valid. I don't know whether I trust earnings over any one-year period. But in Colgate's case, this has gone on long enough that I believe it."

READING FROM THE BACK FORWARD

Robert Stovall scours annual reports the same way he would read a Hebrew newspaper—from the back forward. "I begin by looking at the notes to the financial statement, to see if there are any unusual or potential write-offs, pending patent expirations, or other possible trouble on the horizon," he says. "For example, if it's a mining business, I want to find out about the size and quality of the ore and whether they could move to a lesser-grade quality if necessary. In technology companies, I want to see if there are any upcoming patent expirations, which would give competitors an open door to steal away business. Regardless of what sector you're examining, you want to check whether sales trends are keeping pace with the rest of the industry. If not, you must find out why. You then see whether profit margins are shrinking, expanding, contracting, or staying flat."

Stovall also pays close attention to the accountant's analysis of the financial statements, which often provides some revealing information. One phrase to look out for is any reference to questions about the company's ability to continue as a "going concern." Translated, this means the business is in deep financial trouble and may be forced to declare bankruptcy in the not-too-distant future.

"The last thing I do is read the puff letter from the chairman and look at the pretty pictures that are often included throughout the glossy section up front," Stovall says. That's because he knows first-hand that companies put their best foot forward in the beginning of the annual report, while making the back much more difficult to read. In a former life, as communications director for Dean Witter Reynolds, Stovall was in charge of putting together the company's annual report. "Preparing the annual and quarterly reports was one of the worst tasks I ever had to perform," he contends. "It is essentially a thankless position. The job takes about three months out of the year to complete, including the time required to meet all of the filing requirements as mandated by the SEC. You also need to coordinate all of the numbers with the chief financial officer and triple-check them to ensure accuracy. In my case, I wrote everything, including the chairman's letter. Actually, that was the fun part. I got to put my own thoughts into the chairman's letter. They usually left much of what I prepared alone because they weren't all that interested in it. In essence, I was making policy, even though I wasn't the CEO. Therefore, I never blindly trust what's written in the front of an annual report, because I'm not even sure if it's actually the CEO who is saying it."

START AND END WITH THE NUMBERS

Roy Papp also believes it's important to scrutinize a company's annual report from the back to the front. "I first want to examine the balance sheet, to look at the cash flow and receivables," he says. "Show me a company where sales have barely risen and receivables have gone through the roof, and I'll show you a company that is playing games. That's an early warning sign. I next read the additional notes to see if anything unusual has occurred to mess up this year's earnings. Then I work my way up to the chairman's summary of what's happening with the company."

Whether the chairman eats his own cooking is another thing Papp looks for. This can be found by reading the proxy statement. "I think options are desirable, as long as they can't be redrawn at a lower price," he adds. "In terms of visiting companies, I normally will talk to management on the phone. Unfortunately, it's hard to get through to the chairman or head of the research department any more. You usually wind up talking to an investor relations person and getting the same information as everybody else. Still, such a conversation can teach you something and make you feel more comfortable about your decision."

OTHER SOURCES OF INFORMATION

As first mentioned in Rule Three, Stovall chooses his stocks using a "bull's-eye" approach, which calls for picking companies that stand to benefit from the various themes and trends he picks up on. Once he has his list of candidates in hand, he not only gathers annual reports from each company, but also related research reports prepared by independent brokerage firms. He then reads everything to see if either the company or other analysts have also picked up on these same themes. "Sometimes they do and other times they don't," he admits. "If I find in my readings that I am late in noticing a certain trend, I may drop the idea entirely, because it's important to be early. Other times, if I think I'm on to something that others haven't noticed, I look further at the balance sheet and earnings prospects." Stovall gets his future earnings forecasts from outside services, like First Call, which provide a consensus on what the analyst community expects from the companies going forward.

Elizabeth Bramwell, however, cautions against relying solely on brokerage house research. She prefers to conduct her own investigations and talk with companies directly. "You never know what they're not telling you," she says. "As an investor, you ultimately have to do your own thinking."

DECIPHERING THE FINANCIALS

Now let's dig deeper into the specifics you should look for when examining a company's financial statements. Don Yacktman's ideal company has a return on tangible assets of well above 20 percent (defined as inventory, real estate, and net receivables), plus a cash multiple (after depreciation) of 10 or less. "The companies I purchase each have marvelous economics and, in most cases, are very well managed," he maintains. "In addition, most of my companies generate significant amounts of excess cash and have share repurchase plans in place. They are therefore in a position to enhance shareholder value through repurchasing their own stock at attractive prices."

Yacktman has constructed his database of potential investments one company at a time. Collecting new ideas is an ongoing process. "In a lot of cases, I'll have some broker or client call and tell me about a stock that looks interesting," he offers. "Then I'll examine it to see if it's something worth following. I'm very suspicious of broker recommendations, because they tend to write reports only after a stock has gone up and is highly priced. In that case, I'll mentally say, 'Yes, this company has a good business, and it's something I'd like to own at some point in time, but it's simply too expensive right now.' I'll keep it in the system and follow it until it becomes attractively priced. I followed H&R Block for years. When it sold off part of CompuServe in 1996, H&R Block stock got clobbered to the point where even if CompuServe was worthless, H&R Block was still attractively priced. I bought the stock at those levels."

If the numbers and inherent nature of the business come together, Yacktman takes a look at the general outlook for the industry in which the company is involved. He wants to see how it stacks up next to its competitors and whether its products are likely to remain successful in the future. "As an example, Boeing does a good job of making airplanes," he says. "But I have to tell you I think Coca-Cola has a much better business. Both dominate their respective industries. However, I believe Coke's business is much better because it's more predictable. It is less capital-intensive. One of the problems with a capital-intensive business is that it works fine as long as it keeps up the volume of orders. But once there is a slowdown in demand, it becomes very susceptible. In other words, if a company begins to have problems with its revenue stream, its return on assets is bound to go down rather quickly. The more fixed assets a business has, the more difficult it is to sustain a high return on those assets."

Although debt is definitely taken into consideration, Yacktman contends there's a natural tendency for his companies to be underleveraged. If anything, he's often prodding management to be more aggressive about repurchasing shares and adding debt to the balance sheet. "I think the managers of profitable corporations have a natural tendency to underleverage their companies because it's comfortable and they think debt increases risk. They really don't understand the cost of capital and how debt can be used to lower the cost of this capital," he insists. "I would argue that if you're buying equity at a very low price and taking on reasonable risk, you're not increasing risk, but rather lowering the cost of capital. You have now created a lower hurdle rate for capital expenditures. I like to see companies use their debt capacity, because it reduces the cost of capital. Debt financing is cheaper than equity financing. Having said that, the more debt you put on the balance sheet, the less you should pay out in dividends. Again, to me, the ideal company is one that has no dividend, but an A as opposed to an AAA rating on its balance sheet. That way, if the business slows down, all of the available cash flow can be used toward debt repayment. When examining how much debt a company can handle, the real number to look at is the coverage ratio. In other words, how often does it cover its interest payment?"

Among the most important numbers Elizabeth Bramwell looks for on a company's balance sheet are long-term debt and equity. "I want to see how inventory and accounts receivable are changing from one quarter to another relative to sales," she says. "I ask a lot of questions. Is inventory increasing as rapidly as sales? What's happening to that inventory? Are there accounts receivable? If so, the company may be shipping things but not collecting the money in a timely fashion. Accounting is always very important." Bramwell puts little weight on a stock's price-to-book value ratio, arguing that with companies constantly buying back and issuing new shares, this number isn't as important as it once was. Instead, she pays particular attention to return on capital.

SCREENING FOR FREE CASH

Shelby Davis is starting to use his computer more than he used to. But he's not running momentum screens in search of today's "hot" stocks. Instead, he employs it to analyze and create spreadsheets on the companies he owns and follows. "What I'm really doing is examining various key variables to see what kind of job management is doing," he reveals. "How much free cash flow are they generating?

How much capital do they need to plow into the business to make it grow? What's the maintenance capital spending? If they're generating free cash flow, what are they doing with it? Are they buying back stock? Are they acquiring other companies? Are they using it to make the business grow even faster? I want to know these things."

If company executives ask for his advice, which they sometimes do, Davis tells them to put any extra cash back into the business. "There's been a big change since the Cold War ended and the iron and bamboo curtains came down," he offers. "A lot of companies generating free cash flow now have investment opportunities all over the world. The world suddenly grew five times bigger, from one billion to more than six billion potential customers. It was a huge sea-change secular event, and we're reaping the peace dividend of it right now."

What management does with any free cash flow gives Davis a good indication of how well they are running the company for stockholders and whether or not they're thinking like owners. They weren't in the 1960s, when Davis first started in the investment business. "They were thinking like bureaucrats, sitting on top of companies with lots of internal perks, country club memberships, and all those kinds of things," he reflects. "That's one good result of the leveraged-buyout boom. It forced companies to focus on cash flow, become more efficient, and concentrate on their core businesses. Companies were being taken over by financial buyers who would strip them down to the core and, through the use of leverage, get an enormous return if they were right, because they would buy the company on 85 percent debt. It was like buying a house. You finance 85 percent of your purchase. The difference is you can't strip a house down, whereas you can strip a company and sell off assets, shrink the asset base, and maybe build the earnings, especially by turning around or selling loser divisions."

Davis specifically points to the Dow Jones Company as a good modern-day example of this. Although he didn't own the stock as this book went to press, he was closely monitoring the company's progress. "It has a wonderful product in *The Wall Street Journal*," he insists. "Nobody in the investment business can deny their need to read that paper. Its circulation has been growing for decades. The company's other products, such as *Barron's* and *Smart Money* magazine, are also doing well. Where Dow Jones is losing money is in the electronic news business. It announced plans to spend $650 million over a three-year period on the old Telerate, an electronic pricing and information bank. That thing isn't making any money. Who knows if it can compete with Bloomberg and Reuters? Maybe it can. But it's a real gamble. I would rather see the company close that thing down or sell it and focus on its core business. The company could buy back a lot of stock once earnings go up. That move, in my opinion, would definitely make the price of the stock increase."

UNCOVERING VALUE

While some value-oriented investors pay close attention to a stock's book value, Davis argues that number is virtually meaningless to him. "Unless you're planning to liquidate the company, you really want to look at earnings power," he insists. "My basic thrust is to look at the growth of earnings power, not by quarter or even year-to-year, but whether average earnings three years from now will be higher than they are now."

In order to make that determination, you must rely in part on your own intuition. The rest is raw math. "In insurance companies, which are my specialty, if you believe underwriting can be at a breakeven, and assuming you have more cash every year to reinvest and are receiving dividends on what you've already invested, you'll constantly have a new stream of cash coming in," Davis offers. "So, in a sense, the earnings power of an insurance company is the investment income per share after taxes. Investment income per share is like a compounding machine. It frankly has not been as good lately as when my father first taught me this lesson, because interest rates have been dropping over the past decade. This has caused insurance companies to get into the position where new investment cash is being invested at rates below the embedded rate on the portfolio. By contrast, from the 1950s through the 1980s, the opposite was true."

Back then, investment income was an ever-expanding growth engine. Interest rates were going up, so new cash and dividends were being invested at higher and higher rates. Falling interest rates during the 1990s have been a drag for some insurers, although the strong ones have easily been able to live through it. "American International Group and General Re would have grown faster had they been able to invest their cash at higher rates," Davis contends. "But it sort of balances itself out, because when interest rates go down, reserves usually go up. That's because reserves are mainly invested in bonds, which obviously appreciate as rates fall. Reserves may also become more redundant as inflation drops, which is evidenced by the lower rates. What I'm saying is that if you really get to the heart of the insurance business, you'll find there's a reason it has existed in many countries for so long and been such a compounding machine. I was in Germany several years ago, making a speech at a sales conference. I talked about the virtues of owning quality insurance companies. I mentioned I had owned AIG in the fund for almost 30 years. A man came up to me afterwards and said, 'You know, Mr. Davis, what you said rang true to me, because we have an old saying in Germany that insurance companies are for *holding,* never for *selling.*' He went on to say, 'My family has owned Munich Re and Swiss Re throughout the past 100 years, through two world wars, depressions, and devaluations. They haven't always performed, but they're still around and growing.' The reason is the assets of insurance companies don't become obsolete. I guarantee you that every hard asset on Intel's books today will be obsolete 20 years from now. The two are very different businesses, but a lot of people don't understand that. They always live in the here and now, but the world is constantly changing."

KNOWING WHAT PRICE TO PAY

Elizabeth Bramwell searches for fast-growing companies, but she won't pay just any price for them. "I look at individual valuations relative to the overall stock market, namely the S&P 500, and other companies in the same industry," she says. "I then compare this information to the company's historical valuations and estimated future growth rate. Ideally, you want to find a stock selling at a discount to its growth rate, or at least selling at a multiple to growth that is less than that of the S&P 500. In essence, I'm forecasting the future from the bottom up. But it's also important to look at companies in the context of the world in which we live."

Robert Stovall's first step in evaluating the attractiveness of a stock, in terms of its price, is to see what the company's projected earnings growth rate is compared to its PE ratio. Remember that the ultimate value of a stock is the sum total of its future stream of earnings and dividends. If the growth rate is higher than the PE ratio, that's a good sign. In fact, the higher the better. In other words, all other things being equal, a stock growing at 25 percent a year with a PE ratio of 16 is much more attractive than one growing at 20 percent a year with the same PE. "Next I look at whether the company is experiencing rising sales," he adds. "If sales are going up, but earnings aren't, I want to see whether there's a good chance earnings will catch up to this growth, and if not, why. Therefore, sales per share, which is determined by taking a company's total amount of sales and dividing it by the number of outstanding shares, is an important number. I also want to see if the stock has a dividend, and if so what the yield is. I like stocks that pay dividends because if you're wrong on the timing, the dividends give you extra breathing room while you wait." Of course, most companies don't pay much in the way of dividends anymore, opting instead to invest extra cash in the business or use it to repurchase shares on the open market. For this reason, Stovall keeps a generous helping of convertible bonds and preferreds in his portfolios. Many of these instruments offer yields of between 4 and 7 percent with appreciation potential, albeit not as much as you would enjoy from owning the common stock.

LESSONS OF A GO-GO

As you know, Davis learned a great deal about how *not* to invest while buying go-go stocks during New York Venture's early years. "I was picking them the same way many younger managers do today, namely by saying a stock is cheap if it's selling for twice its growth rate," he says. "My attitude was if the multiple was one or two times the growth rate, regardless of what that was, it was OK. But the higher multiple means the stock is more vulnerable to any downdrafts. In addition, you have to question the sustainability of these high-growth rates. People throw huge numbers out, but a growth rate is meaningful only if you can guarantee it will last for a long time. Otherwise, it might be a short-term anomaly. I was ignoring the length of these growth rates thinking they were symptomatic of the future. I learned the hard way that's not always the case. High-return and high-growth businesses are great. But because of that, they attract competition. High returns bring money toward the business, and high-growth rates tend to breed opportunity. However, it usually takes a few years for this to show up, and that can catch novice investors off guard. I've seen it with the fast-food restaurant chains, steak houses, bowling alleys, hospital chains, nursing homes, and HMOs. Coffeehouses could be next, unless Starbuck's is the unique one. There's always the odd one that can make it. However, almost any high-growth group breeds imitators."

THE BOTTOM LINE

Before buying any stock, you should first call the company's investor relations department and ask for the latest annual and quarterly reports, forms 10-K and 10-Q, proxy statements, and any additional research reports they might have. With these documents in hand, pay special attention to the balance sheet. Is there plenty of cash on hand? At what pace are sales and earnings growing? How much debt has been taken on, and what is the money being used for?

You can use this information, not only to determine whether the company is financially strong, but also to figure out whether its current stock price is a bargain or too expensive based on the underlying fundamentals.

Rule *11*

DON'T SPREAD YOURSELF TOO THIN

All smart investors know that you should never put all your eggs in one basket when it comes to investing in stocks. Diversification is the name of the game. Spreading your bets over a handful of companies and industries not only reduces risk, but also the price volatility of your overall portfolio. That's because when one industry is out of favor, you can continue to profit from another of Wall Street's current darlings. "I think of a portfolio as a beautiful garden," reveals Shelby Davis. "Not every plant is in bloom all the time. This is why you want to own an assortment of good companies."

Nevertheless, owning too many companies is also a mistake. You don't want to overdiversify either. Your goal should be to keep enough stocks in your portfolio to control risk, but not enough to cripple your returns. The problem with owning too many companies is that if you have one or two winners, they won't matter much if they're just a small percentage of the overall picture.

THE "MAGIC" NUMBER

Roy Papp keeps around 30 stocks in each of his mutual funds, which he contends might be too many for an individual portfolio. "I believe in diversification," he says. "Mathematicians have told us for years that you need 13 stocks for theoretical diversification. I think you really need 20 to 23 myself, though with a large fund I keep around 30. You're probably thinking that the average mutual fund has around 60 to 80 stocks, and you're exactly right. The reason is they don't have any faith in their choices. They are closet indexers. If they want to be closet indexers, they need about 80 stocks. That makes little sense to me. Would you be a happy client if I told you I've got a great stock that's the seventy-ninth best idea on my list? Of course not. But that's what happens when you buy a fund with so many holdings. The more stocks you own the weaker your results. You get closer to the index every time you add another name. If that's your goal, fine, especially since 80 percent of active managers can't beat the index. But I believe it can be done if you pick the right companies."

REMAINING FOCUSED

Don Yacktman is another big believer in concentration. He did some back-testing, which showed if he had stuck with a smaller number of names in his flagship Yacktman Fund, he could have considerably beefed up its overall results. So in 1997, he launched a new fund, called Yacktman Focused. It is a nondiversified offering that usually holds no more than 15 of his favorite ideas. "Some feel this approach increases risk, but I would argue it actually lowers it," Yacktman insists. "Overdiversification is a symptom of poor or superficial research. If you feel comfortable with the knowledge bank you have and can find only a handful of good companies selling for 50 cents on the dollar, or whatever your discipline might be, why should you steer away from your course and buy lesser companies at a higher price?"

DIVERSIFY WITH BONDS

To Robert Stovall, diversification means more than spreading your equity holdings across a wide range of companies. It also means owning some bonds and convertible securities to cushion volatility.

"I buy Treasuries even for my younger clients," he says. "It adds to liquidity. I would never have a 100 percent equity portfolio, but that's me. I want to reduce risk and add to income. It's what most of my clients demand. Even if you don't need any income, I think there is still room for bonds. Of course, fixed-income portfolios will move in price along with interest rates. If you want to be more aggressive, sprinkle in some convertibles as well. Adding these instruments to your portfolio will smooth out its performance." Not everyone agrees with Stovall's strategy of holding bonds even for younger investors. As previously mentioned, Yacktman has one client in her nineties who is almost fully invested in equities. However, if tempering market volatility is of concern to you, sprinkling a few fixed-income securities into the mix should do the job.

PRUNE THE WEEDS

Earlier, Shelby Davis compared a diversified portfolio to a beautiful garden. Part of your responsibility as the caretaker is to keep an eye on your crop of stocks and make sure everything is growing as expected. If not, you must be prepared to take action. "Your job as a gardener, or portfolio manager, is to weed the garden of a few mature plants every year, plant a few new seeds, and, with luck, enjoy flowers that bloom sequentially," Davis insists. "In other words, once in awhile you must add one holding here, sell another there, or replace yet another here. The fact that you get a constant rotation in the market is fine with me. It's nerve racking, but that's why I keep an eye on my Bloomberg terminal. When something rotates out of favor, it may create an opportunity. The most difficult part of this job is deciding when to lighten up on one of my positions. That's always tricky."

Knowing when to sell is tricky indeed, and in Rule Twelve we'll discuss how to know when it's the right time to bring out the hedge trimmers in your portfolio.

THE BOTTOM LINE

Keep a well-diversified portfolio of 20 to 30 companies from many different industries. This will reduce your overall risk, while making sure you have broad exposure to a well-rounded number of sectors.

Rule 12

KNOW WHEN TO SAY GOOD-BYE

The focus of this book has been to give you advice for identifying and buying winning growth stocks for your investment portfolio. However, it's equally important for you to know how and when to "sell" one of your holdings. Letting go is never easy. After all, if you've done your homework right, you have spent a lot of time researching and getting to know each company in your portfolio. Saying good-bye can be tough.

STOVALL: BE READY TO SELL BEFORE YOU BUY

Robert Stovall calls deciding when to sell a stock the single-most trying chore investors face. Still, it is something you will have to deal with. While your goal should be to own the companies you choose forever, the reality is you must never become complacent. Instead, you should be prepared to let go if your reasons for buying in the first place either change or, better yet, come to pass and you make a lot of money in the stock.

In Stovall's case, he often determines when he's going to sell a stock before he ever buys it. "I always set price targets," he explains. "These price targets are based on a number of factors, including earnings expectations, the company's current and historical PE ratio, price-to-sales ratio, the market's PE ratio, and the dividend yield (which has become less important in recent years as corporations use free cash for reinvestment instead of paying it out to shareholders)." Here's an example. Let's say Stovall finds a stock selling for a PE of 17. He might calculate that, based on its past record, it really merits a PE of 22. When he buys this undervalued company, he sets a target price of 22 times earnings. Once it reaches that level, he knows it's time to sell.

Stovall notes that during the 1990s, the biggest mistake investors have made is selling too early. "That's certainly been my problem," Stovall admits. "The market keeps hurdling one historical barrier after another, and that's something you have to watch out for." Stovall tries to keep from making this mistake by constantly referring to his sector analysis research and reviewing the historical price ranges for various industry groups. Once he learns that a stock he owns is trading at the high end of its historical range, he often decides to cut back on it or entirely eliminate his position. In other words, if he knows that historically auto stocks have traded within a PE range of 9 and 13 times earnings, once General Motors sells for 14 times earnings, he may decide the stock is overpriced and thus a candidate for sale. In this case, it is the overall industry PE that drives his decision.

Like everyone else we've met in this book, Stovall relies heavily on fundamental analysis, or good hard research, although he often pays attention to technical indicators as well. If a stock's chart pattern begins to unravel, he'll often unload his position, even if he believes the fundamentals are still in place.

YACKTMAN'S THREE RULES OF SELLING

According to Don Yacktman, it's time to sell a stock when:

1. The share price of a good company approaches its private market value (as defined in Rule 1 of this book).

2. The fundamentals deteriorate.

3. A better business is available for the same price or less.

Sticking with these guidelines requires discipline and occasionally leads to disappointment. For instance, the market doesn't know the number Yacktman has calculated for a company's private market value. Therefore, even though one of his holdings might reach that magic number, its shares could still keep going up. This is something that happens frequently during bull markets. It's what's known as a stock's "opportunity cost," or the potential profits an investor loses from being on the sidelines in cash. Even though this premature selling can cause his performance to temporarily suffer, Yacktman insists he must stick with his discipline of getting rid of stocks that he deems to be overvalued.

"My decision to sell based on price really isn't as canned as it might sound," Yacktman insists. "It's more of a comfort index. When a stock reaches a point where I begin to think it's too expensive, or I'm getting increasingly nervous about it, I have to let go. It comes back to that principle of getting the highest return consistent with a minimal amount of risk. The further a stock increases in price relative to its value, the more risky it becomes. Also, in taxable accounts, I do keep tax liability in mind. If you have a stock with a huge gain that would trigger a large tax liability, you might hold on to it longer than you would in a tax-deferred account."

Of course, a company's private market value does change as the years go by, but the figure isn't revised upward in Yacktman's book as often as you might think. "I don't alter it very much," he says. "I adjust the cash flows quarterly. But the stock's capitalization rate rarely changes. It would take a major move in interest rates or attitude for the number to go up or down significantly."

As noted, Yacktman will also sell a holding if the long-term fundamentals deteriorate, if a similar high-quality business can be found at a lower price, or if a better company comes along and he needs to free up some cash to buy it.

PAPP'S REASONS FOR PULLING THE TRIGGER

To say that Roy Papp hates to sell a stock is an understatement. "My goal is to buy a company I never have to get rid of," he notes. In the real world, that's not practical. While his turnover is low, Papp does trade around his positions every once in a while. Among other things, he'll let go of stocks it was a mistake to buy in the first place. "Another reason is if the industry or company has changed," he says. "I'll give you a perfect illustration. One of my largest holdings over the last ten years has been Albertson's, the supermarket chain. This was a very well-run company, with enormous profit margins compared to the competition. The industry it operated in was in shambles and full of debt. Albertson's was different. But the company no longer has the ballpark to itself. Safeway and others have gotten their acts together and are now formidable competitors. As a result, Albertson's is struggling. The company isn't going down the tubes, but it won't continue to grow by 15 percent a year. Therefore, it's not a stock I want to continue to own for the long term.

"I'll give you another one," he continues. "Have you ever heard of a company called Bush Wellman? It had one product that was unique. It manufactured beryllium. There were only two plants in the world that made this metallic element. One was in the Soviet Union and the other was in the United States. If there was ever a monopoly, this was it. There were two problems, though. The U.S. government decided that having too much beryllium in the air could kill people. Then, when the Cold War with Russia ended, demand for this product went way down. Before, it was a perfect monopoly. Now it wasn't worth a hill of beans. There was a change in the industry."

The third reason Papp sells a stock is if it gets too expensive. "Before I buy a company, I determine what I feel its intrinsic value is," he says. "I want to buy it at least at a 10 to 25 percent discount from what I think it's really worth. That's not always possible. Sometimes you have to buy at or slightly above intrinsic value, and that's all right. But if it goes 50 percent above that mark, I'm out. Keep in mind that intrinsic value gets altered every three months, because the earnings and prospects are constantly changing. I also believe that when you view the market, you have to view it through the windshield, not the rearview mirror. Therefore, on September 30, I start using next year's earnings estimates. The market usually sells at a multiple based on where it thinks things will be six months out. If you're looking through the rearview mirror, you're looking at history. As I've said before, changes are accelerating in our business. You can't afford to look at history as a primary yardstick."

DAVIS: THINK LONG TERM, BUT KNOW WHEN TO FIRE YOUR PARTNERS

When you get to know a company as intimately as Shelby Davis does, the decision of when to move on becomes even more difficult. "People ask me what my holding period is. I say when I go into something, I hope it's perpetual. But it can't always be that way," Davis maintains. "My average turnover is 15 to 20 percent a year, which means I own a stock for about five to eight years. One thing I learned in the late 1960s is that you can be right about a high-multiple stock and have it go up 50 or 300 percent. However, that likely won't last forever. My biggest winner at that time was Memorex. I first bought it for around $20 in early 1960. It kept going up and up, until it hit $168. The company was competing head-on with IBM, which wanted to squash it. Once interest rates started going up, the stock came spiraling down. You don't know where it's safe to buy when the multiple is that high. I began buying some more at $70, after it had dropped more than 50 percent. Pretty soon it was down to $40. That's when I ended up selling at a loss. I went from having a triple to a loss. It ultimately sank to $3. The problem with a high-multiple stock, in my mind, is that if the market turns down, you don't know where the floor is. It's hard to have an instinctive feel for that. If a stock trades for 30 times earnings, that's a 3 percent earnings yield. If it drops to 20 times earnings, that's only a 5 percent earnings yield. In either case, that's not very competitive if interest rates move up to 8 percent or more.

"Sometimes you sell because of a secular shift in the growth outlook for an industry," Davis continues. "For example, oil and gas went sour on me in the early 1980s, and I finally recognized those stocks weren't going back up any time soon. The supply-and-demand equation was too unequal. A second reason is more personal. If a company disappoints me on a regular basis, I begin to believe the management is a bluffer, not a doer. I always say to my kids, 'Say what you mean and mean what you say.' It's a pretty good rule. If one of my companies doesn't mean what it says, I begin to lose faith in it. I like honesty, even if the facts aren't favorable. Along those lines, I want to see accurate numbers. If I smell bad accounting or sense any fraud, I'll get out. That tells me the people in charge are of low quality and unfit to be one of my partners. Remember, my premise is that I'm a partner in a business when I own the stock. Management is the operator of my business."

Other times, things may be fine with a company he owns, but Davis gets the sense he's better off in cash because the overall market is too exuberantly priced. "Nobody talks about this anymore, because it's been so long, but sometimes you have to cut back on your holdings because you feel more comfortable on the sidelines," he adds. "If you feel the risk-free rate on bonds is going up considerably, you know PE ratios will come down. My marketing department wouldn't be happy if I raised a lot of cash in my funds. But I would still do it if I felt we were running into long-term trouble with the market. I wouldn't take it all out, maybe 20 percent or so. I'd write to my shareholders and say I was no longer thinking as much about beating the market averages on the way up, but rather building insurance protection by squirreling away cash in the event of a fall. Even Warren Buffett got out of the market once. He returned money to his shareholders in the late 1960s, and it turned out to be a pretty wise move."

A final reason Davis will abandon a holding, and one you already know is shared by his colleagues, is if he finds a more compelling stock in which to invest his money. "As an example of that, I built up a position in a couple of paper stocks in 1995 and sold out about a year later after they failed to perform," he offers. "I didn't lose anything, but decided that even though there would likely be another shortage of paper in the future, the industry really hasn't been that great to investors over the past 30 years. So I decided to move the money into several brokerage stocks instead. While both are volatile areas, I feel the brokerages will grow faster. The demographics are more favorable."

BRAMWELL: A FREQUENT TRADER

Elizabeth Bramwell has a slightly heavier hand than Stovall, Yacktman, Davis, and Papp. She trades around 60 to 90 percent of the positions in her portfolio each year. "I'd like to hold a stock for at least 18 months to take advantage of the 20 percent long-term capital-gains tax rate," she says. "However, the small- and mid-cap stocks I tend to buy are volatile and may require more frequent trading." Given these inherent risks, she also keeps a highly diversified portfolio, owning an average of 80 different stocks at any given time, well above the 30 or so recommended by those who stick with larger names.

The primary reasons Bramwell moves out of one holding and into another are because a company's fundamentals deteriorate, a stock becomes excessively priced relative to its future growth potential, the macroeconomic outlook turns bleak, or she finds better places to put her money.

THE BOTTOM LINE

While you should go into every stock position with the intention of holding on forever, sometimes it is necessary to sell. Here are some good reasons to let go:

- The company's fundamentals begin to deteriorate.
- The stock meets your price target.
- You find a better company at a lower price.
- There is a secular shift in the industry that's bound to negatively impact the stock.

ELIZABETH R. BRAMWELL

$\mathcal{W}$hile Shelby Davis was practically born speaking the language of bulls and bears, Wall Street was never a part of Elizabeth Bramwell's childhood vocabulary. The frequent topic of discussion in her home was music. Her dad was an organist who conducted five different choirs, while her mom ran the house and took care of Elizabeth and her younger brother. "My parents never talked about business," she says. "I didn't even know what a mutual fund was until I got out of college." Bramwell describes herself as a shy late bloomer who graduated from high school at the age of 17, a year younger than most of her classmates. She was awarded a scholarship to attend college and initially thought about becoming a doctor. But by the time she graduated from Bryn Mawr, she was tired of school and didn't want to spend several more years studying to be a physician. "I was a chemistry major," she notes. "However, if I had to do it over, I would have majored in history or economics instead."

WRITING THE FACTS

With her degree in hand, Bramwell went off to Washington, D.C., where she had an opportunity to write a question-and-answer column that was syndicated to 75 regional newspapers across the country. "I answered readers' queries," she explains. "Questions had to be factual and ranged from which president had the most children to what was the fastest animal. If I didn't know the answer, I would research it. The column was originally started in the early 1920s. That's when it had its heyday, before the development of radio and TV. At one point, the column was carried by some 300 newspapers. By the time I got there, it was used basically as filler, although it ran regularly in such big newspapers as the *Washington Star.* I put together eight questions for each day of the week."

Bramwell found this job through a friend at Bryn Mawr, whose mother had worked on the column out of college a generation earlier. "The woman who wrote the column before I came along wanted to take a leave of absence to write a book. After interviewing me and at the very end checking my handwriting to get a sense of my personality, she hired me," Bramwell says. "She was a great teacher and very wise woman. I learned how to write newspaper style, using the inverted pyramid. I didn't realize at the time that there were different ways of writing and that the way you write term papers is different from the way you write newspaper articles. I learned how to write succinctly, striking out all the adjectives, and putting the most important things first, in case the reader didn't finish the whole article. It was the best writing course I ever had. I also learned how to research and back everything with written documentation. Among the many sources I referred to was a phenomenal morgue of old newspaper clippings."

COLUMBIA BOUND

After 18 months of responding to inquiring minds, Bramwell returned to New York, edited chemistry books for John Wiley & Sons, and began to question the direction of her career. Her roommate worked for the investment department at Chemical Bank, and another college friend was at the Harvard Business School. In her mind, their lives were more exciting than hers, so she decided to explore other options. "I started taking night courses at City College's Baruch School of Business, studying subjects such as accounting and security analysis," Bramwell says. "The investment business was exciting, measurement was quantitatively objective (in that stocks went up or down), and I decided that a master's in business administration was the degree for me, even though there weren't many women working on Wall Street at that time. However, I wasn't excited about writing the yearlong thesis that Baruch required. So I went up to Columbia University's Graduate Business School and told the dean of admissions that I wanted to transfer to Columbia. I started my first class in September 1966 and graduated with an MBA in finance a year later."

Bramwell loved her time at Columbia. "The students there knew why they were going to school," she says. "They had a game plan in mind for their lives and were seeking knowledge that could be applied. That's still true today." Bramwell was one of only three women out of a class of around 100. "Women didn't have that many opportunities back then," she points out. "My Bryn Mawr classmates went into teaching, medicine, law, or government. There was also an undercurrent that anything to do with the private sector was bad. For me, it was fun being a pioneer and having no role models."

Among her classmates at Columbia was a red-headed, freckle-faced man named Mario Gabelli. The two would subsequently cross paths many times throughout their careers and would eventually work together. "We had an accounting course together my first year and other classes in subsequent semesters," Bramwell says. "Columbia didn't have as many students then as it does now. The faculty and deans' wives served us tea every afternoon in a spacious first-floor lounge that has now become a busy, crowded cafeteria. It was a great way to get to know your classmates. I made several friends at the school as a result, many of whom I still have to this day."

STARTING ON WALL STREET

After earning her MBA, Bramwell became an analyst at Morgan Guaranty Trust Company. Mario Gabelli joined Loeb Rhoads. Although they were at separate firms, they followed several of the same companies. "While our research overlapped, he was on the sell side and I was on the buy side," she says. "I went into Morgan's investment research department and started covering leisure time, entertainment, and specialty retailing. The bank was in the process of expanding its investment universe from large-cap stocks, such as Sears Roebuck, IBM, and General Motors, to smaller companies. It was a time when small-cap funds were being launched. Young companies like Home Depot and McDonald's were just starting out. Two of the earliest stocks I followed were American Greetings, which is still an independent company, and Lenox china, which isn't."

Personal computers didn't exist at that time, and analysts worked largely off printed annual and quarterly reports. They also attended company meetings. "We used slide rules during my first year and a half on the job," Bramwell recalls. "When calculators were initially introduced, they were the size of today's personal computers. The bank kept them in a special room. The creation of handheld calculators was revolutionary. They accelerated the numbers-crunching process immensely. The same thing has happened in recent years with computers, which have dramatically changed the way I work. The analytical process remains the same, however. I still put my data together using the format I followed at Morgan. Among other things, I keep track of quarterly changes in sales, income, and profitability. One reason I think momentum investing has become so popular is that it's so easy to retrieve this data electronically today. You can get information and react to it instantly. You couldn't do that when I started out. Investing was a slower, cerebral process. These days you don't have that luxury. If you don't act quickly, you may lose your opportunity."

SWITCHING SIDES

After Morgan Guaranty, Bramwell joined the sell-side research boutique of William D. Witter. For a short time, one of her colleagues at the firm was former Columbia classmate Mario Gabelli. "I covered specialty retailing and leisure time," she says. "I was first runner-up in the *Institutional Investor* poll in 1975 and 1976, largely for work I did on Disney. I had conducted the supporting research on this company for Morgan Guaranty. The stock became one of the trust department's largest holdings. We bought Disney before Disney World opened in September 1971 and saw our investment multiply several times from our original cost. My long-term earnings forecasts came out remarkably on target."

Bramwell made stock recommendations to William D. Witter's institutional clients. (Buy-side analysts work for such institutions as mutual funds, bank trust departments, and money management firms. They look for equities to recommend to their internal portfolio managers. Sell-side analysts, on the other hand, often influence the purchasing decisions of those on the buy side. They are viewed as experts in the industries they cover and are employed by the brokerages and investment banking firms that bring various issues to market.) "On the sell side, there is a lot of marketing involved," Bramwell explains. "You're constantly out visiting institutional money managers. I think being on the buy side starting out is preferable, because you're exposed to a greater number of industries and companies."

William D. Witter was acquired by Drexel Burnham in 1976. Bramwell then joined the buy-side research department at Bankers Trust. She became head of a group that followed everything from railroads to photography. She also looked for special situations, potentially attractive stocks the bank's clients didn't already own in their portfolios. But when her second child came along in 1978, she went on maternity leave and never returned. "Although the research was exciting, I'd had enough of internal meetings and wanted to take some time off," she says.

HEDGING HER CAREER

After a year at home, a Wall Street friend introduced her to the manager of a new hedge fund who was looking for a research analyst. "I joined the fund on a part-time basis for six years, and it was great," she says. "We had about $10 million when I started, and while I was there it grew to around $60 million. We had a portfolio of 25 to 30 stocks and focused on growth companies with strong fundamentals."

Meanwhile, Bramwell's college classmate, Mario Gabelli, went out on his own soon after William D. Witter was acquired. Originally he started a firm that sold research to institutional investors. Before long, an executive at one of the companies he was researching wrote him a check and asked him to manage his money. That was the spark Gabelli needed to branch out into the full-fledged investment management business.

THE GABELLI CONNECTION

Gabelli has always been a popular value player. His favorite professor at Columbia was Roger Murray, who followed in the footsteps of Benjamin Graham. "When Gabelli first started to manage money, he did well buying companies based on their private market values, defined as what an informed businessperson would pay for the entire business," Bramwell observes. "To see why this worked so well, you have to go back to the Carter administration, when PE ratios were in the single digits. We had inflation that got up to 13 percent, and interest rates were in the high teens. Cable and cellular companies, with their monopolistic and duopolistic industry structures, were just beginning to emerge. A lot of them sold below their private market values and Gabelli saw that. When the public market price is less than the private market value, you can arbitrage the difference by buying the stock at a huge discount from what the company is worth to an informed buyer. It was a phenomenal opportunity, and Gabelli made good money for his investors. The environment has since changed. I think we're now in an age where the public market value is likely to be higher than the private market value. But this process worked back then."

During the 1980s, private market values were often determined by looking at similar transactions within like industries. For example, if a food company was bought for 20 times forward earnings by an outside acquirer, the assumption was that other food companies were worth the same multiple. Therefore, it was relatively easy to compute a company's private market value if you could estimate forward earnings and what similar competitors were being bought out for.

Gabelli's impressive early performance at selecting undervalued stocks, combined with his media savvy, got him a lot of attention from numerous financial publications, including *Barron's*. In no time, he became a celebrity investment manager, and his firm started to grow. In 1985, he asked Bramwell to become his director of research. She joined him that November. Gabelli soon found himself inundated with requests from individual investors who read about him in the press and wanted him to manage their money. Most of these folks had relatively small accounts, which are most effectively handled through a single pool, like a mutual fund. So the Gabelli Asset Fund was born the following year.

GABELLI GROWTH

Mario Gabelli was clearly making a name for himself as an expert at picking stocks based on private market valuations, but this shrewd businessman knew he needed more than just one fund and investment style to build an investment empire. With Bramwell's help, he developed a plan for starting an entire fund family. The first logical addition was that of a pure growth fund, which Bramwell would manage. It was a perfect complement to the value-oriented Gabelli Asset Fund. Bramwell wrote the original investment policy for what became the Gabelli Growth Fund. She was named as its sole portfolio manager in the initial prospectus.

Gabelli Growth was launched in April 1987. The market was already up about 20 percent for the year, and Bramwell was an unknown entity. Like any fund, Gabelli Growth couldn't be listed in the paper until it had 1,000 shareholders or $25 million in net assets. It didn't reach the 1,000-shareholder mark until August 1988, 16 months later. As a result, the fund and Bramwell got little media exposure at first, because few people knew either existed. "Fortunately, I made some good macro calls in the fall of 1987," she says. "I had about 40 percent of the portfolio in cash by mid-October. When the market went down, that allowed me to have a great fourth quarter relative to everybody else." Bramwell believes the crash of 1987 was partially caused by short-term traders who abruptly sold after hearing that the Ways and Means Committee of Congress was considering a plan to eliminate the tax deductibility of interest expense for merger-and-acquisition debt, thereby significantly changing the investment carrying cost. In her opinion, this selling created a snowball effect, leading to the abrupt fall. She felt, however, that specific underlying company fundamentals generally remained strong.

Given that, Bramwell went out and bought several distressed IPOs, including Budget Rent-a-Car and HWC Distribution, a wire-supply company. "They were particularly stressed because after the crash investors sold their biggest losers at year-end for the tax write-offs," she says. "In the first half of 1988, I was fully invested. Other investors were waiting to see what would happen and held a lot of cash. The IPOs I bought started to take off. The fund was up 39 percent in 1988 and 40 percent in 1989. Gabelli Growth became the number-one equity fund in the nation over the three-year period ending in August 1990." That strong performance attracted attention. The fund began garnering top recommendations from various investment magazines, newsletters, and financial advisers, which led to increased assets.

THE STAR MANAGER VERSUS THE BOSS

Although it had his name on the cover, Mario Gabelli himself was not directly involved with the fund. "I was cited in the prospectus as the portfolio manager from day one," Bramwell points out. "I was president of the fund and chaired all meetings of the board of directors. Mario wasn't even on the board for the first five years. I made all of the investment decisions." The media took notice when Bramwell outperformed her boss. A 1989 article in *Forbes* was headlined "Top stock picker Mario Gabelli faces stiff competition from one of his own employees." And, in what turned out to be a prophetic statement, *The Wall Street Journal* wrote the following about the Gabelli Growth Fund on August 3, 1989: "With its solid performance it probably should be called the Bramwell Fund. Maybe it will be some day." This obviously put a strain on the working relationship between Gabelli and his star manager.

Bramwell ran the fund without any internal support until 1991, when Gabelli gave her one dedicated analyst. By then, the fund's assets had grown to some $300 million. Bramwell invested in a universe that was almost entirely different from the rest of the Gabelli organization. By the time her lone analyst left in January 1994, the fund had grown to $700 million. Gabelli stalled on hiring a replacement, leaving Bramwell alone once again. "He then mandated that I immediately move from my office in New York City to his new head-quarters in Rye, which is a one-hour drive from Manhattan," Bramwell contends. "Analyst meetings were becoming more important, and they were held in Manhattan. I told him I couldn't spend my day riding back and forth on the highway during trading hours to attend those meetings and that the fund's performance would suffer. That didn't affect him. The last straw was when I went off to a lunch put on by one of the companies in my portfolio in February 1994 and came back to find that he had changed the locks on my office door." Bramwell abruptly quit her job on February 10, 1994, and quickly began laying the foundation for the next phase of her career.

ON HER OWN

It's not that Bramwell wanted to part ways with Gabelli. As she puts it, leaving the Gabelli Growth Fund was like abandoning a child. Besides, she earned a great salary. Her bonus in 1993 alone was $750,000. "My compensation was open-ended," she explains. "I got a percentage of the management fee after expenses. No one expected it to turn into such a big fund. I was not planning to leave. I even bought shares of Gabelli Growth in January 1994. I wouldn't have done that if I were planning to go." Nevertheless, she felt there was no other option, given the lack of support.

"I had always worked for somebody else and decided that if I were going to do anything, I was going to work for myself," she insists. "I wanted to prove I could start up a business and succeed. It was a mountain I needed to climb." Her first step was to register her new firm, Bramwell Capital Management, with the Securities and Exchange Commission. A woman attorney who read in the paper about her breakup with Gabelli offered to help write Bramwell's fund prospectus, while preparing and filing the necessary forms with the SEC. Meantime, a friend found some temporary office space for her to work out of, until she could locate a place of her own.

Gabelli was not happy about Bramwell's departure. He sued to get 1993's $750,000 bonus back, claiming it was an advance on future earnings. Since she was gone, he argued, she should return it. Bramwell filed a countersuit, and the case went to binding arbitration with the National Association of Securities Dealers. "We had this agreement that if I were to leave, I'd be paid six times my last month's compensation," she says. "Also, I had not been paid out on stock I owned in Gabelli's two companies, Gabelli Group and Gabelli Securities." The NASD ultimately rendered a judgment in Bramwell's favor. She wound up receiving a settlement worth around $1 million.

After a few months of getting organized, Bramwell found permanent office space in a modest complex in the heart of Fifth Avenue's shopping district. It's a historic building that boasts several art galleries as its primary tenants. She has a great view of Central Park. If your vision is good, you can also see the street she grew up on—West 67th. "I moved into my new office in June 1994," she says. "I couldn't even put in a phone system until then. I never realized how important that was. I then began assembling a team of people to work with me."

Most investment advisers start their money management firms with a few large accounts and over time work their way up to establishing a mutual fund. That's how Gabelli did it. Bramwell, however, chose a different path. "My recognition was with the general public, as the Gabelli Growth Fund had blossomed to more than 60,000 individual shareholders," she says. "Starting a fund immediately was the way for me to go, although it's not the normal route managers usually take."

BIRTHING BRAMWELL GROWTH

One person who was especially helpful to Bramwell as she got her new firm off the ground was Don Yacktman. He invited her to come out to Chicago and spent the morning giving her advice, particularly on how to structure her fund and investment advisory firm. He had been down the same road a few years earlier and warned her about some of the pitfalls along the way. Another friendly voice was Ralph Wanger of the Acorn Funds. He also started his own firm after leaving Chicago's Harris Associates. "Don and Ralph paved the way for me to go out on my own," Bramwell says. "They were both very nice about advising me as I was getting organized. Their success was encouraging, but starting a new business was still challenging."

A Slow Start

The prospectus for the Bramwell Growth Fund became effective on August 1, 1994. By the end of September, the fund had amassed only $5 million in assets. By year-end, that number jumped to around $13 million. "I was disappointed that the fund grew so slowly because the break-even point in this business is high," Bramwell admits. "Fortunately, we attracted some media attention, and the performance was good. There's a lot of interest in mutual funds, and there are more and more magazines and TV shows that need fresh news material. Start-up funds have an advantage, since they are a new subject to cover. That's helpful because advertising is expensive." Still, she expected more money to come in at the start, especially given her past high visibility.

Once Bramwell was able to get her fund included in various no-load, no-transaction-fee mutual fund supermarkets, including those operated by Charles Schwab and Fidelity Investments, assets started flowing in at a faster pace. Additionally, it didn't hurt that in her first year out, not only was the overall stock market doing well, but the fund's performance was also several percentage points ahead of the S&P 500. However, she made a costly error during the fourth quarter of 1995 by moving into telecommunications stocks at the wrong time, just before investor disenchantment with mobile-telephone equipment companies surfaced. She ultimately pulled out and cut her losses short. Nevertheless, her performance suffered.

The Landmark Ruling

Bramwell set a precedent when the SEC issued a "no-action" letter that, in essence, allowed her to refer to her track record from Gabelli Growth in the Bramwell Growth Fund's prospectus, not only in the first year, but also thereafter. "As a result, it has become substantially easier for fund managers in general to go out on their own and refer to their past records," she points out. "People come up to me at conferences and thank me for facilitating the process of starting their own businesses. It's very gratifying."

More fund companies have since begun using management teams, instead of individuals, to muddy who is really in charge of making the day-to-day investment decisions for the portfolio. This strategy makes it harder for managers to leave and claim the record at their former fund was solely their own. "I think that's excessively paranoid," Bramwell offers. "As far as I'm concerned, the more competition the better. That's what keeps the market liquid."

BEATING THE INDEX

The pressure to outperform the S&P 500 is always on every fund manager's mind. It's a bogey that has gotten more difficult to beat. Studies show some 80 percent of all active portfolio managers now turn in results below that of the computer-run S&P 500 index funds. "It's not the same old index that it used to be," Bramwell maintains. "It used to be easier to beat, because it didn't change that much. Today it contains growth stocks such as Microsoft and Dell. If those companies keep growing by 25 percent or so a year, they will continue to drive up the index. Although the index is supposed to be representative of the whole market, it is increasingly dominated by the top 25 stocks. I believe it's also important for investors to compare the performance of their managers to a peer group. In my case, that could be the Lipper Growth Fund Index. Going forward, as valuations rise and the thrust of new investors going into index funds as their initial investment levels off, I believe the market will broaden and active managers will be better able to beat the S&P in the future."

A GROWING BUSINESS OF HER OWN

Bramwell Capital Management has grown into a firm of seven, including three analysts besides Bramwell. Assets total more than $500 million, $150 million of which is in the Bramwell Growth Fund. The firm also subadvises Selected Special Shares, a small-company growth fund, for Shelby Davis's company.

Your first impression after entering Bramwell's firm is that it's anything but an upscale investment boutique. Although she's recently doubled her work space, making the quarters a little less cramped, the reception area is full of fund prospectuses, with nary a couch to sit on. The entire place is covered with boxes containing annual reports and other material that has found its way inside. It looks as if Bramwell and her staff save everything, and to some degree that's true. Bramwell acknowledges she's a pack rat of sorts, preferring to keep stuff she even *thinks* she might want to review down the line, rather than tossing it out and living to regret it. "I hate to throw anything away," she says. "You never know when you might want to go back and look at one of these companies."

This is something that happens more often than you might imagine. The day I visited Bramwell, she had just purchased shares of furniture component maker Leggett & Platt. Her rationale for buying it was that the company was an effective consolidator. It had followed a successful acquiring strategy that served to eliminate redundant costs and leverage distribution. She first bought shares of this company back in the 1980s. She has been in and out of it several times since. "I know the management and have been following the company for a long time," she says. "It's a seasoned operation. The problem is companies often go through plateau periods, where growth starts to slow down. As an investor, you have two options. You can either stick with them through the tough times, or you can sell out and buy something that looks better. After I sell a stock, I usually continue to follow it, looking for a chance to buy it again at a more favorable price. Many analysts stop following a stock once they sell it. The problem with that is you have to start your research from scratch when you ultimately decide to revisit the idea."

Bramwell's private office is full of reports and books, such as *Investment Biker* by Jim Rogers, *First Things First* by Stephen Covey, and *Thriving Up and Down the Free Market Food Chain* by Arthur Lipper III. As I walk inside and observe her library, I ask why she doesn't have any of *my* investment titles on the shelf. She tells me she does, and promptly pulls out one of my books from the crowded space.

Bramwell was on the phone when I arrived, listening to a conference call with one of the companies she owns. As the CEO talked, she thumbed through the research reports and newsletters that covered her desk. In between, she kept a close eye on her computer, watching the continuous price changes for the stocks in her portfolio. This is just another typical morning at Bramwell Capital.

USING IPOS

Unlike the other growth stock managers I interviewed, Bramwell selectively utilizes IPOs. As I mentioned, picking up newly issued

IPOs after the 1987 Crash contributed to her early strong performance at Gabelli Growth. There is no shortage of new companies
looking for investors on Wall Street. In fact, Bramwell's office is covered with preliminary prospectuses (known in the industry as Red
Herrings) for many of these stocks. "I scan them, and if I'm interested, I'll do further research and go to the company's road show,"
she says. Bramwell attended one such meeting the day I visited her
office. It was for At Home, an Internet-related startup that wasn't
expected to have any earnings for at least one year. She found its
presentation much too slick and decided to pass. Nevertheless, to
show you how volatile IPOs can be, At Home's offering price was
set at $10.50 a share. It opened at $24.87 and reached a peak of
$27.50 before closing at $17 on its first day of trading.

LONG-TERM PERSPECTIVE

Bramwell believes that being in the business for three decades gives
her the advantage of having a historical perspective. In addition, she
emphasizes that learning to keep your emotions out of the process
and not becoming attached to the stocks in your portfolio are important lessons for investors to grasp. "If you don't know this, you can
get killed," she cautions.

FAMILY LIFE

Bramwell's husband, Bill, is a retired attorney. They have two children, a son and daughter, who are in college. While she speaks
openly of her adventures on Wall Street, Bramwell is reluctant to talk
about her family. "They don't like the publicity, and it's better that
they have their own identities," she says. To balance her high-
charging job of chasing stocks, she spends her weekends enjoying
outdoor sports, such as tennis, golf, skiing, hiking, and canoeing. "I
played varsity field hockey, badminton, and basketball at Bryn
Mawr," she adds, noting that fierce competition on the playing field
is a good background for competing in the investment arena.

ELIZABETH R. BRAMWELL'S
top 10 GROWTH STOCKS

FOR THE 21ST CENTURY

1. Colgate

2. Dell Computer

3. General Electric

4. Home Depot

5. Automatic Data Processing

6. Lucent Technologies

7. Merrill Lynch

8. Microsoft

9. Pfizer

10. Robert Half International

Index